THE

CHARTER, CONSTITUTION, BY-LAWS,

AND

OFFICES OF DEVOTION

OF THE

Protestant Episcopal Society

FOR THE PROMOTION OF

EVANGELICAL KNOWLEDGE.

New-York:
NO. 11 BIBLE HOUSE, ASTOR PLACE.
1856.

ADDRESS

OF THE

PROTESTANT EPISCOPAL SOCIETY

FOR THE

Promotion of Evangelical Knowledge.

A Society, with the above name, having been organized during the present session of the General Convention of the Protestant Episcopal Church in these United States, by several of the Bishops, Clergy, and Laity of said Church, it becomes a matter of obvious propriety that they should submit to their brethren and friends the views by which they have been governed in their work. They invite your attention

I. FIRST, TO THE RIGHT TO ORGANIZE.

The Association which we have formed involves action on the voluntary principle. On this point we enter into no argument. We have acted on the already recognized right thus to organize. The right, among Episcopalians, to hold differing opinions—within the limits of orthodoxy in the faith, and of loyalty to the Church—carries with it the right to maintain these opinions, and to associate for their maintenance. Several of the most important of our religious societies are organized on the voluntary principle.*

We assert for ourselves the right to organize on the same basis. Permit us now to detain you a few moments upon

II. SECOND, THE REASONS FOR ORGANIZING.

These have a relation to the object of our association; and this object leads us to the use of the press. Our reasons, then, for organizing for the religious use of the press are resolvable into two. We organize

1. First, because error is spreading through our Church.

It is not necessary, at this point, to enter into particulars. Unhappily we shall be too well understood by the mere allusion. We will therefore but say, in the general, that we refer to errors against which our judgments and our consciences constrain us to bear a solemn and most earnest testimony; errors touching both doctrine and the Church; both the way and the means of salvation.

With us the question is—not whether men may not hold important truths in connection with these errors—but whether these errors, spreading with the lapse of ages, and moulding the mind of successive generations, do not put saving truth more and more out of sight, till finally they leave countless multitudes without that whereby the Holy Spirit renews and sanctifies us in Christ Jesus; and whether, if operating without an antidote, they have not a

* The General S. S. Union, the New-York Tract Society, and the various Bible, Tract and Homily Societies are voluntary institutions.

present and immediate tendency to jeopard the salvation of the soul? This is the question which we have to consider; and our consideration obliges us to answer it in a way which, in our judgment, renders some such organization as the present imperative. As we have "learned Christ," we hold these errors to be dangerously corrupting to a pure Gospel and a pure Church, and deeply perilous to "a good hope through grace." We can not, for an hour, give place to the plea that they are errors in words more than in things. In our best judgments, they affect the vital parts of the religion of Christ. We organize

2. Second, because without organization we are, and must be, instrumental in the propagation of these errors.

By our involuntary influence, by the implied sanction of our names, and by the indirect contribution of our means, we are, under our ordinary modes of action, constrained to aid in disseminating views, against which our consciences have solemnly bound us to testify. At present, the stream of error, far too inadequately opposed, runs through every portion of our Church. Except to a limited extent, we can not check its flow. With a power which at present it is difficult to resist, the press among us is subsidiary to the spread of a most perilous infection; and by our silence and want of organization, we label the poison as "GOOD MEDICINE" for our families and our parishes. Except when its character is already known, we can not buy a book for the family till we have read it; nor purchase a dozen for a Sunday-school library till we have studied perhaps fifty. We must have an organization for publishing, selecting, and sanctioning such books and tracts as we approve, and for furnishing them to our families and our parishes through our own recognized depositories, and under our own recognized imprint. By these means, we may most reasonably hope to prevent the silent and gradual disappearance of evangelical views from the Church to which we belong, and which we have been taught to love. Without these means, we labor against most formidable disadvantages. We favor a silence, in which error yields most certainly and most abundantly its hundred-fold fruits. We must have an organization, around which we can rally under the standard of our Church, and in whose name we can promote what we hold to be the unadulterated Gospel of Christ. We proceed now to exhibit

III. THIRD, THE PRINCIPLES OF THE ORGANIZATION.

Our Society is based on the maxim that the press, in the hands of a truly faithful ministry, and of an intelligently pious laity, is one of the mightiest weapons for the maintenance and defense of truth. With this, mainly, must the power of a corrupt press, in the hands of the various ministers of evil, be met and broken. The importance of a pure and healthful Christian literature to the purity and healthfulness of religion and of the Church, can not easily be over-stated. The principles then, which through the press we seek to disseminate, are :

1. First, as to DOCTRINE, distinctively EVANGELICAL.

We use this term in its well-understood sense, as indicating the leading and fundamental doctrines of the glorious Reformation. Our system of doctrine will readily be recognized by a statement of a few of its particulars.

Scripture, the sole rule of faith; not Scripture and tradition in joint rule: *Man*, an utterly lost and helpless sinner; and *Christ*, a most free and sufficient Saviour: *Pardon*, the direct gift of Christ to every one that "believeth with the heart;" with no intervention other than that needed to bring him to faith; not dependent on a priestly or any human intervention for the forgiveness of sin: *Justification*, a gracious act of God, received by faith without works; not an inward character in man, consisting of faith as one of a catalogue of justifying graces: *Renovation*, the work of the Holy Spirit in the regeneration of man, operating mainly through the Truth, and making us "new creatures" in Christ: *Sanctification*, distinguished from justification, as the fruit from the seed; not blended with justification as making therewith one whole of inherent righteousness.

2. Second, as to the *Church*, our principles are distinctively PROTESTANT EPISCOPAL.

Here, also, the system which we adopt will be easily distinguished by a few of its features.

The Church, "the blessed company of all faithful people:" *Episcopacy*, as having existed "from the apostles' times:" The *Sacraments*, divine signs and seals, pledges and means of grace to faith; not standing miracles, whereby Christ is made incarnate in His members: *Jesus*, the immediate High Priest and sole Intercessor in behalf of every individual believer; not approached through the necessary medium of any ministerial intervention: *Worship*, according to our Liturgy, simple and scriptural; not loaded with human inventions and unauthorized ceremonies.

Such, brethren and friends, are the reasons for our organization, and the principles on which we are organized. Without entering into further detail, or into any labored appeal, we conclude by saying frankly, that, among those who coöperate with us, we do not expect identity of opinion. Our invitation is to all, and only those who, for *substance* of faith and practice, agree in the stand which we have here taken. We seek the sympathy, the prayers, the coöperation of all, and only those who feel bound of God in their consciences to perpetuate the true Evangelical faith, and the really Protestant character of the Church of our fathers. We would apply the principle of a freely acting spiritual affinity; one of the main principles in the hands of God for keeping alive in the world true faith, love, and holiness. Surround us, then, in our sacred association, with the living atmosphere of your prayers; strengthen us, in our arduous work, by the willing contribution of your means; and thus, for the sake of Him who hath our vows, aid us to keep burning on earth, and to spread brightening through the world, the lights of a pure faith in a purified Church.

New-York, October, 1847.

CHARTER.

AN ACT TO INCORPORATE THE

PROTESTANT EPISCOPAL SOCIETY

FOR THE

Promotion of Evangelical Knowledge.

Section 1. Be it enacted by the Senate and House of Representatives of the Commonwealth of Pennsylvania in General Assembly met, and it is hereby enacted by the authority of the same, that J. H. Fowles, William Suddards, Richard Newton, Thomas H. Powers, Matthew T. Miller, and Arthur G. Coffin, together with the other persons belonging to, or comprising the said Protestant Episcopal Society for the Promotion of Evangelical Knowledge, and their successors, (who shall become members of the Society according to the By-Laws,) be, and they are hereby made, and constituted a Corporation and body politic in law and in fact, by the name, style, and title of "The Protestant Episcopal Society for the Promotion of Evangelical Knowledge," and by that name shall have perpetual succession, have a common seal, make contracts, may sue

1*

and be sued, plead and be impleaded, in any court of record, or in any other place whatever; and may also take and hold any real or personal estate conveyed to them by gift, grant, bargain and sale, devise, bequest, or other alienation whatsoever; and sell and convey the same, provided that the clear yearly value of the lands, tenements, or other real estate of the said Corporation, shall not exceed the sum of three thousand dollars.

Sec. 2. The object of this Society shall be to promote Evangelical knowledge by the publication of Tracts, Sunday-school, and other books. The affairs of the Society shall be under the direction of a Board, consisting of a President, Vice-President, Secretary, Treasurer, and Managers, elected tri-annually. The Board, twelve of whom shall form a quorum, shall meet annually, at such time and place as they may appoint, and elect an Executive Committee, which shall consist of eight members, four of whom shall be Laymen, upon which Committee shall devolve all the powers of the Board during its recess. Until the first election shall be held in pursuance hereof, the officers of the Society, as at present organized, shall be the officers of this Corporation; and no failure to hold an election for, or to elect any of said officers shall be deemed a forfeiture of any of the corporate privileges hereby conferred; but the same shall continue unimpaired thereby, and on such failure or failures, the officers of the preceding year shall continue in office until their successors are duly elected. No person shall vote in the election of the Board who has not been a member of the Corporation at least three months before the time of such election, and the Board shall have the power to provide for, and regulate the admission of persons, being citizens of the United

States, as members of the Corporation. Five members of the Executive Committee shall constitute a quorum for the transaction of business, and shall have power to appoint such officers, clerks, and assistants under them, as shall be necessary for executing the business of the Corporation, and shall be capable of exercising such other power for the well-ordering and conducting of its affairs, as shall be determined by the By-Laws; *provided always*, that the said By-Laws shall not be repugnant to the Constitution and Laws of the United States, or of this Commonwealth.

Sec. 3. The Legislature may at any time alter, amend or repeal the privileges hereby granted.

William F. Packer,
Speaker of the House of Representatives.

William Williamson,
Speaker of the Senate.

Approved the Third Day of March, One Thousand Eight Hundred and Forty-Eight. Francis R. Shunk.

Secretary's Office,
Harrisburg, March 16, 1848.

Pennsylvania.

[seal.] I do certify that the above, and foregoing, is a true copy of the Act of Assembly now on file in this Office.

In testimony whereof, I have hereto set my hand, and caused to be affixed the seal of said Office the day and year above written. J. Miller,
Secretary of the Commonwealth.

CONSTITUTION

OF THE

PROTESTANT EPISCOPAL SOCIETY

FOR THE

Promotion of Evangelical Knowledge.

ARTICLE I.

This Society shall be denominated the Protestant Episcopal Society for the Promotion of Evangelical Knowledge.

ARTICLE II.

The object of this Society shall be, to maintain and set forth the principles and doctrines of the Gospel embodied in the Articles, Liturgy, and Homilies of the Protestant Episcopal Church, by the publication of Tracts, Sunday-school, and other books.

ARTICLE III.

Any person approving the objects of this Society may become a member of the same by the annual contribution of one dollar. Any person, by paying fifty dollars at one time, shall be a member for life.

ARTICLE IV.

This Society shall meet triennially at the time and place of the meeting of the General Convention, and shall, at each triennial meeting, elect a President, Vice-Presidents, Secretary, Treasurer, and a Board of Directors, and also transact such other business as may be brought before it. At every triennial meeting the transactions of the preceding three years shall be reported.

ARTICLE V.

The Bishops of the Protestant Episcopal Church in the United States, who may signify their approval of the objects of this Society, shall be *ex-officio* Vice-Presidents of the same, and members of the Board of Directors.

ARTICLE VI.

Upon the Board of Directors shall devolve all the powers of the Society requisite to the transaction of its ordinary business ; they shall meet annually at such time and place as themselves shall appoint: twelve members of the Board, regularly convened, shall constitute a quorum for the transaction of business: they shall enact By-Laws for the Society, and have power to fill vacancies in their own body, when such vacancies occur between the Triennial meetings of the Society: and they shall annually elect an Executive Committee, upon whom shall devolve all the powers of the Board during each annual recess of the same. This Executive Committee shall consist of not less than four nor more than six *clerical*, and of not less than four nor more than six *lay* members; *Provided*, nevertheless, that in addition to the members elected, the General Secretary and the Treasurer of the Society shall be *ex-officio* members of said Committee.

ARTICLE VII.

Any association formed on the principles of this Society, and annually contributing to its treasury, shall be considered an auxiliary, and the President and Secretary, for the time being, of such auxiliary, shall be *ex-officio* members of the Board of Directors.

ARTICLE VIII.

All meetings of the Board of Directors, and of the Executive Committee, shall be opened with prayer.

ARTICLE IX.

The Constitution shall not be altered except at a triennial meeting, and by a vote of two thirds of the members present.

BY-LAWS.

ARTICLE I.

The original Constitution of this Society, so far as it is consistent with its Charter, shall form part of the By-Laws thereof, and be subject to alteration only as provided in the eighth article of that Constitution.

ARTICLE II.

The Executive Committee shall meet, as soon as practicable after the annual meeting of the Board of Directors, for the purpose of electing their Chairman, Recording Secretary, Corresponding Secretary, General Agent, and Editor; and also the following standing committees, namely, a Committee on Publication, and a Committee on Finance and Accounts.

ARTICLE III.

Stated meetings of the Executive Committee shall be held on the last Thursday of every month. Special meetings may be called by the Chairman, or in his absence by the Recording Secretary, on the written request of two members.

ARTICLE IV.

At all meetings of the Executive Committee five members shall constitute a quorum for the transaction of business; and the following shall be the order of proceedings, namely:

1. Prayer.
2. Reading and approving the minutes.
3. Reports and communications from officers of the Society, and of the Executive Committee.
4. Reports of standing committees.
5. Reports of special committees.
6. Special orders.
7. Unfinished business.
8. Miscellaneous business.

ARTICLE V.

The Chairman shall preside at all meetings of the Executive Committee, and shall be invested with the powers, and perform the duties usually devolving upon presiding officers. In his absence, a Chairman *pro tempore*, with like powers and duties, may be appointed.

ARTICLE VI.

The Recording Secretary shall have the custody of the seal, charter, and by-laws of the Society, and the records of the Executive Committee. He shall, under the direction of the Chairman when present, and in his absence on the written request of two members, give due notice of the time and place of all meetings of the Executive Committee, and shall attend the same. He shall keep accurate minutes of the proceedings at such meetings, and engross the same, when approved by the Committee, upon its journal. He shall, immediately after the same, give notice to the several officers and committees, of all votes, orders, resolves, and proceedings of the Executive Committee affecting them, or appertaining to their respective duties.

ARTICLE VII.

The Corresponding Secretary shall have charge of the general correspondence of the Society, and report the same to the Executive Committee at its stated meetings. He shall coöperate with the Committee on Finance and Accounts in devising and carrying into effect plans for increasing the funds of the Society; and shall, from time to time, in correspondence and personal addresses, present the objects of the Society, and its claims upon the Church and the public.

ARTICLE VIII.

The General Agent shall have the charge of all the property of the Society not under the care of the Recording Secretary or Treasurer. He shall keep an accurate account of the books received, and of those distributed or sold. He shall conduct the business correspondence of the Society; keep an account with individuals, and auxiliary and other Societies, doing business with the Executive Committee; and pay over weekly, to the Treasurer, all moneys coming into his hands for account of the Society. He shall superintend the printing of the Society's publications, and be responsible for their mechanical execution. He shall attend the meetings of the Executive Committee, whenever notified and requested so to do; and generally carry out the instructions of that Committee in relation to all business pertaining to the operations of the Society.

ARTICLE IX.

It shall be the duty of the Editor of the Society to compose, select, and revise books and tracts for publication, and to present the same, with his recommendation thereof, to the Committee on Publication. He shall inform the Executive Committee, at each of its stated meetings, of all original matter sent to him for publication by the Society, with the names of the authors, and the general contents and character of the matter; and shall, when requested by the Executive Committee, forward to the Committee all such matter. It shall require a vote of two thirds of all the members of the Executive Committee either to adopt for publication any such matter not recommended by the Editor, or to reject any matter recommended by him. The Editor shall, when convenient, attend the meetings of the Executive Committee, and Committee on Publication; and by his advice and coöperation within the sphere of his appropriate duties aid in the accomplishment of the objects of the Society.

ARTICLE X.

The Treasurer shall have the custody of all contracts and securities of the Society. He shall receive all moneys due or belonging to the Society; and shall disburse the same, for account of the Society, on the warrant or order, in writing, of the Executive Committee, signed by the Chairman; and until so disbursed, all moneys received by him for the Society shall, immediately upon their receipt, be deposited and remain in some Bank in the city of New-

York, and the account thereof kept in the name of the Society. He shall pay, out of the funds of the Society in hand, all orders and bills, approved by the Executive Committee and signed by the Chairman. He shall attend the meetings of the Executive Committee, and of the Committee on Finance and Accounts, when notified and requested so to do; and shall present to the Executive Committee, at each stated meeting, a statement, in writing, of the receipts and disbursements for the intervening time; and shall annually prepare his accounts, to be examined and audited by the Committee on Finance and Accounts, and presented to the Executive Committee at its last meeting preceding the annual meeting of the Board of Directors. His books and papers shall be considered as the property of the Society; and, as such, shall at all times be open to the inspection, and under the control of the Executive Committee; and, at the expiration of his term of office, shall be delivered over to his successor in office.

ARTICLE XI.

The Committee on Publication shall consist of four members; and it shall be their duty to examine all works referred to them by the Executive Committee, or presented to them by the Editor, and recommended by him for publication; and they shall recommend such of them as they may approve, to the Executive Committee for its final action.

ARTICLE XII.

The Committee on Finance and Accounts shall consist of four members; and it shall be their duty to make all contracts in behalf of the Society, involving the expenditure of money; attend to the pecuniary concerns, generally, of the Society; devise and execute plans for increasing its funds; and propose to the Executive Committee all such agencies as, in their judgment, are requisite for the efficient prosecution of the objects of the Society. They shall examine all bills and accounts previous to their being submitted to the Executive Committee for approval. They shall annually, at the last stated meeting of the Executive Committee preceding the annual meeting of the Board of Directors, present a full and accurate account of the stock, property, and funds belonging to the Society, and also an account of the Society's indebtedness, with a statement of its resources and means for meeting the same. They shall audit the Treasurer's annual accounts, so that they may be presented to the Executive Committee, at the meeting last above-mentioned.

ARTICLE XIII.

All standing committees shall, immediately after their election, organize themselves by the appointment of a chairman and secretary. They shall meet at least once a month, and as much oftener as business may require. They shall keep regular minutes of their proceedings, which shall be presented to the Executive Committee for approval, at each of its stated meetings.

ARTICLE XIV.

All books and tracts sold or distributed in the name of the Society, and under the sanction of the Executive Committee, shall bear some distinctive mark or label, indicating the approval of the latter; and no book or tract shall be published by the Executive Committee in the name of the Society, which has not been examined by the Editor and a majority of the Committee on Publication ; and to the publication of which the assent of at least three of the Bishops who are members of the Society has not been obtained.

ARTICLE XV.

Alterations in the By-Laws, except Article I., may be made by the affirmative vote of a majority of the Executive Committee, at a stated meeting thereof, notice of such alterations having been given at a previous meeting of the Committee, and in the notice of the stated meeting at which they are adopted.

OFFICERS

OF THE

PROTESTANT EPISCOPAL SOCIETY

FOR THE

PROMOTION OF EVANGELICAL KNOWLEDGE.

President.

RIGHT REV. WILLIAM MEADE, D.D.

Vice-Presidents.

Rt. Rev. B. B. SMITH, D.D.,	Rt. Rev. JOHN JOHNS, D.D.,
" " C. P. M'ILVAINE, D.D.,	" " M. EASTBURN, D.D.,
" " S. ELLIOTT, D.D.,	" " ALFRED LEE, D.D.,

Right Rev. H. W. LEE, D.D.

Board of Directors.

CLERICAL.

C. W. Andrews, D.D., Va.,	K. Goddard, Pa.,
H. Anthon, D.D., N. Y.,	C. Goodrich, D.D., La.,
Wm. R. Nicholson, O.,	M. Gallagher, W. N. Y.,
L. P. W. Balch, D.D., Md.,	W. Horton, Mass.,
W. H. Barnwell, S. C.,	Samuel Cooke, N. Y.,
G. T. Bedell, D.D., N. Y.,	H. V. D. Johns, D.D., Md.,
E. H. Canfield, D.D., N. Y.,	S. C. Brinckle, Del.,
J. T. Brook, D.D., O.,	R. B. Duane, Pa.,
L. Bull, D.D., Pa.,	A. Jones, D.D., N. J.,
C. M. Butler, D.D., O.,	George D. Cummins, D. C.,
D. A. Tyng, Pa.,	W. B. Stevens, D.D., Pa.,
C. D. Cooper, Pa.,	E. Neville, D.D., N. Y.,
N. B. Crocker, D.D., R. I.,	R. Newton, D.D., Pa.,
B. C. Cutler, D.D., N. Y.,	E. W. Peet, Iowa,
T. R. Chipman, N. Y.,	W. N. Pendleton. Va.,
T. F. Fales, Mass.,	J. Peterkin, Va.,
C. P. Gadsden, S. C.,	C. C. Pinckney, S. C.,

J. PRATT, Me.,
W. PRESTON, Conn.,
E. REED, S. C.,
G. W. RIDGELY, Del.,
W. A. SMALLWOOD, Ill.,
G. A. SHELTON, N. Y.,
W. W. SPEAR,
J. S. STONE, D.D., Mass.,
H. STRINGFELLOW, Va.,
W. SUDDARDS, Pa.,
J. TRAPNELL, R. I.,
S. H. TYNG, D.D., N. Y.,
J. A. VAUGHAN, D.D., Pa.,
A. H. VINTON, D.D., Mass.,
J. R. WALKER, D.D., S. C.,
J. S. C. GREENE, Mass.

LAY.

WM. APPLETON, Mass.,
W. H. ASPINWALL, N. Y.,
L. R. ASHURST, Pa.,
R. W. BARNWELL, S. C.,
W. C. BEE, S. C.,
L. BRADISH, N. Y.,
F. H. DEANE, Va.,
E. W. DUNHAM, N. Y.,
D. K. ESTE, O.,
F. O. WATTS, Mass.,
B. HOWARD, Mass.,
J. P. INGLE, D. C.,
H. M. BASH, Md.,
W. E. MARTEN, S. C.,
C. C. MEMMINGER, S. C.,
ROBERT ORR, Pa.,
C. MORRIS, Pa.,
J. S. MORSELL, Md.,
R. C. NEILSON, Md.,
W. F. BULLOCK, Ky.,
STEWART BROWN, N. Y.,
JOHN BOHLEN, Pa.,
W. H. MCFARLAND, Va.,
J. N. CONYNGHAM, Pa.,
H. COPE, Pa.,
R. H. CUNNINGHAM, Va.,
W. M. GOODRICH, La.,
E. W. PEGRAM, Md.,
F. T. PEET, N. Y.,
THOMAS H. POWERS, Pa.,
FRANCIS WHARTON, Pa.,
J. SANDS, N. Y.,
B. STORER, O.,
J. G. TOLFORD, Me.,
G. T. WARDWELL, R. I.,
P. WILLIAMS, Va.,
W. WHITLOCK, N. Y.,
F. S. WINSTON, N. Y.,
D. B. TRIMBLE, M.D., N. J.,
S. G. WYMAN, Md.

Executive Committee.

Rev. B. C. CUTLER, D.D.,
" H. ANTHON, D.D.,
" E. NEVILLE, D.D.,
" E. H. CANFIELD, D.D.,
" S. COOKE,
" G. T. BEDELL, D.D.,
Hon. L. BRADISH,
Messrs. S. CAMBRELING,
S. BROWN,
E. W. DUNHAM,
J. B. HERRICK,
HORACE WEBSTER, LL.D.

Editor, Rev. C. W. ANDREWS, D.D., Shepherdstown, Va.
Corresponding Secretary, Rev. H. DYER, D.D., No. 11 Bible House, New-York.
Secretary of the Board, Rev. WM. SUDDARDS.
Treasurer, Mr. F. T. PEET, 47 Chambers street, New-York.
The Executive Committee meet regularly on the last Thursday in each month.

FORM

OF A

BEQUEST TO THE SOCIETY.

I GIVE and bequeath to the Protestant Episcopal Society for the Promotion of Evangelical Knowledge in the United States of America, incorporated by the State of Pennsylvania, in the year one thousand eight hundred and forty eight, the sum of   to be applied to the uses of said Society.

PRAYERS.

Offices of Devotion.

Let the words of my mouth, and the meditation of my heart be always acceptable in Thy sight, O Lord, my Strength and my Redeemer.

Let us pray.

O Lord! show Thy mercy upon us;

Ans. And grant us Thy salvation.

O God! make clean our hearts within us;

Ans. And take not Thy Holy Spirit from us.

O Eternal God! Infinite in greatness and in holiness! unto whom all hearts are open, and from whom no secrets are hid: Fill our minds with reverent thoughts of Thy dread majesty, and affect our souls with abasing views

2

of our own unworthiness; that we may never draw near Thee with our mouth, and honor Thee with our lips, while our hearts are removed far from Thee.

We are not worthy to lift up our eyes to heaven. Our iniquity is great and our transgressions multiplied; our best love to Thee is cold, and our best obedience defiled. Create and make in us new and contrite hearts; affect us with a godly sorrow for all our sins; and fill us with a lively faith in Christ our Saviour. We beseech Thee, also so to lead us in the knowledge and acknowledgment of Him who is The Way, The Truth, and The Life, that we may obtain of Thee, the God of all mercy, perfect remission and forgiveness; and so to guide the motions of our wills, and to cleanse the thoughts of our hearts by the inspiration of Thy Holy Spirit, that we may perfectly love Thee and worthily magnify Thy Holy Name.

Grant us, we pray Thee, the Spirit of Love and of power, and of a sound mind. Shed abroad Thy Love in our hearts by the Holy Ghost. May the love of Christ constrain us to live not unto ourselves, but unto Him that died for us. And may we have such love for the souls of men, that being affectionately desirous of them, we may be ready to impart not the Gospel only, but our own lives also, in labors and in sacrifices for their salvation.

In the work of this our special calling, endue us with power from on high. Dwelling in our hearts by faith, may Christ be made unto us the Power of God. May the weapons of our warfare be mighty, through God, to the pulling down of strongholds. And guided by wisdom from above, may our influence be in demonstration of the Spirit and of power, and tend to bring every thought into captivity to the obedience of Christ.

Make our hearts, also, sound in Thy statutes. Open our understanding that we may understand the Scriptures; and that, having a right judgment in all things, we may continue unto the end, steadfast in faith, joyful through hope, and rooted in charity, through Jesus Christ, our Lord. *Amen.*

Almighty and everlasting God, by whose Spirit the whole body of the Church is governed and sanctified; Send down on this, Thy spiritual family, Thy manifold gifts of grace.

Heal the divisions and hush the contentions of Thy Church, by purifying her from all error and superstition, all false doctrine and persecuting tempers; and by filling her more and more with the mind of her Divine Head; His lowly and loving mind, His mind for sacred toil and for heavenly peace. Make her thus the true Fullness of Him that filleth all in all. Enrich her with that love which is the bond of perfectness, and with that faith which worketh the bond of Love.

Replenish her with spiritual life, and with men consecrated to the dissemination of that life; with holy Truth, and with men ready to suffer in defense of that Truth. And thus endowed, fill the earth with her praise. Let the fullness of the Gentiles come in, and so all Israel be saved through that glorious Deliverer, who shall turn away ungodliness from Jacob; Thy Son, Jesus Christ our Lord. *Amen.*

Almighty God, the Fountain of all wisdom, we implore Thy special blessing on this Association. Instituted for the defense and propagation of the Gospel of Truth, may it be divinely qualified for its work. May every individual Member, Officer, and Agent, be fully a partaker of the grace of life, richly endued with wisdom from on high, and mightily strengthened for every good work. And may all our joint counsels and labors have heavenly guidance and reach heavenly results. May our earnestness in defending Truth, and in combating Error, be an emanation from God; a spirit strong and steady, patient and persevering. May we not be so zealous for truth as wickedly to violate peace; nor so long for peace as to be virtually indifferent to truth: may we be neither easily disheartened by appearances of present failure; nor unduly elated by prospects of future success; but, giving ourselves to our work in Thy steadfast fear and love, may we pursue our way trustingly, diligently, perseveringly: looking to Thee for all needed blessing, and depending on Thee for all desired acceptance.

Let Thy Holy Spirit be with us, and graciously preside over our present deliberations. Direct us in *all* our doings with Thy most gracious favor, and further us with Thy continual help; that in all our works, begun, continued, and ended in Thee, we may glorify Thy

Holy Name, and finally by Thy mercy obtain everlasting life; through Jesus Christ our Lord. *Amen.*

Our Father, who art in heaven, hallowed be Thy Name. Thy kingdom come. Thy will be done in earth, as it is in heaven. Give us this day our daily bread. And forgive us our trespasses as we forgive those who trespass against us. And lead us not into temptation, but deliver us from evil: for Thine is the kingdom, and the power, and the glory, for ever and ever. *Amen.*

The grace of our Lord Jesus Christ, and the love of God, and the fellowship of the Holy Ghost be with us all evermore. *Amen.*

A Prayer for the Chief Officers of the Society.

O Lord Jesus Christ! Thou great Shepherd of the sheep; Vouchsafe, as to all our bishops, so especially to the President and the Vice-Presidents of this Society, Thy heavenly blessing. Endue them richly with holy love and tenderness, wisdom and firmness, patience and earnestness. Imbue their hearts with the Spirit of Christ. Make them fearless and faithful witnesses unto Him at all times, and in all places. May they restrain no divine Truth, and sanction no opposing Error. May they lay hands suddenly on no man ; but faithfully and wisely make choice of fit persons to serve Thee in the sacred ministry of Thy Church. May their personal influence be always holy; and their hearts ever favored with a true enjoyment of the hope of eternal life ; through Thy merits, O blessed Jesus ! who art, with the Father and the Holy Ghost, One God, world without end. *Amen.*

A Prayer for the Committee on Publications.

Blessed Lord ! who lovest the Truth, even as Thou lovest Thyself; shed on this Committee such a portion of Thy Spirit, that we may love Thy Truth more than we love ourselves. Help us, in all sincerity, to say, Oh ! how I love Thy law. It is my meditation all the day. How sweet are Thy words unto my taste ;

yea, sweeter than honey to my mouth; that having this relish for Thy Word, our souls may ever dwell in its light, and our labors never debase its purity. Preserve us from all error, both in doctrine and in practice; and let all our efforts be blessed to the result of filling Thy Church, and finally the world, with the truth of the Gospel; with the knowledge, the love, and the likeness of God in Jesus Christ our Lord: to whom, with the Father and the Spirit, be honor and glory for ever. *Amen.*

A Prayer for Special Occasions.

Almighty and Eternal God! Thou art wisdom and strength. In our ignorance and weakness, we betake ourselves to Thee. In view of the important concerns which are now to engage our solicitous regards, grant us Thy special guidance, that we may attempt nothing contrary to Thy holy will, and accomplish nothing without Thy crowning blessing. Setting the Lord always before us, may we earnestly desire, and wisely pursue, what is most agreeable to Thee. May Thy cause take no detriment from our counsels, and Thy name no dishonor from our measures. In particular, may our present action promote the welfare of Thy Church, and the progress of Thy Truth; that so, gaining wisdom under Thy guidance, and dispensing good from Thy fullness, we may at last, with all our services, find acceptance through Thy mercy, in Jesus Christ our Redeemer. *Amen.*

Order of Proceedings.

1. Prayer.
2. Reading and approving the minutes.
3. Reports and communications from officers of the Society and of the Executive Committee.
4. Reports of standing committees.
5. Reports of special committees.
6. Special orders.
7. Unfinished business.
8. Miscellaneous business.

STATEMENT

OF THE

DISTINCTIVE PRINCIPLES

OF

The Protestant Episcopal Society

FOR THE PROMOTION OF

EVANGELICAL KNOWLEDGE.

PUBLISHED UNDER DIRECTION OF THE EXECUTIVE COMMITTEE.

NEW-YORK:

DEPOSITORY, 22 JOHN STREET.

1850.

THE PRINCIPLES OF THE ORGANIZATION.

[*Extract from the Society's Address of November*, 1847.]

Our Society is based on the maxim, that the press, in the hands of a truly faithful ministry, and of an intelligently pious laity, is one of the mightiest weapons for the maintenance and defence of truth. With this, mainly, must the power of a corrupt press, in the hands of the various ministers of evil, be met and broken. The importance of a pure and healthful Christian literature to the purity and healthfulness of religion and of the church, cannot easily be overstated. The principles, then, which, through the press, we seek to disseminate, are—

1. First, as to DOCTRINE, distinctively EVANGELICAL.

We use this term in its well understood sense, as indicating the leading and fundamental doctrines of the glorious Reformation. Our system of doctrine will readily be recognized by a statement of a few of its particulars.

Scripture, the sole rule of faith; not Scripture and tradition its joint rule: *Man*, an utterly lost and helpless sinner; and *Christ*, a most free and sufficient Saviour: *Pardon*, the direct gift of Christ to every one that "believeth with the heart;" with no intervention other than that needed to bring him to faith; not dependent on a priestly or any human intervention for the forgiveness of sin: *Justification*, a gracious act of God, received by faith without works; not an inward character in man, consisting of faith as one of a catalogue of justifying graces: *Renovation*, the work of the Holy Spirit in the regeneration of man, operating mainly through the Truth, and making us "new creatures" in Christ: *Sanctification*, distinguished from justification, as the fruit from the seed; not blended with justification as making therewith one whole of inherent righteousness.

2. Second, as to the *Church*, our principles are distinctively PROTESTANT EPISCOPAL.

Here, also, the system which we adopt, will be easily distinguished by a few of its features.

The Church, "the blessed company of all faithful people:" *Epis-*

copacy, as having existed "from the apostles' times:" The *Sacraments*, divine signs and seals, pledges and means of grace to faith; not standing miracles, whereby Christ is made incarnate in His members: *Jesus*, the immediate High Priest and sole Intercessor in behalf of every individual believer; not approached through the necessary medium of any ministerial intervention: *Worship*, according to our Liturgy, simple and Scriptural; not loaded with human inventions and unauthorized ceremonies.

STATEMENT

OF

DISTINCTIVE PRINCIPLES.

This Society was organized at a meeting of several of the Bishops, and a respectable number of the Clergy and Laity of the Protestant Episcopal Church, during the session of the General Convention in the year 1847. At that time a brief statement of the distinctive principles of the Society was presented to the public. The subsequent appointment of a new officer, as General Secretary, whose whole time is to be devoted to the affairs of the Society; and the consequent removal of the seat of its operations from Philadelphia to New-York, present a fit occasion for a somewhat fuller enunciation of the principles on which the Society is based; and as the hope is indulged of an increasingly liberal patronage in support of its operations, it is no more than right that the Church should be put in full possession of the views, by which the Society proposes to govern itself.

Without further preface, then, these views may be

presented under the two great divisions of religious teaching,—

The Elements of Christian Theology;

and,

The Constitution of the Christian Church.

I. The Elements of Christian Theology.

In themselves, these are identical with the whole and true body of the doctrines of the Gospel. In relation to these doctrines, the Society desires to be known as, Distinctively Evangelical. It starts not on its course under the banner of Calvinism, of Arminianism, of Lutheranism, or of any other human School for training in religious controversy. It wishes to move under the single banner of Christ and his Gospel. It would be known as *simply and distinctively Evangelical.*

Under this head, however, it is not necessary to the purposes of the following Exposition, to set forth a complete Body of Divinity. What the Society understands by *distinctively* Evangelical, may be made to appear by stating and illustrating those points, which have had a leading influence in its organization.

The religious doctrines of any individual Christian, or of any body of Christians, so far as those doctrines are intelligently received and held, take their distinctive character from *the Rule of Faith* which they adopt; that is, from the authority, to which they appeal in settling and proving their doctrines. The same is true of the views taken of the Constitution of the Christian Church. Hence the necessity of defining, at the outset, *the Rule of Faith*, which the Society adopts. This, indeed, is not strictly one of the *doctrines* of Christ's religion. Nevertheless, being a guide to the determination of those doctrines, it may with propriety head the list of the Society's Distinctive Principles.

1. On this point, then, the Society takes the well known ground of *The Bible, as the sole Rule of Faith;* in distinction from the equally well known ground of *The Bible and Tradition as the joint Rule.*

Strictly speaking, Divine Testimony is the only authoritative rule of faith. This Testimony, whereever it may be certainly and clearly found, is decisive in all questions of religious truth. It admits of no appeal, or doubt. The Divine Testimony was communicated in olden times, by "holy men, who spake as they were moved by the Holy Ghost." Being thus infallibly secured against error, the communications of these men were unquestionable Truth. Originally their communications were transmitted to others both by *writing* and by *word of mouth;* and, in either case, they were perfectly reliable. Their *written* communications from God, safely handed down from age to age, we now possess in the several books of the Canonical Scriptures. These Scriptures, therefore, are Divinely authoritative in all matters of Faith. From the nature of the case, however, the *oral* communications of inspired men were strictly confined to those whom they originally addressed. When transmitted by these latter, either orally or in writing, they ceased to be the *oral* communications of the Divine Testimony by inspired men; and passed into the form of a *professed report* of such communications; true, only in proportion as they were truly reported. But, as all such reports, in passing from man to man, and from age to age, are liable to deep corruption, or to total loss, even these have become wholly untrustworthy. Indeed, we have no evidence that any of them, as they came from God, have ever reached our times. Hence it is manifest that the Canonical Scriptures alone remain as the Church's Rule of Faith. They are the only standard of Divine authority, to which we can appeal in settling and proving the true doctrines of Christianity.

But the Church of Rome, having overlaid "The faith once delivered to the Saints" with various corrupt and corrupting dogmas, and being unable to defend her additions by a fair appeal to the Bible; holds that this sacred Book needs an infallible Interpreter, and that this interpreter is her own infallible self. She claims to hold certain ancient traditions,—the alleged *oral* teachings of the Apostles,—which have been handed down in several of her ancient writings, or embodied in a portion of her peculiar observances. These Traditions she regards as of equal inspiration, and therefore, of equal authority, with the Canonical Scriptures: and with this assumed *character* of those *Traditions*, she attempts to bolster her claims as an Infallible *Interpreter* of these *Scriptures*. With *her*,—not the Bible *alone*, but the Bible and Tradition *jointly*, are the Rule of Faith: the Bible and Tradition; each of equal inspiration and authority; the *latter* necessary to the right interpretation of the *former;* and *herself* possessed of sole, exclusive right to use the one in settling the sense of the other.

With this monstrous and fallacious claim there are, unhappily, in our own Church, not a few, who more or less deeply sympathise; and from whom this Society is constrained most emphatically to differ. To admit that the alleged Traditions are of co-ordinate inspiration and authority with the Canonical Scriptures, and in this character necessary to a right interpretation of those Scriptures, is, in effect, to place Tradition *above* the Bible: inasmuch as that which interprets, is of higher rank than that which is interpreted. This accounts for the practical regard for Tradition, and the virtual disregard for the Bible, which so notoriously characterize the Church of Rome, and which she cherishes notwithstanding the total want of proof that her Traditions have any Inspiration; notwithstanding the manifest corruptions and falsehoods with which they abound; and notwithstanding the demonstrable truth, that, instead of being either less obscure, or more accessible, they as really need interpretation as the Lively Oracles themselves, and for all practical purposes, are far less easily approached.

For Tradition, in the sense of our thirty-fourth Article, this Society cherishes the proper regard. It considers Tradition as entitled to conscientious respect, whenever embodied in such "Ceremonies of the Church as be not repugnant to the Word of God, and as have been ordained and approved by common authority." It goes farther, and regards *written* or *historic* Tradition as useful in ascertaining what were the actual teachings of the ancient Christian authors, and the actual decisions of the ancient Christian Councils, whether these teachings and decisions were agreeable or contrary to the Word of God;—nay, as valuable, like all other appropriate *human* aids, in attaining to a clearer understanding of the true sense of the divinely inspired and authoritative Scriptures. But, of these sacred writings the Society acknowledges no infallible interpreter save the Scriptures themselves, and that Holy One by whom they were inspired. It abides by the declaration of our sixth Article, that "Holy Scripture containeth all things necessary to salvation; so that whatsoever is not read therein, nor may be proved thereby, is not to be required of any man, that it should be believed as an article of faith, or be thought requisite or necessary to salvation."

2. After thus indicating our Rule of Faith, the first doctrinal point which strikes our view, is that moral character and condition of man, by which both Redemption and Revelation were rendered necessary. On this point, then, the Society holds, that *man is an utterly lost and helpless sinner;* in distinction from the doctrine that he is able to save himself, or even by works done "before Justification," to make himself "meet to receive grace,—or, as the School-authors say, *deserve* grace of congruity."

By our doctrine on this point, we do not mean that man, by the fall, became *paralyzed*, either physically or intellectually; or that, even *morally*, he became incapable of being moved to what is right and good:—but we mean that, by the fall, every man has derived a *corruption*, or *infection of nature*, whereby he is so entirely gone from original righteousness, that of his own nature he is inclined to evil; the flesh lusteth always contrary to the Spirit; he cannot turn and prepare himself, by his own natural strength, to faith and calling upon God; but is dependent entirely on the prevenient grace of God to give him so much as a good will, and to work in him after that will has been given. We mean, moreover, that, as such actual transgression and the corruption of nature by which it is induced, "deserve God's wrath and damnation," every man, as a sinner, is *lost,* "a child of wrath," in himself without either holiness or hope of salvation. Moreover, as a sinner, thus involved in guilt and defilement, is unable either to "find a Ransom" for himself, or to cleanse his own nature from pollution, his ruin, so long as he is left to his own resources, is *irreparable.*

On this point, therefore, we hold and shall teach, that, in himself, *man is an utterly lost and helpless sinner.* Both for pardon and for purification he is wholly dependent on the mercy of God through the Sacrifice of His Son and the gift of His Spirit. The idea that, by his own "works before Justification," that is, by "works done before the grace of Christ and the inspiration of His Spirit," he can make himself "meet to receive grace, or, as the School-authors say, *deserve* grace of congruity;" and still more, the idea, that by his own self-discipline and culture, he is wholly able to deliver himself from the curse and the corruption of sin; are no where to be found in the Bible, and cannot by us be regarded otherwise than as a part of the falsehoods of a vain and deceitful Philosophy.

3. The lost and helpless condition of man as a sinner naturally turns our thoughts to the necessity and the character of a *Redeemer.* On this point, the doctrine of the Society is:—*Christ, a most free and*

sufficient Savior; in distinction from the theory, that His Redemption is limited either in the offer to be made of its benefits, or in its adequacy to the wants of mankind.

That our Redeemer is "mighty," that He is "able to save to the uttermost," and that he pleads with touching earnestness, "Come unto me, all ye that labor and are heavy laden, and I will give you rest;" we have in express terms the Divine testimony. That His Gospel with its included offer should be preached "in all the world," and "to every creature," is also the explicit injunction of its Author. We are, moreover, taught that "whosoever will may come," and that "he that cometh shall in no wise be cast out." In distinction, therefore, from those who restrict the offer of that salvation which Christ hath perfected; or limit in any degree the value of that atonement which He has made; or teach the inadequacy of that atonement to the saving of all mankind, if all would receive it on its prescribed terms; or insist on any moral qualification in the sinner as a prerequisite to an interest in the offered blessing; the Society maintain that *Christ is a most free and sufficient Savior;* needed of all, suited to all, sufficient for all, and most urgently offered to all, "without money and without price." God's purpose of election bars no one, who will, from coming to Christ, and receiving the fulness of His salvation.

4. Such being the character of the Savior whom we need, the question at once occurs; how are we to become *partakers* of the salvation which He brings? And by way of answer in part to this question, the

Society holds that "*Pardon is the direct gift of Christ to every one that believeth with the heart*"; in distinction from those who teach the necessity or the use of a Priestly intervention for the forgiveness of sin.

St. Paul affirms that "in Christ we have Redemption through his blood, even the forgiveness of sins." And St. Peter testifies, "Him hath God exalted with His right hand to be a Prince and a Savior for to give repentance to Israel and forgiveness of sins." That this forgiveness, therefore, was purchased by the sacrifice of the body and blood of Christ, and is now His gift, no one, with whom we have to do, is likely to gainsay. Yet there are among us those who maintain that Christ dispenses this gift, not *directly*, but *representatively*; that, for this purpose, He has constituted a Priesthood, and once for all, committed to that Priesthood the power, not merely of declaring on what terms sin may be forgiven, but of actually conveying this forgiveness; that a sinner, desiring to obtain it, must apply, not directly to Christ, but intermediately to the Priest; that he must go to the Priest, not simply for instruction and encouragement, but for forgiveness itself; that, on being satisfied of the penitence of the applicant, the Priest is empowered to give absolution; and that this is done by the administration of Baptism, or, if the applicant have been already baptized, then, on a satisfactory confession to the Priest of the particular sins committed after Baptism, by formally dispensing to him a pardon of the sins confessed.

This system of the necessity, or use, of a Priestly intervention for the forgiveness of sins, the Society regards as utterly unscriptural and thoroughly pernicious. In the language of Dr. Barrow, the aim of this system of particular confession is, "that the Priests may have a mighty awe on the consciences of all people, may dive into their secrets, and may manage their lives as they please." "And what," asks that learned divine, "doth a like particular absolution intend, but to set the Priest in a lofty state of authority above the people, as a judge of their condition, and a dispenser of their salvation?"

The proper office of a Christian Minister is that of an authorized and responsible teacher and guide, not that of a Priest in the Jewish sense of the term. His service is, to be a helper to the people's faith and joy, by such instructions as shall lead them to the Savior, and make them realize that, by faith in Him, they may obtain a free forgiveness, and that, in the right use of divinely-ordained means, they may attain to the full life and comforts of true godliness. On those, who "believe with the heart," full remission is bestowed by Christ Himself. The act of Remission is exclusively His. The assurance of this remission is given, primarily and authoritatively, in His inspired Word; secondarily and declaratively, by the lips of His commissioned ministers. By them, also, the *Seal* of this remission is given in the divinely appointed Sacraments of the Church. *But other Priestly intervention* for the forgiveness of sins the Society can never recognize. The language of Christ to the weary and heavy laden is, not "Come to the *Priest*," but "Come unto *me*." To arrest a returning sinner by interposing a Priest as a necessary or needed medium of favorable communication, without whose intervention pardon cannot ordinarily be had, is an absurd and mischievous perversion of the ministerial office. It is as absurd as if a sign-board were used to barricade the path, instead of standing by the way-side and rightly directing the inquisitive traveler; and it is as mischievous as it is absurd; for it robs Christ of His glory, ruins the souls of men, and inflates an aspiring, self-aggrandizing Priesthood. The history of Christianity is a vast repository of evidence to the deep, manifold and destructive evils, into which this anti-Evangelical dogma has plunged the Church.

5. But mere *Pardon* is not all that sinners need. They require full *Justification.* By way, therefore, of further answer to the question: How do we become partakers of the salvation, which Christ has offered? the Society holds that *Justification is a gracious act of God, grounded on the perfect righteousness of Christ, and received by faith without works;* in distinction from those, who teach that it is, in part at least, a *merited* act of God, grounded on an inward character in man, or on faith as one only of a catalogue of justifying graces.

So far as there is a difference between Pardon and Justification, it may be thus expressed. The former is simply a gracious removal of *penalty.* The latter is an equally gracious restoration to *favor. Pardon* is purchased by the *Death* and Passion of Christ, suffering in the sinner's *stead. Justification* is procured by the whole *Righteousness* of Christ, obeying to the sinner's *benefit.* Pardon and Justification are but parts of the one great work of God in applying to the sinner His one great gift of Redemption: connected, not disjoined; received at one and the same time by one and the same act of faith, not successors to each other through different operations of the mind. When we speak of Pardon, however, we look most to the *sufferings* of Christ; and when we speak of Justification, we look most to the *obedience* of Christ. The point may perhaps be cleared by reference to the case of a person attainted of treason, by human law, and under sentence of death, disfranchisement and confiscation of estate. The supreme Executive, moved by proper considerations, may grant a *pardon*, and thus remove the adjudged penalty of death. By this act the convict simply escapes *suffering*. He is not *executed* as a traitor. It is plain, however, that his escape does not place him on the footing of one who has always been loyal to his country. From the removal of the death-penalty, it does not follow that he is, in all respects, to be treated as though he had never violated the law. His escape from execution through the clemency of his ruler does not put him in favor as a candidate for rewards. He goes free of his country's *vengeance;* but this entitles him not to his country's *honors*. To reach the latter, he must either be proved innocent of the crime for which he was condemned, or receive an act of special grace from the Government, reaching beyond the mere clemency of pardon, and restoring to him the enjoyment both of his citizenship and of his estates. Now, what this latter act, under a human government, as restoring the traitor to his country's favor, would be to the executive act of clemency in merely removing the temporal penalty annexed to his crime; such, under the divine government, is Justification, as restoring the sinner to the full favor of God, when compared with pardon, as simply releasing him from the eternal penalty which his sins deserve. Christ has suffered in the sinner's *stead;* by faith in Christ the sinner is admitted to *pardon;* his sins are forgiven, and so he escapes everlasting punishment. But this is not all. Christ has also wrought out a perfect righteousness for the sinner's *benefit;* by the same act of faith the sinner *receives* this benefit; he is *justified;* he is restored to favor with God; he is treated as if he had never sinned; he is made "a joint-heir with Christ" of eternal glory.

Justification is more than exemption from the punishment of sin. It is full restoration to the favor of God. The individual, who receives the benefit, is *truly* regarded and treated as if he had never sinned.

To say that the act, which thus exalts the believer, is the act of *God*, is but to affirm what from the nature of the case must be obvious, and what Holy Scripture expressly declares: "It is *God* that justifieth." It is more important to state what we mean when we call it the *gracious* act of God. By this, then, we do not mean that the act is without adequate consideration. This neither is, nor can be true, consistently with the Law and Character of God. To reconcile the act with these, some suitable provision must have been made. Accordingly we find that such a provision has been made in the perfect righteousness of Christ; that perfect *obedience*, whereby He "magnified the Law and made it honorable." This, we apprehend, was spoken, not of the ground of the sinner's *pardon*, but of that of his *justification.* Hence the prophet declares: "The Lord is well pleased," not for his *sufferings'*, but "for his *righteousness'* sake. He will magnify the Law and make it honorable." God *was* pleased with the sufferings of Christ, as the ground of the sinner's *pardon;* but that was not the idea then in the prophet's mind. Isaiah was evidently setting forth the ground of the sinner's *justification;* and therefore he says, "The Lord is well pleased for his *righteousness'* sake." By His *righteousness*, Christ magnified the Law and made it honorable. He rendered a magnifying, honoring obedience to the Divine Law. By faith, this obedience is counted, or made available, to the sinner's *benefit.* For the *sake* of this all-deserving righteousness, God *justifies* the true believer; regards and treats him as though he had never sinned; makes him "a joint-heir with Christ" in the glories of Heaven. Now, we call this justification a *gracious* act, because, in receiving it, no *meritorious* consideration is furnished by the justified believer himself. To *him*, the act is, and, from his condition as a sinner, *must be*, "of grace" and not "of works." An adequate consideration has, indeed, been rendered; not, however, by the insolvent sinner himself, but by his all-sufficient Savior. "*Christ* is the end of the law for righteousness", or justification, "to every one that believeth." The demands of the law were met to the uttermost by the righteousness of Christ; and now, God's act of justification, grounded on that righteousness, is, to the believer altogether of grace. The boon is received "without money and without price." The heart's reception of Christ and reliance on Him, as set forth in the Gospel, constitute true, evangelical *faith;* and, with this faith, by Divine appointment, justification is immediately and inseparably connected. This great benefit is not a fruit of any merit in faith *itself;* this, from its very nature, is a self-renouncing grace: nor is it a fruit of any certain *effects* of faith, in its foreseen, meliorating operation on the character of man; this would contradict St. Paul's teaching, and make justification of "*works*" and of "*debt*"; but it is a fruit of the righteousness of Christ alone, of which faith is the heart's reception, and which, through faith, God reckons to the believer's benefit, or accounts it his. The benefit is not, in any part, a *merited* grant, grounded on an inward character in man, or on faith as one of a catalogue of justifying graces: it is wholly "a *gracious* act of God, grounded on the perfect righteousness of Christ, and received by faith without works."

The teaching of St. James, on this point, does not conflict with that of St. Paul. When the former speaks of works as justifying, he is manifestly treating of works as evidences that faith is not *dead,* but *living, fruitful.* He does not represent works as *meriting,* in *any* measure, the sinner's justification in the sight of God. Indeed, the doctrine of human merit, in this connexion, is second to no other error in its pernicious tendency.

6. But the sinner, who, by faith, relies on the sufferings and righteousness of Christ as his ground both of pardon and of justification, is no longer in his natural state. He is, what the Bible denominates, "a new creature." He is "not in the *flesh,* but in the *Spirit.*" He is the subject of that new and spiritual

life, which is needed in order to his enjoyment of God. On this point the Society holds, that *Regeneration is the work of the Holy Spirit, operating mainly through the Truth, and making us new creatures in Christ;* in distinction from those, who teach that it is the work of the Spirit, rendering operative the water of Baptism, and therewith making Christ incarnate in our natures.

The indispensable *necessity* of a spiritual change in our nature, not slight and superficial, but deep and thorough, to fit us for rightly engaging in the service of God on Earth, and for fully enjoying His presence in Heaven, is clearly the doctrine of our Church, based on the authority of the Sacred Scriptures. This necessity arises from the introduction of *sin.* Whilst, as a violation of the Divine Law, sin involves us in guilt and liability to punishment, it is also the "corruption" of our nature itself, whereby "every man that naturally is engendered of the offspring of Adam is very far gone from original Righteousness, and is of his own nature inclined to evil; so that the flesh lusteth always contrary to the Spirit," and is, therefore, without a spiritual change, incapable of spiritual happiness. The *change,* thus rendered necessary, is, by the inspired writers, expressed in strong and striking language: "If any man be in Christ he is a *new creature.*" "You hath he *quickened*"—or made alive—"who were *dead* in trespasses and sins." The *power,* by which this great change is wrought, is not any *created,* but a *divine* energy. Hence the Evangelist: "Born, not of blood, nor of the will of the flesh, nor of the will of man, but of *God.*" The *exercise* of this divine power in the sinner's "new birth unto righteousness" is specially ascribed to the *Holy Ghost.* Hence the subjects of this change are said to be "born of the *Spirit.*" In effecting His work, this adorable Person in the Godhead moves in mysterious sovereignty. "The wind bloweth where it listeth, and thou hearest the sound thereof, but canst not tell whence it cometh and whither it goeth: so is every one that is born of the Spirit." To limit his operations to any particular time, or place, means or mode, would be great presumption. The doctrine of the Church of Rome, that Regeneration is ordinarily wrought by the Holy Spirit in and by the Water of Baptism, after the mode of what is termed grace "*ex opere operato,*" or grace from the work wrought, grace from the working of the Baptismal water itself, is no where taught in the Word of God, but is, on the contrary, repugnant to its plain import.

The question here is, not whether the Holy Spirit, by His own direct agency, ever regenerates either the infant or the adult *at the time of Baptism?* on this point different opinions are entertained; but, whether He ever makes *the Water* of Baptism his instrument, forming *Christ* in that Water (as in a new material matrix,) and thence making Him incarnate in all the Baptized? This, fairly eliminated and thrust forth from its inclosure of dark words, is the doctrine now so current even in our own Church; and this, we hold, is not merely without warrant from Scripture, but wholly repugnant to its teachings.

The ordinary *means* by which the Spirit operates in making us "new creatures," are various. But His grand instrumentality is, doubtless, *the Truth* as revealed in the Holy Scriptures, or otherwise suggested to the mind. "Of His own will *begat* He us *with the*

Word of Truth." "Being *born again*, not of corruptible seed, but of incorruptible, *by the Word of God*, which liveth and abideth forever."—James i., 18; 1 Pet. i. 23.

The *effect* of this agency of the Holy Spirit is "*a new creation*;" not the mere possibility of such a result, a something which may or may not occur, but really and actually "*a new creation*;" and this work unfolds itself in those graces, and in that holy obedience, which evince its *reality*, and, apart from which, where the *possibility* of such development exists, to suppose the new birth is most dangerous assumption.

7. The new birth of the Spirit is the true beginning of the divine life in the soul. It is, however, no *more* than its beginning. All growth in grace, all ripening in godliness, is but its necessary subsequent development. On this point, the Society holds, that *Sanctification is the believer's growth in holiness, and that it differs from Justification as truly as the fruit differs from the act of planting its seed;* in distinction from those who teach that Sanctification is merely Justification in progress, and that it makes, in connexion *with* Justification, one whole of inherent Righteousness.

The Church of Rome, and those among us who sympathize in her error, use language on this point which virtually confounds the two benefits of Justification and Sanctification; language which makes them practically one and the same thing, viz: a spiritual change wrought in the sinner himself, making him personally just and holy, and constituting that *inherent* righteousness, in consideration of which he obtains the favor of God. Thus, while professing to rely on the atonement of Christ, they, in fact, substitute another, and an altogether false ground of acceptance.

That Justification and Sanctification are intimately and inseparably allied is readily conceded. It cannot be otherwise; because *faith* is at once the instrument of the former and the root of the latter. Nevertheless, the two are distinguishable, and it is of the utmost importance to understand in what the distinction consists. The points of difference between them are various, and have an important bearing on the Christian life. These points may be thus briefly stated.

Justification, then, and Sanctification differ, 1st, in their *causes*. Justification comes by the Righteousness of *Christ;* Sanctification, by the agency of the *Holy Ghost*. 2d, in their *effects*. The effect of Justification consists in our external restoration to the favor of God, and the bestowment on us of a covenant title to eternal life; that of Sanctification, in the removal of our inbred corruption, and the renewal of the divine image in the soul. 3d, in their *locality*. Justification is an act of God, done amid the solemnities of His court in *Heaven;* Sanctification is a work of the Holy Spirit, wrought on the dispositions of our inner man on *earth*. 4th, in time and *degree*. Justification lies at the *beginning* of the Christian life, and, except in its consequences, does not extend beyond it, but is instantaneous and complete upon our first exercise of cordial faith; Sanctification begins where Justification ends, runs throughout the Christian life, and is partial and progressive, from measure to measure, until it reaches its perfection in glory. In short, Justification is God's act *for* us, through the righteousness of His *Son;* Sanctification is His work *in* us, by the power of His *Spirit.* The former is our *title* to Heaven; the latter is our *education* for Heaven. In the one God acts *alone;* in the other He brings us to co-operate *with* Him. To thrust ourselves *into* the former would rob God of His glory; to keep ourselves *out* of the latter would perpetuate our incapacity for bliss.

The principle of these distinctions, and the testimony of our Church in their favor, may be seen in her 11th and 12th Articles, and more largely in her two Books of Homilies. For our present purpose, however, a few passages from the Articles will suffice. In the 12th Article it is said: "Good works are the *fruits* of faith, and follow *after* Justification." In their full sense, "good works" are *Sanctification* itself; and it is evident that they cannot be the same with that of which they are *fruits;* nor the same with that after which they *follow.* It is also evident that they cannot be, in any sense, the meritorious *cause* of justification. No one of these things is possible, unless it be possible for *fruit* to be the same with its *root;* or for *consequent* to come before *antecedent;* or for *effect* to produce its *cause.* Again, the 11th Article speaks on this point in a very clear and decided tone. "We are justified by faith *only,*" or "are accounted righteous before God, *only* for the merit of our Lord Jesus Christ, by faith." This is sufficiently definite. But, not content with affirming the *Truth* on this point, the Article proceeds formally to repudiate its opposing *error,* by adding, "and *not* of our own *works* or *deservings.*" That is, *Sanctification* is no part of the ground, or consideration, on which we are *justified* before God. As such ground, or consideration, *Christ's* righteousness stands *perfect* and *alone. Ours* adds nothing to *His*, and takes no part in making up our title to glory: "*Only* for the merit of our Lord Jesus Christ, by faith." To this "doctrine, most wholesome and full of comfort," we adhere, against that whole mass of error with which Rome and her sympathizers would obscure and cover so vital a truth. For *Justification*, the truly enlightened Christian gives thanks and praise, as for something past, perfect, and complete. For *Sanctification*, he still longs and labors, as for something yet future, imperfect, and to be completed.

Such, then, are the distinctive principles of the Society on those main points, which are strictly *Doctrinal*, or belong to the department of *Christian Theology*. There are other theological truths, which we readily acknowledge to be common both to us and to those from whom we differ. But because they are thus common, it is not necessary that they should be particularized. It is enough to say that those, which have been stated, touch the very vitals of Christianity; and that, if they have been stated in conformity with the Truth, they sweep away, at a stroke, half of that vast aggregate of corruptions and of superstitions, with which past ages have overlaid the fabric and hidden the glory of the Gospel and the Church of God.

II. The Constitution of the Christian Church.

Having dwelt at sufficient length on the points of Christian Theology, we proceed, now, to exhibit our views on the Constitution of the Christian Church.

As, in the former department, then, we expressed our wish to be known as distinctively *evangelical*, so, in this, we would take our stand as distinctively *Protestant Episcopal.* In exhibiting our views of the Church, several distinct points will necessarily pass under review.

1. And first, *The Church itself.*

On this point, our Society holds, that *the Church is "The blessed company of all faithful people,"* or of all true believers in Jesus, abiding in communion with Christ, by a living faith. Of all and only such, does the Church, as "the Body of Christ," consist. This Church is made visible *to men* under the form of "Sacraments duly administered according to Christ's ordinance, in all those things that of necessity are requisite to the same." This we hold, in distinction from those who teach that the Church, as "the Body of Christ," is composed of all professing Christians, who are united together under a particular external ministry, to which exclusively is committed and confined the power of *making* and ministering the Sacraments.

The word, *Church*, it is well known, has various meanings, both in Sacred Scripture and in uninspired writings. It is here used in the sense intended in the Creed by the phrase, "*Holy Catholic Church.*" This is well described, and, for all practical purposes, sufficiently identified, in the language quoted from our Communion Service: "The blessed company of *all* faithful people;" and this description may be suitably amplified in the appropriate language of Dr. Barrow, in his "Discourse concerning the Unity of the Church." "The whole body of God's people that is, ever hath been, or ever shall be, from the beginning of the world to the consummation thereof, who, having (formally or virtually) believed in Christ, and sincerely obeyed God's law,—shall finally by the meritorious performance and suffering of Christ be saved, is called *The Church.*" Again: "This is that one Body into which we are all baptized by one Spirit; which is knit together and compacted of parts affording mutual aid and supply to its nourishment and increase; the members whereof do hold a mutual sympathy and complacence; which is joined to *One Head,* deriving sense and motion from it; which is enlivened and moved by *One Spirit.*"

In perfect keeping with this, and as a farther illustration of the Society's views, may be cited the following passage from "A Treatise on the Holy Catholic Faith and Church," by Dr. Thomas Jackson; whom even Tractarian writers characterize as one of "the best and greatest minds" which the English Church "has nurtured." Speaking of the Church in its Catholicism, he says: "This Church is a true and real Body, consisting of many parts, all really, though mystically and spiritually, united into One Head; and by their real union with one Head, are all truly and really united amongst themselves. The union is wrought between both by a power supernatural, superartificial, by a wisdom infinitely surmounting the highest reach of human policy. That this Church is a true Body, the Apostle, who in his lifetime was a true member of it, and, under Christ the Head, a chief master-builder for his skill, and yet withal, a most painful laborer in fashioning or squaring the parts or materials of this structure, hath left registered: 'I rejoice in my sufferings for you, and fill up that which is behind of the afflictions of Christ in my flesh for His Body's sake, which is The Church.'—Col. i., 24. Every one, then, is so far a member of Christ's Church as he is a member of Christ's Body. He that is not, in some sort, a member of Christ's Body, can be in no sort a member of His Church. He that is a true, live member of the one, is a true, live member of the other. He that is but an equivocal, analogical, hypocritical, or painted member of the one, is but an equivocal, analogical, hypocritical, or painted member of the other."

Indeed, it would be necessary to re-write the whole Bible, as well as the most important parts of English ecclesiastical literature, before that restricted view of the Church could be maintained, which limits this Body of Christ to those, who hold communion with one form only of an external ministry. So far as our Church is concerned, she recognizes, in her 19th Article, the Sacraments as connecting us with the Visible Church, in "those things only which are of *necessity* requisite to the same:" and she no where teaches that her own form of the ministry is among the *necessary* requisites to the administration of a Sacrament. In truth, she instructs us that there are cases, when a man, if he have *a true and lively faith*, may "eat and drink the body and blood of our Savior Christ profitably to his soul's health, although he do not receive the Sacrament with his mouth." (Rubric, Communion of the Sick.) The force of this language consists, not in depreciating the value of the outward form, but in showing that, after all, it is the inward faith which really incorporates into Christ.

2. The *Priesthood* of the Church.

On this point the Society holds that *Jesus Christ is the sole and immediate High Priest and Intercessor in behalf of every individual believer;* in distinction from those who teach that He has left a true and effective Priesthood upon earth, through the medium of which He must be approached and apprehended.

The ambiguity so often noticed of the term, *Priest*, in our language, has occasioned no little confusion; favoring thus the ends of those, who hold and have introduced into our Church, many serious errors. The word has a double signification. 1. It is a contraction of the word, *Presbyter*, and denotes simply a *minister* in the Christian Church. Such is its import *in all our Services.* 2. It is a translation of the Hebrew and Greek term, which denotes one duly authorized to offer *Sacrifices* and to make *Intercession.* Such were the *Priests* under the Law. In this sense, however, the term is *never*, in the Scriptures, applied to a minister of Christ. The Priests under the Law were typical of Christ and His work. When He appeared upon Earth and finished that which their office and their service signified, their typic Priesthood, having answered its end, ceased. Since that period, as there is but *One Sacrifice*, that which Christ "offered once for all," so there is but *One Priest*, Jesus, "who ever liveth to make intercession for us" in Heaven. And as, to attempt any *propitiatory Sacrifice*, other than that "One Offering of Christ," or to attempt any manner of iterating His Sacrifice, would be to deny its sufficiency, so, to constitute any *Priestly Intercessors*, other than that glorious one, who officiates in His own everliving person and presence before the throne, would be to reflect on His Intercession as inadequate to our needs; and thus doubly to dishonor his whole Mediatorial office and work.

Such, in effect, is that Sacerdotal System, which Rome has artfully matured, and which sympathizers with Rome in our Church attempt to imitate; a system, which practically fills the mind's vision with the *Church*, to the displacement or the concealment of *Christ;* allowing supplicants no direct access to Him, but confining their approach to the mediation of a human Priesthood, through rites of their own administration; as if the sincere and fervent prayers of the individual Christian, offered in the name of Christ, would not be accepted, but must needs pass through a sort of preparatory intervention!

In distinction from a system which thus robs Christ of His true prerogative and glory, and believers of their great privilege and comfort, the Society holds that we have but ONE Priest, the great, the true High Priest; that He officiates, not on earth, but in Heaven; that, nevertheless, by faith, he is present to all and each of His true disciples; and that, by the indwelling of His Spirit, He is building up all and each, as "living stones," into that glorious Temple, in which, when perfect, He will forever dwell. We have a Priest, not mortal but immortal; not atoning for himself, but unspottedly pure; not anointed with an earthly chrism, but hallowed by the unmeasured Spirit; not presenting earthly things, sacrifices bloody or unbloody, essentially poor and mean, but offering His own most precious Sacrifice, a thing of heavenly power and of exhaustless value; not of any earthly lineage or succession, nor clad in symbolic robes like those of Aaron, but of Divine generation, and ministering in the Heaven of heavens, and in his own essential holiness;—"a High Priest *forever* after the order of Melchisedec."

Our address and exhortation shall ever be in the animating spirit of the Apostle to the Hebrews:—"Seeing, then, that we have a great High Priest, that is passed into the Heavens, Jesus the Son of God, let us hold fast our profession; for we have not an High Priest which cannot be touched with the feeling of our infirmities; but was in all points tempted like as we are, yet without sin. Let us therefore come boldly to the throne of grace, that we may obtain mercy and find grace to help, in time of need."

3. The *Ministry* of the Church.

It has already been remarked, that we consider the term *Priest*, in all our services, as simply a contraction of the word *Presbyter*. As, therefore, except in this sense, we recognize no human *Priesthood* in the Church, we value the more justly the appointed *Ministry* of the Church. The true and only *Head* of this body being in Heaven, we prize the more highly the due and well-subordinated *servants* of the body on earth. On this point, the Society holds, that *The Ministry of the Church is Episcopal, as a reverent following of the Apostles, and needed for the best welfare of the Church;* in distinction from those who teach that it is Episcopal, as a mystic Sacrament from Christ, and necessary to the *existence* of the Church.

The preface to our Ordinal states: "It is evident to all men, diligently reading Holy Scripture and ancient authors, that, *from the Apostles' times*, there have been these orders of ministers in Christ's Church, Bishops, Priests, and Deacons." The wise moderation in which this is expressed is worthy of all praise. It teaches, that, on the point of the Ministry, our Church is organized in conformity with the Apostolical Model; and it implies, that such a Ministry is essential to the completeness of the Christian Church, and best adapted to the ends of the Gospel. But these views, while they furnish the strongest reason for maintaining our own polity in its fulness and integrity, and render adherence to it—unless under *sinful* terms of Communion—a matter of conscience, involve no necessity of denouncing those, who, on this point, differ from ourselves.

That Episcopacy is essential to the *being* of a Church, so that under *no* circumstances of exigency, can a Church *exist* without it; and that, therefore, all societies not in connexion with a Bishop episcopally consecrated, are no part of the Catholic Church; their ordinances being invalid, and their members with no hope of salvation, save in what are called "The uncovenanted mercies of God;" we do not hold and shall not teach. Where the fundamental truths of Christianity are held, Christ Jesus loved in sincerity, and the fruits of the Spirit plainly manifested; though we may lament a want of completeness in the Ministry, and pray and labor that the defect may be supplied, yet, we neither dare nor desire to say of such, that they are not of "The blessed company of all faithful people;" "members of the mystical Body of Christ," which is His Church. The late Bishop White over and again affirmed such to be the views of the Communion, of which he was so distinguished an ornament, and pronounced all beyond to be mere private opinion. In this, too, he but repeated what was before maintained by the learned Archbishops Usher and Wake, the judicious Hooker, and many other dignitaries of the Church of England.

It is only necessary, on this point, to add, that, while our views of the Church lead us to regard her Ministry as distinctively *Episcopal*, they also lead us to cleave to her position as no less distinctively *Protestant.*

Protestantism, it is true, is not an article of "the faith once delivered to the *Saints.*" In our view, however, it *is* an article of the *practice* now demanded of *Christians.* We long, as ardently as others, for the time, when the *whole* Church of Christ may rest together on the *one* base of *really* Catholic Truth. But, so long as the Church of Rome exists in her present character, as a vast body of usurpation and corruption, claiming to be, not only a Church, but *The* Church, exclusive and condemnatory of all other Churches, we shall be constrained, not only in many points of faith, to *differ* from her, but also, with unconceding distinctness of practice, to *protest* against her. As we deem it the chief glory of the Reformation that it has made our own Church *evangelical* in her *doctrine*, so we deem it but a secondary glory that it has made her *Protestant* in her *Episcopacy.* In all her ranks, she is bound to stand up, in word and act, *a living Protest* against the false claims and the fatal corruptions of that persecuting Hierarchy, from which God once granted her a safe, though a bloody separation.

4. The *Sacraments* of the Church.

To the Ministry appertain various functions. Besides those of preaching the Word, exercising discipline, and generally caring for the souls committed to its charge, is that of administering *the Sacraments* of the Church. On this point the Society holds, that *The Sacraments are divine signs and seals, pledges and means of grace, whereby Christ is continually set forth to His people's faith*;—in distinction from those who exalt them as mystic marvels and powers, sources and channels of grace; making them, instead of signs, the very grace which they signify; and instead of pledges, the very grace which they pledge; working by an intrinsic efficacy, independent of the faith of their recipients, and making Christ continually incarnate in his people's *humanity*.

"A Sign," says St. Augustine, "is a thing, which, besides the appearance which it presents to the senses, causes something else, different from itself, to come into the mind." Some signs have a *natural* significancy. Thus, smoke is a sign of fire; and paleness, of disease. Others have none but an *arbitrary* significancy: that is, they are signs only by positive appointment. Such were the rainbow, and the scarlet thread, mentioned in the Bible. When the Sacraments are called signs, it is not meant that they are such of their own *nature:* they are *made* signs by positive appointment. And yet, they are not without a certain suitableness, arising from some of their properties, to represent the things which they signify. They are, likewise, not merely *audible*, but also *visible* signs: and as they are appointed by the authority, not of *man*, but of *God*, they are, still further, *divine* signs.

Such signs are found both in the Old Testament and in the New:—in the former, Circumcision and the Passover; in the latter, Baptism and the Lord's Supper. The things signified,—Christ and all the benefits of his Death and Passion,—are the same under both dispensations; and hence St. Paul attributes the Sacraments of the Old Testament to believers under the New, and those of the New Testament to believers under the Old.—(1 Cor. v., 7; x. 1. 4; Col. ii. 11.)

We know not that there was any absolute necessity for Sacramental signs. God's Word, in which the identical things signified are taught in a variety of ways, certainly constituted an adequate representation. But, of His superabundant grace, He has, from the beginning, added to His Word the more impressive mode of exhibiting Divine Truth by affecting signs.

> "Segnius irritant animos demissa per aures
> Quam quæ sunt occulis subjecta fidelibus."—

——— Thus what is primarily communicated, by language, through the ear, is, secondarily presented, in the Sacraments, to the eye:—and it not unfrequently happens that "the *eye* affecteth the heart" when the *ear* has left it unmoved. In reference to this mode of teaching, and because of substantial identity in the things taught, some of the fathers called the Sacraments "Visible Words." The peculiar impressiveness, however, of this mode of teaching arises from the circumstance that it is addressed—not to *one* sense only, but to *several.* We are so constituted that what addresses itself simultaneously to various senses, affects us more powerfully than that which is offered to but *one.*

Being thus, by divine appointment, *Signs*, the Sacraments are still further, and by the same appointment, *Seals.* Under this aspect, their purpose will be understood by a reference to the common mode of *covenanting.* In this proceeding, the attestation, or ratification of the parties is effected by the annexing of their respective *Seals* to the writing, in which the covenant is expressed. In law, these seals are necessary to the full validity and binding effect of the engagement.

In the covenant of grace, the contracting parties are God and His believing people. The terms of this covenant are fully set forth in Holy Scripture : on God's part, the free gift of pardon, justification and eternal life ; and on the part of each believer, faith in His atoning Son and in the Word of Promise by Him, attested by practical obedience and true holiness of life.

Of this covenant, the Sacraments are the appropriate *Seals*, and they are of mutual action. Appointed by God's authority, they most strongly confirm the promises of His grace ; and received by the believer, they attest his reception of the offered benefits, and bind him to the rendering of the required performance.

It would, however, be wrong to suppose that these Seals were really needed to bind *God* to the performance of His promises. His Word, *in itself,* is sufficient, and needs no confirmation. The design of these Seals, therefore, has a gracious reference to *our* natural slowness of faith, weakness of purpose, and proneness to distrust. In this view, they are of peculiar value. To be able to realize that God has not only passed His Word, but also confirmed it by that, which has the force of an oath, "that, by two immutable things, in which it was impossible for God to lie, we might have strong consolation," leaves nothing to be desired or conceived by even such weak creatures as we are, by way of filling us with an assurance of God's favor and goodness towards us. And such, in the experience of those by whom they are rightly used, are the Sacraments, considered as Seals of the Covenant of grace.

Thus used, they have a still further effect. They are not only Signs and Seals, but also *Pledges*, of grace.

A *Pledge* is more than a Seal. It is an *earnest*, a *foretaste*. The Hebrew and Greek word, by which the idea is expressed, means, a part payment, by way of assurance that the whole amount stipulated, shall in due time be received. Thus, as Christians, we are said to be "*Sealed* by that holy Spirit of promise, which is the *earnest*," or pledge, "of our inheritance." The *sealing*, here mentioned, is the *effect*, or *fruit* of the Spirit; not any outward *sign* of that effect. So far, then, as the Sacraments are, as described in our Catechism, "*Pledges* to assure us" of the grace of Christ, they are so, not in their *outward forms* merely, but in those *inward fruits* of the Spirit, by which, in the experience of the true believer, they are accompanied. To such, these graces of the Spirit are "*first fruits*," *earnests*, an early instalment, giving the faithful Christian not only a sweet assurance, but also a witness in kind, of the blessedness which is in store for him.

That the Sacraments are also *means* of grace will not be questioned by any who seriously and intelligently receive them. How, and under what circumstances, they *become* such means is an inquiry, which has been variously answered. Some have supposed that, by the consecrating act of the *priest*, so called, they receive and possess an energy, by which they *impart* the grace signified; operating, when endowed with this marvelous power, after the manner of spiritual *causes*. Others have held that they become, by such consecrating act, *channels*, in which the signified grace is contained, and *through* which that grace is conveyed to the recipient. On both these theories, the efficacy of the Sacraments depends, not on the right dispositions of the recipient, but on the mysterious power, which resides in, or is conveyed through, the Sacraments themselves. All that is indispensable to their effect is that the recipient oppose no bar to their operation; in other words, that he be not living in positive unbelief, or in any deadly sin. The Sacraments themselves, by the act of consecration, are supposed to become instinct with mysterious activity, and to operate as a sort of mystic marvel or power, a kind of supernatural source or channel, of grace to the soul; the result of which is—*to make the Manhood of Christ incarnate, or incorporate, in the whole human nature of His members.* This effect is supposed to flow, not from the *material* substance itself of the Sacramental elements, but from the *Manhood*, or *Person* of Christ, which, by the act of Consecration, becomes the *Essence* of the Sacraments.

We find, in the Bible, nothing to authorize such views of the nature and effect of the Sacraments. But we do find that both the *faith* and the *repentance* of the recipient were required in order to *Baptism;* and that some of the early Christians were severely censured for conduct, in regard to the *Lord's Supper*, which implied that they were strangers to the dispositions proper to its right reception. They, who had not faith, or spiritual perception to "discern the Lord's Body," or to perceive the difference between a common meal and that religious feast, which symbolized the Body of Christ, "ate and drank damnation to themselves." Indeed, from the whole view of the subject, furnished by the Bible, it appears evident that the Sacraments have a wholesome and saving effect on those only, whose hearts God has previously prepared for their right reception. They are, equally with the *Word*, addressed to *faith*, and to the appropriate religious affections which *accompany* faith, and which show that the Holy Spirit has opened the understandings and renewed the hearts of their receivers. The *manner* in which grace is communicated, is evidently the same, whether in the Word, or in the Sacraments. Both are of Divine appointment. Both present to the mind the same Divine Truths. In both, these Truths are addressed to the understanding, the faith, and the affections: and the difference in the *measure* of effect produced by each, so far as there *is* a difference, seems to spring from the fact, that Truth in the *Word* is carried by the Spirit through the Ear, or through the Eye, used *alone;* while Truth in the *Sacraments* is carried by the Spirit through several senses, *simultaneously* used.

What is now said applies to the administration of the Word and the Sacraments to adult recipients of each. How the Holy Spirit operates, if He ever operate, on the soul of the unconscious Infant in Baptism, is not manifest. Some think that the faith of the *parents* stands in the place of the faith of the *child.* Others have held that the baptized *child itself* has, or may have, faith. Others, still, believe that the *prayer* of faith on the part of the Church avails, and is answered when the child comes to understand and feel the truths symbolized and sealed in its baptism. It is enough for us to deny that, in the baptism of infants, the spiritual grace of regeneration invariably accompanies the outward sign, and to confess that, both in Baptism and in the Lord's Supper, the Sacraments are divine *means* of grace; and that "in such only as worthily receive the same have they a wholesome effect, or operation;" being blessed by the Holy Spirit in his own way and time.

As to the alleged effect of the Sacraments in making the *manhood* of Christ incarnate, or incorporate, in the whole human nature of his members, we hold that the Bible, interpreted on sound principles, teaches no such notion. That there is a *union* between Christ and his members is a plain and precious truth of Inspiration. His indwelling in them is taught in express terms; and its intimacy and importance are illustrated by striking and beautiful imagery; such as that of the Vine and its branches; the Corner-Stone, and the temple which it supports; the Head, and the body which i informs. But, in this union, Christ is expressly said to "dwell in our hearts by *faith*," not by incarnation or incorporation. Intimate and vital as it is, this union is *spiritual* in its nature, being formed and furthered by the exercise of a lively *faith*. It is most appropriately symbolized in the Lord's Supper, which, while it is a commemoration of the Death of Christ and a sign and seal of the blessings thereby purchased, is also a representation of our union with Him; and, where *faith* is exercised, it is that union in *real* and *active* existence. But to suppose that this union, because *real*, amounts to an incarnation, or incorporation of the manhood of Christ in the whole human nature of his members, is to sensualize and degrade the relation. This union no more involves the incarnation of Christ in his members than the union of believers with one another involves their *mutual* incarnation. In both cases, the union is real and spiritual, and of both the Lord's Supper is a simple and most significant visible representation. The doctrine of the continual incarnation of Christ in his members involves the *essence* of the absurd dogma of the Transubstantiation of the Elements in the Sacraments.

5. The Worship of the Church.

This is her stated incense of prayer and of praise; and on this point, the Society holds, that, in order to the highest edification, *Public Worship should be Liturgical, simple and Scriptural;* in distinction from those, who would cumber it with human inventions, superstitious forms, and corrupting ceremonies.

Without saying that our Liturgy is *faultless*, we freely confess that we have yet to discover anything which so fully commends itself to our judgment, taste, and religious affections. Some are satisfied with modes of public worship, which to us appear even too severely simple; while others, in their craving for the sensuous and the showy, have cumbered their ritual with a weight of inappropriate and often puerile ceremonies. Many of these, too, however attractive to the natural man, are unedifying to the renewed mind, inconsistent with the genius of Christianity, and corrupting to the Gospel of Christ. Our Reformers, guided by a spirit of piety and of wisdom, which peculiarly qualified them for their great work, happily avoided both extremes. They have transmitted to us a Liturgy sober, solemn, devotional, and rich in Scriptural truth; sufficiently simple for children in Christ, yet full and lofty enough for those who have attained the mental and spiritual maturity of advanced Christians. These appropriate services we love too well, willingly to see them disfigured and travestied by association with a system of symbolic attitudes, and of manifold manipulations, borrowed and brought back upon us from that corrupt Communion, which our fathers so righteously and resolutely renounced. Nor are we willing that our Scriptural Liturgy, so suited to the best religious instruction, should be degraded by sharing its office in this particular, with divers material fixtures and arrangements, both within and without the Sanctuary; constituting collectively what has been reverently termed "a holy teaching architecture." It would be quite as sensible and as commendable to attempt the use, in connexion with our modern art of Printing, of the dark Hieroglyphics of an early age, invented to lock up knowledge in the breast of Pagan priests, or to impart it with a painful slowness to the untaught multitude; as it is to think of reintroducing the shadowy symbolism of former days in connexion with the use of our plainly teaching Liturgy, now that books and schools, pastors and teachers, are engaged in communicating to even the *commonest* minds, and with such admirable facility, despatch, and efficiency, the grand, but simple truths of our religion. And this would be saying *enough*, if that symbolism taught nothing but these truths. When, however, we find it constructed on the principle of teaching what we regard as dangerous *corruptions* of these truths, we must say, still further, that the attempt to re-introduce it in connexion with the use of our Liturgy, is not merely absurd, but, in an awful degree, mischievous. Such childish, yet deep studied expedients, which not only imply the inadequacy of incomparably better modes of teaching, but, in many instances, tend to insinuate pestilential doctrinal errors, will find no countenance in the publications and influence of this Society. We regard them as both *causes* and *symptoms* of a spiritual corruption, to defend the Church from which no labors and no sacrifices can be too great. Experience, historical and living, shows that, where this system of symbolism prevails, and, in proportion to its prevalence, its allied errors exist, or will make their way: "A Priesthood, itself Sacramental, and conveying grace by right, and salvation to souls as a dependency to office; the very houses of God, instead of possessing that *relative* sanctity, which alone befits them, and no more, will become Sacramental too: grace will be limited by walls; the Divine presence, localized; and that holiness transferred to carved wood and sculptured stone, which only belongs to the living temples of the Holy Ghost. Men will reckon with Almighty God, and pay for forgiveness by the *satisfaction* and *atoning* power of mortification and bodily discipline: all will look *out*wardly instead of inwardly; and, as *one* Sacrament admitted them, by the mere power of the consecrating act, into the Church, and made them children of God, so outward services and a *material* Church will sustain them through life, and *another* Sacrament, equally outward, will seal their peace, and be their *Viaticum* to Heaven and their title to the inheritance of the saints in light." (Garbett's Bampton Lectures, vol. i, p. 251—2.) Then the avowed purpose of certain Tractarian agitators, more intelligent and more audacious than many whom they mislead, will be accomplished; our Reformed Church will, indeed, be "un-protestantized," and will need but the *formality* of a reconciliation with Rome. Then, the false brethren, now, we hope, comparatively few, who are, in some instances, driven by force of circumstances, to separate from those whom they are beguiling, would possess the power at which they aim; and it would remain for us and our children either to conform to their corruptions, or to suffer, as their tender mercies might dictate, *for conscience' sake.* As we have no desire to contend with such results, we are determined neither to overlook the *tendencies* to them, nor to leave these tendencies unresisted. Enough has already occurred, and more is daily occurring, to rouse us to energetic action in defence of our most holy faith. We yield to the exigencies of the occasion, and give ourselves, without faltering, to the solemn work, to which God in His Providence has called us.

Having thus plainly stated the distinctive principles of our Society, we have only to add, in language used on another occasion, "Our invitation is to all those, who for substance of faith and practice, agree in the stand which we have defined. We seek the prayers, the sympathy, and the co-operation of all, who feel bound of God in their consciences to perpetuate the truly Evangelical faith and the really Protestant character of the Church of our fathers. We would apply the principle of a freely acting spiritual affinity, one of the main principles, in the hand of God, for keeping alive in the world true faith, love, and holiness. Surround us, then, in our Sacred Association, with the living atmosphere of your prayers; strengthen us, in our arduous work, by the willing contribution of your means; and thus, for the sake of Him who has our vows, aid us to keep burning on earth, and to spread brightening through the world, the lights of a pure faith in a purified Church."

CONSTITUTION

OF THE

PROTESTANT EPISCOPAL SOCIETY FOR THE PROMOTION OF EVANGELICAL KNOWLEDGE.

ARTICLE I. This Society shall be denominated the Protestant Episcopal Society for the Promotion of Evangelical Knowledge.

ART. II. The object of the Society shall be, to maintain and set forth the principles and doctrines of the Gospel embodied in the Articles, Liturgy, and Homilies of the Protestant Episcopal Church, by the publication of Tracts, Sunday School and other books.

ART. III. Any person approving the objects of this Society may become a member of the same by the annual contribution of one dollar. Any person, by paying fifty dollars at one time, shall be a member for life.

ART. IV. This Society shall meet triennially at the time and place of meeting of the General Convention, and shall at each triennial meeting, elect a President, Vice Presidents, Secretary, Treasurer, and a Board of Directors, and also transact such other business as may be brought before it. At every triennial meeting the transactions of the preceding three years shall be reported.

ART. V. The Bishops of the Protestant Episcopal Church in the United States, who may signify their approval of the objects of this Society, shall be *ex-officio* Vice Presidents of the same, and members of the Board of Directors.

ART. VI. The Board of Directors shall meet annually, at such time and place as themselves shall appoint, and elect an Executive Committee, which shall consist of four clerical and four lay members, upon which Committee shall devolve all the powers of the Board during its recess. The Board shall enact By-laws; and twelve members, at any meeting regularly convened, shall constitute a quorum for the transaction of business.

ART. VII. Any association formed on the principles of this Society, and annually contributing to its treasury, shall be considered an auxiliary, and the President and Secretary, for the time being, of said auxiliary, shall be *ex-officio* members of the Board of Directors.

ART. VIII. All meetings of the Board of Directors, and of the Executive Committee, shall be opened with prayer.

ART. IX. This Constitution shall not be altered except at a triennial meeting, and by a vote of two-thirds of the members present.

Officers of the Society.

President.

Rt. Rev. WILLIAM MEADE, D. D., Virginia.

Vice Presidents.

(See Article V. of the Constitution.)

Secretary.

Rev. WILLIAM SUDDARDS, Philadelphia.

Treasurer.

FREDERICK T. PEET, New-York.

Directors.

(The Board consists of ninety-seven Clergymen and Laymen, and the Bishops who approve of the objects of the Society.)

Executive Committee.

Rev. B. C. CUTLER, D. D.
Rev. L. P. W. BALCH, D. D.
Rev. H. ANTHON, D. D.
Rev. G. T. BEDELL,

Messrs. F. S. WINSTON,
LUTHER BRADISH,
GEORGE N. TITUS,
STEWART BROWN.

General Secretary and Editor.

Rev. JOHN S. STONE, D. D., 22 John street, New-York.

General Depository—22 John street, New-York.

F. G. FISH, *General Agent.*

Auxiliary Societies.

Massachusetts (Depository at Boston); New-York and its vicinity; Western New-York (Depository at Rochester); Pennsylvania (Depositories 178 and 193 Chestnut street, Philadelphia); St. Andrew's Church, Wilmington, Del.; Maryland; Georgetown, Md. (Depository); All Saints' Parish, Fredericktown, Md.; Virginia (employing a Colporteur); South Carolina (Depository at Charleston); Louisiana (Depository at New-Orleans); Cincinnati (Depository); Gambier, O.; Louisville, Ky.; St. Louis, Mo.

☞ *Persons addressing the Society will please add "22 John street."*

VITAL TRUTH

AND

DEADLY ERROR.

"I marvel that ye are so soon removed from Him that called you into the grace of Christ unto ANOTHER GOSPEL: WHICH IS NOT ANOTHER; but there be some that trouble you, and would pervert the Gospel of Christ." GAL. i, 6, 7.

"To be IMPUTED and to be INHERENT differs no less than God and man, Trent and Heaven." BP. HALL.

CINCINNATI:
H. W. DERBY & CO, PUBLISHERS.
1853.

CINCINNATI:
C. A. MORGAN & CO., STEREOTYPERS,
HAMMOND ST.

TO

ALL THE PEOPLE OF CHRIST,

AND ESPECIALLY

TO MY BRETHREN OF THE PROTESTANT EPISCOPAL CHURCH,

This humble Contribution

TO THE

MANIFESTATION OF THE TRUTH AS IT IS IN JESUS,

IS AFFECTIONATELY INSCRIBED.

VITAL TRUTH AND DEADLY ERROR.

SECTION I.

INTRODUCTORY REMARKS.

If man be indeed a depraved being, it might be anticipated that nothing could pass through his hands without risk of perversion. This expectation has been confirmed by experience. The history of the Church is as much occupied with the relation of heresies within, as of persecutions without. And the past history and present aspect of Christendom alike declare that the "name" of heresy is "Legion," and that there is no one doctrine in the whole circumference of Christianity which may not be the point of departure at a tangent from the system of revelation. All such perversions, however, like the doctrines themselves, may be embraced in two classes, those relating to God and those relating to man. Error in doctrines of the former class produces a change in the *body* of the Scripture system, and is at once apparent as a different system. Error in those of the latter is a departure from its *vital spirit*, and may lie hid under the *same body and substance*, an unseen and unexpected decay; and hence is the more dangerous of the two. Yet such is their mutual connection, that what begins with error respecting man and the application to him of what is recorded

Religious error two-fold.

of God, tends ever on to a perversion also of the doctrine concerning God. The violation of the *spirit* of the Gospel leads on to a change in its *substance;* and *secret error*, if uncounteracted, becomes at last *open heresy.* It is against these *inward diseases* that the Church of God needs to be most diligently warned; not only because of their dangerous secrecy, but because it is here that the innate corruption of the human heart has its spontaneous development. Left to itself, it breeds error here as surely as dead flesh breeds corruption. Heresies respecting God are of a different origin. When not the ultimate result of these inward decays *sloughing off* some of the outward members, they arise from some impulse given to the intellect by outward circumstances, such as the force of a heathen education or the mutual repulsion of theological controversy.

Error stereotyped. As these errors respecting the doctrine of man and his relation to God are the spontaneous growth of the human heart, it is natural to expect, and we actually discover, a fundamental identity in the errors of successive generations. Indeed, we find *just two species of error* perpetually recurring, under aspects somewhat modified, it is true, by the circumstances of their birth, but always recognizable. Both originate in the self-righteousness of the heart; but one takes the form of *unbelief*, the other the form of *superstition.* Under the Jewish dispensation they were represented in the Sadducees and Pharisees. Paul opposed them under the names of "Greeks" and "Jews." And so, through various names and stages of development, we may trace them down to the present time. They often exist when least suspected. We may ourselves be running into them unawares.

It is therefore proposed here to sketch these errors in their present aspect, to place them in contrast with 'the truth as it is in Jesus,' and, without going into any argument on their respective merits, leave it to be *felt* by every reader, which is in accordance with the word of God; after which it is proposed to note the precise point of divergence from the truth, and exhibit the tendency of each to changes in the very substance of divine revelation. It is not supposed necessary to give references for all the quotations which may be made in the prosecution of this plan, as the design is not to fasten the imputation of error upon individuals, but clearly to set forth existing systems of belief. It may be premised, however, that the quotations are entirely from writers of standing in either the Protestant Episcopal Church of this country or the mother Church of England. Plan of the essay.

SECTION II.

TRUE SYSTEM OF THE GOSPEL STATED.

Before proceeding to the exhibition of these erroneous systems, let us get a clear view of that system which the apostle Paul has called '*the gospel of Christ*,' as distinguished from 'another gospel.'

They have, of course, much in common. The doctrines of a Trinity of persons in the one God, and of the Incarnation, the vicarious Death, and the Mediatorial Reign of the Eternal Son, lie at the foundation, and form a part of each of these systems. The same, indeed, may be said of the doctrines of Natural Religion. How far all agree.

True view of man's nature. 'The Gospel of Christ' declares man to be in a state of ruin—ruin both as to his destiny in the future and his moral condition in the present. For his own actual transgressions he is lost, under the eternal condemnation of Him who has said, 'The soul that sinneth, it shall die.' Moreover, his nature is corrupt. It was born corrupt; as a descendant of Adam he has inherited his fallen nature, a nature as sure to develope into evil as the acorn to germinate into the oak. His "original sin standeth not in the *following* of Adam;" it is "the fault and corruption of his nature," "whereby he is very far gone from original righteousness, and is of his own nature inclined to evil, so that the *flesh lusteth always contrary to the Spirit.*"* His "condition is such that he cannot turn and prepare himself of his own natural strength and good works to faith and calling upon God."† Yea, so entirely has he fallen, that he is "of his own nature, fleshly and carnal, corrupt and naught, sinful and disobedient to God, without any spark of goodness in him, without any virtuous or godly motion, only given to wicked thoughts and evil deeds."‡

What he needs and how provided. Such being man's condition, he needs both a ransom from condemnation and a cleansing from corruption. God has found him the ransom in the blood of His own Son; incarnate, that He might be our surety, suffering under the load of our sin, dying as the victim of our disobedience, and rising from the dead that He might 'lead captivity captive,' and 'receive gifts for men.' The cleansing is accomplished by the operation of God the Holy Ghost upon the sinner's

---

* Art. IX. † Art. X. ‡ Homily for Whitsunday.

heart, turning him from sin to holiness by making him a new creature in Christ Jesus. Both these blessings, the ransom and the cleansing, come to him as the free and sovereign mercy of the God he has offended. They are a divine gift to man, unpurchased and undeserved. The tidings that God is thus reconciled to man by the death of His own Son, and ready to take away the enmity of our carnal hearts by the Spirit of His grace; that He is willing thus to restore us, pardoned and renewed, to our forfeited inheritance of 'life and immortality,' are those 'good news from a far country' which entitle Christianity to its distinguishing name of GOSPEL (*good spell*,) and make it indeed 'glad tidings of great joy' to perishing man. These tidings it is which the Christian ministry has been commissioned to 'preach to every creature.'

The name Gospel, *evangelium.*

But Christ's work for the sinner does not save mankind in the gross, but by individual application. How then is that life-giving application to be made by which the sinner gains an interest in his Saviour? The sins of men were 'laid upon' Christ, or so reckoned as his that He bore the penalty which was due. He took the sinner's place, and was dealt with as though He were Himself the transgressor. So, in return, are the merits of His sufferings and righteousness laid upon the sinner, or so reckoned as his that he reaps their reward. He appears in judgment represented through Christ. The acceptance with God and the title to eternal life earned by his surety are passed over unto him. He is "*accounted righteous* before God." The availing cause of his being thus "accounted" is "only the merit of our

The work of Christ how applied.

Lord and Saviour Jesus Christ."* The instrumental medium of its imputation is "Faith," "the only *ordained mean* and *instrument* by which we thus receive, apprehend" and "apply to ourselves the fruits and merits of Christ's death."† Do we ask why? Because faith, (says Bp. Horsley,) "is the *first principle* of that communion between the believer and the Divine Spirit, on which the whole of our spiritual life depends." Is it further asked, What is here meant by faith? We reply: "The right and true Christian faith, is not only to believe that holy Scripture, and all the foresaid articles of our faith, are true; but also to have a *sure trust and confidence in God's merciful promises to be saved from everlasting damnation by Christ.*"‡ "And yet that faith doth not shut out repentance, hope, love, dread, and the fear of God, to be joined with faith in every man that is justified; *but it shutteth them out from the office of justifying.* So that although they be all present together in him that is justified, yet they justify not altogether."‡

The nature of saving faith.

How acquired.

To this "faith" man "cannot turn and prepare himself by his own natural strength and good works."§ 'It is the gift of God.' God the Holy Ghost must apply unto us the work which God the Son hath wrought. The one hath done all *for* us; the other does all *in* us. We must 'be born of the Spirit!' That great change from death to life, the regeneration, conversion, or new birth of the soul, is by the power of the Holy Ghost, operating on the soul according to the laws of its own being—the action of mind on mind—the Infinite on the finite. However it may be with a soul undeveloped,

* Art. XI. † Homily on the Passion. ‡ Hom. on Salvation. § Art. X.

the operation of the Spirit of God on a mind matured accords with the prayer of Jesus, 'sanctify them through thy truth: thy word is truth.'* We are 'born again by the word of God, which liveth and abideth forever.'† Hence the Christian ministry was 'sent to preach'—to proclaim truth, and that truth 'the Gospel.'‡ Hence also the Spirit, invisible in essence as 'the wind blowing where it listeth,'§ can be recognized only in the effects of divine truth upon the mind: as it happened in the case of Cornelius and his company, 'while Peter yet spake these words, the Holy Ghost fell on all them who heard the word.'||

Truth's order and the soul's experience.

The doctrines of the cross are the instrument of the Spirit for the soul's conversion. 'The preaching of the cross is the power of God.'¶ Yet the unawakened sinner esteems it 'foolishness.' He rejects the salvation because he feels not the danger. 'The law is the schoolmaster to lead' such an one 'to Christ.'** It must go before the Gospel to the individual sinner, as it did to the world, to cry with trumpet tongue in the wilderness of sin, 'prepare ye the way of the Lord, make his paths straight,' before 'the crooked' can 'be made straight,' 'and the rough' 'be made smooth,' and the blind soul 'see' and receive 'the salvation of God.' It must shine on the opened eye in unattainable glory as a rule of life. It must thunder in the startled ear its curse upon transgression. The crystal battlements of Heaven's holiness and the smoking furnaces of Hell's retribution confront the awakened soul. The heights of the former it cannot climb; the dread alternative of the

The Law.

* John xvii, 17. † 1 Pet. i, 23. ‡ 1 Cor. i, 17. § John iii, 8
|| Acts x, 44. ¶ 1 Cor. i, 18. ** Gal. iii, 24.

latter it cannot shun. Then 'by the law comes the knowledge of sin.'* The extremity of his guilt, the certainty of his condemnation, are alike unveiled. The proud rebel is crushed like a worm; the haughty despiser of mercy now cries in alarm, 'what must I do to be saved?' Now Sinai's thunders have done their work; The Gospel. a ministry of love must follow. The sinner, fleeing 'the wrath to come,' is led by the Spirit unto Calvary; he sees a cross upreared, and there hangs on it *his Saviour.* 'Tis there his sins are laid; and love and justice speak with mingled voices from that sacred tree. He sees a love which revives his hopes; he beholds a justice which quickens his sense of guilt. The very sight which cheers him humbles him; and while it conveys a hope of pardon, reveals more fully his desert of condemnation. He is destroyed, yet quickened; he dies, and yet he lives—dies in himself, lives in Christ. He is 'dead, and his life is hid with Christ in God.'† In himself he is all ruin; in Christ he has life and peace.

New feelings. As the Holy Spirit preaches this 'Gospel of salvation' to the despairing sinner, the new life divinely inwrought into his being begins to appear. As the child of nature comes into the world a weeping babe, so he draws his first spiritual breath amid the tears of repentance. His strong convictions of sin settle down into sighs of contrition, and the terrors of condemnation are lost in a deep sense of moral defilement. The same accents of mercy which assuage his alarm deepen his sorrow. 'The *goodness* of God leadeth him to repentance.'‡ 'Cast down, yet not destroyed,' he makes his humble supplication for pardon, and cries out with the Publican,

---

* Rom. iii, 20. † Col. iii, 3. ‡ Rom. ii, 4.

'God be merciful to me, a sinner!' 'CHRIST CRUCIFIED' arrests his eye. How glorious, how divine a Redeemer! 'Full of grace and truth.' 'The Lord our righteousness.' 'Tis all for him. He gazes; he listens; he believes. On that dear head he lays his sin; *his* for judgment no more. All God's promises of mercy to those who believe in his Son he believes. In that Son, as one able and willing to save, he also believes. And conscious that he has experienced the faith, he believes that he has received the forgiveness and adoption which were promised. Faith in God's word conducts him to Christ. Faith in Christ appropriates the merits of His work; and faith in God's word, again, assures him that his own name is now 'written in the Lamb's Book of Life.' But he has other evidence than this. By faith the Spirit has united him to Christ, and by this union he is not only justified, but born again. 'The last Adam is a quickening spirit.' While he knows, by faith in God's word, that he has passed from condemnation to acceptance, he knows by experience, that he has 'passed out of darkness into marvellous light.' A mighty transformation has been wrought within him. His eyes discern spiritual things. His heart loves them. Satan's slave is free. The lover of sin now flies her embrace. The man 'without God in the world' rejoices in God as the center and sun of his being. 'Old things are passed away; behold, all things are become new.' He is 'a new creation in Christ Jesus.'* The dawning consciousness of these things ushers in a bright and blessed morning on the soul, till now in midnight

*2 Cor. v, 17.

gloom. A peace, tranquil as the Sabbath morn, sheds its serene influence over the mind. A hope glowing with anticipations of heaven lights up his path. The joys of a conscious reconciliation and sonship to God tune heart and voice to thankful praise. With self-distrusting but resolute spirit, the new-born soul starts forward on its course of obedience to God.

Confession of Christ.

His first desire is to confess Christ before the world in the sacraments which He has ordained for that purpose. He exclaims with the eunuch, 'See, here is water: what doth hinder me to be baptized?' With public vows to God, and faith in the mercy pledged by the rite, he receives the seal of the covenant, and with "faith confirmed and grace increased by virtue of prayer to God,"* like the eunuch, he goes 'on his way rejoicing.' Weak and empty, he has found one who 'filleth the hungry with good things,'† and out 'of his fullness' does he 'receive grace for grace.'‡ Faith working in him, and the spirit of God, by his faith, 'worketh by love,' 'purifieth the heart,' and 'overcometh the world.' All duties become delights, all ordinances means of grace; and, looking ever unto that Lord, of the memorials of whose dying love he rejoices to partake, to be 'the Finisher,' as he has been 'the Author,' of his faith, 'with open face beholding, as in a glass, the glory of the Lord, he is changed into the same image, from glory to glory, even as by the spirit of the Lord.'§ Thus are all the people of Christ 'builded together for an habitation of God through the Spirit.'‖ Thus they become 'strength-

---

* Art. XXVII. † Luke i, 53. ‡ John i, 16.
§ 2 Cor. iii, 18. ‖ Eph. ii, 22.

ened with might by his Spirit in the inner man, Christ dwelling in their hearts by faith;' they rise above the region of doubt, overcome their fears, grow 'rooted and grounded in love,' and are increasingly 'filled with all the fulness of God,'* till they pass from grace to glory, and 'see face to face, and know even as also they are known.'†

Characteristics.

The whole design and tendency of this system is to "exalt the Savior, humble the sinner, and promote holiness." It strips all pretence of merit or strength from man, and makes salvation 'the free gift' of God. It leaves man no ground of boasting, no room to glory. 'Christ is all, and in all,'‡ the 'alpha and omega, the beginning and the end.'§ This is, indeed, 'the Gospel of the grace of God,' joyful tidings of his free mercy to sinners. It says, in every part, 'By grace are ye saved through faith, and that not of yourselves; it is the gift of God: not of works, lest any man should boast.'‖

SECTION III.

A LEGAL CHRISTIANITY EXPOSED.

How made.

The first system which I would place in contrast with that Gospel of Christ, which has now been exhibited, may be described as a *legalized Christianity*—a hybrid religion, resulting from a confounding of the two dispensations, combining the *promises* of

---

* Eph. iii, 16–19. † 1 Cor. XIII, 12 ‡ Col. iii, 11.
§ Rev. i, 8. ‖ Eph. ii, 8, 9.

the Gospel, as a dispensation designed for fallen beings, with the *terms of acceptance* which obtained under the law, as a dispensation adapted to holy beings. The general character of this scheme may be more distinctly set forth by two statements, which Bishop Horsley says had passed into maxims with the clergy of his day: "That it is more the office of a Christian teacher to *press the practice* of religion upon the consciences of his hearers than to inculcate and assert its doctrines;" and "that *practical religion and morality are one and the same thing;* that *moral duties* constitute the whole, or by far the better part, of *practical Christianity.*"* The same general view of the nature of the Christian dispensation has thus been more fully expressed by one of its advocates: "As the corruptions with which the Gospel has been intermingled, by the fraud of some and the ignorance of others, shall be purged away, Christianity will become again, as it was at the beginning, *nothing more than a rule of life.* The practice of its duties will be the test of faith, the standard of interest, and *the only condition on the performance of which immortality will be expected.*" The benefits which, according to this view, the believer receives from Christ, have been declared to be, "Redemption from a state of certain condemnation and restoration to a state of possible salvation, together with a gracious provision of assistance to make that salvation sure." "But whether this state of possible salvation through Christ may become a state of actual salvation to the believing party, must depend upon the

General character.

Salvation by works.

Bishop Horsely's Charge, 1790.

use made of the means vouchsafed for that purpose." These means are further defined in the declaration that "*obedience to the moral law*" is "*necessary to bring fallen man into a state of acceptance with God*, by qualifying him for the salvation which has been purchased." Hence, all the benefit a believer gets from Christ is to be "*put into a way* of being eternally happy, *if all things go on well*."

Baptism the foundation.

The foundation of the soul's interest in Christ, according to this system, is laid in baptism. "If there have been subjection to this in infancy, it was then the party began to be recognized, in the eye not of man only, but of God, as a Christian." "In baptism, duly performed on the suitable subjects of it, these become the subjects of Christ's spiritual kingdom, *in the most ample sense of the expression*." In that ordinance, "divine favor is assured for the present, and divine aid pledged for the future." *If the aid be unimproved, there ensues a fall from grace*." According to this view, baptism really *amounts to justification*. And indeed, some of this school have not hesitated to call "the admission into Christianity our first justification;" to declare "the word justification *synonymous* to baptism," and that it "belongs to all professed Christians without exception." By baptism, then, all are brought into acceptance with God, and it depends upon themselves whether they continue therein, or "fall from grace." In that rite also occurs the change which gives corrupt nature the ability to maintain acceptance with God; and all that is necessary is to develope by education what was then given. Hence we are told, that "young persons therein made 'members of Christ, children of God, and inher-

Development of the baptismal germ.

itors of the kingdom of heaven,' if, in consequence of a religious education, and religious impressions made on their minds, they do not *fall into what may be called a state of sin*, *need nothing* that comes under the idea of a *subsequent conversion*;" and a rebuke is given to what is called "the error of those who instruct baptized persons leading virtuous lives, and not neglecting the exercises of devotion, that there remains for them the necessity of a regeneration, until which they are the children of the devil, and liable to the judgment of God in another life." If, indeed, there should unhappily be "a fall from this state, it can only be recovered by repentance."

Repentance seldom needed.

But if there should not be such a fall, which is contemplated, not only as a possible, but as a frequent event, all repentance, or, at any rate, all deep humiliation, all searching sorrow for sin, all but some general sense and acknowledgment of frailty, would seem to be excluded; for there is this objection made to the system here exhibited as the true Gospel, that "in the educating (according to it) of baptized infants, until of an age susceptible of conversion, it is difficult to conceive in what way they are consistently to be trained up to the worship of God. The only prayers suited to them," (if their regeneration in baptism be denied,) "are those in harmony with 'God be merciful to me a sinner.' It is otherwise on the ground here taken." This, then, is a *fatal objection*, in the view of those who hold a legalized Christianity! We have been accustomed to regard this prayer as one that the Christian should daily offer, even to the end of his pilgrimage. But "it is otherwise on the ground here taken." God help us, if the anguished heart and trembling lips of the tempted Christian, who finds this the only suitable expression of his wants, cannot "consistently" engage in "the worship of God!" "Justification," we are told further, whether begun in infant baptism or obtained in later years, "is supposed variable, sometimes increasing, sometimes decreasing." To be 'justified by faith' is variously explained. The general notion of faith, as concerned in our justification, is an assent to the truth of Christianity. According to some, it is "an allowance that Jesus is the Messiah." According to others, "'faith only' means an *honest principle;*" or "obedience to the whole religion of Christ, including both belief and practice;" or "the complex of all Christianity;" or "faith in the *concrete*," "faith as comprehensive of all Christian duties." And this faith justifies, not because it unites us to Christ, or is the instrument through which we apply His merits to ourselves, or complies with "the precept of relying on Christ's merit for justification;" but because it "*implies true holiness in the nature of it*," because it *includes* "the other evangelical graces," or because, "like love and repentance, it is a fundamental cause of obedience." "It saves us no otherwise," it is declared, "than by being a spring and principle of our obedience." And this view of faith is accompanied by a strong repugnance to the use of the expression, justification by faith, and a strong disposition to enforce "the necessity of *recommending ourselves* to the mercy of God, and *rendering ourselves worthy* of the mediation of Jesus Christ by holiness of living, and by an abhorrence of vice." And a zeal against the supposed antinomian tendencies of the doctrine of justification by faith leads the advo-

Justification not permanent.

Notions of faith.

cates of this view to speak much of "good works as the condition of salvation," as "not merely effects, but *coefficient conditions* with faith;" to group all together in the declaration that "faith, repentance, and good works, through the operation of the Spirit, are the conditions upon which God engages to vouchsafe justification;" and even, forcing James into an unnatural opposition to Paul, to affirm that "a man is said to be *justified by works*, because good works are *the condition*, according to the divine appointment, established in the Gospel covenant as requisite and necessary to his justification; that is, to his obtaining remission of sins through Christ, and acceptance into the divine favor."

Works bro't in.

Evidences.

The evidences by which, upon this scheme, a man is to test his hopes of salvation, are of a corresponding character. It has a decided repugnance to "what are called experiences" in religion, as wanting in soberness of mind, and tending to spiritual pride. "We make no scrutiny into them," says one, but "require such evidence as may be the result of *profession and conduct.*" Accordingly, a *serious desire* of the Christian ordinances is esteemed sufficient warrant for the applicant's admission; and the works of his life, to the rejection of any experience and consciousness of his soul, are made the criteria of his condition, to the Christian himself, as well as to others.

Such is the scheme of a legalized Christianity. It is what an inspired apostle would call, "Another Gospel, which is not another." "Another," for it is fundamentally diverse from "the Gospel of Christ;" yet "not another" *Gospel;* for it is *no Gospel.* 'The glad tidings of great joy' to burdened sinners have disappeared, and they are left, poor guilty creatures as they are, to '*work out their own salvation with fear and trembling,' as best they can.*

SECTION IV.

A CEREMONIALIZED CHRISTIANITY UNVEILED.

THE second scheme to be contrasted with 'the Gospel of Christ' is a vastly more ingenious and complicated system, and far better fitted to impose upon an awakened soul. It may be described as a *ceremonialized Christianity*, a system which elevates the outward and prescriptive in religion above the inward and spiritual, by making it the indispensable and invariable means to its attainment.

Union with Christ through the Church, the fundamental principle.

The fundamental principle of this system is thus stated: "Since it is *by aggregation to the body of the faithful that we become members of Christ*, therefore our personal blessedness is the *result of that family union*, which gives us a share in its collective rights."* "Our union with the manhood of Christ, or our participation in His presence, is brought about in our union with the Church, which is His body mystical;"† so that "all the ordinances of the Church, its hallowed things, places and persons—its worship and sacraments—are a series of instruments whereby the sanctified manhood of the Mediator diffuses itself as a life-giving seed through the mass of hu-

* Wilberforce on the Incarnation, p. 350. † Ib. p. 243.

manity:"* with this radical distinction, however, that "sacraments differ from all other means of grace in that, whereas other things *result from* union with Christ, *they*, on the contrary, *conduct to it*."† In answer, then, to the question, "How can God's image be created anew in the soul?" it is said, "If man had never fallen, it had been sufficient to inherit it: fallen as he is, there must be the gift of a new life." "This new life had its commencement in the fact of the Incarnation." "Out of this beginning arises the whole system of this Christian life. And this heavenly influence is extended to us in

Baptism.

baptism." "The basis of our spiritual growth is to be laid in it."‡ "The soul's regeneration, like the body's growth, is a protracted process, which the whole of life is not too long to complete. But . . . in that holy rite this process is begun. For there are men joined by heavenly agency to Christ, that the life of their souls may from that day forth have its development."§ A further "development" takes place in *con-*

Confirmation.

firmation. In that rite "through the instrumentality of His minister, the new Head of man's race receives His younger members into *closer union*, and *confirms* those graces which at baptism have already flowed into them from Himself. Thus is a natural mode of converse with God exalted into *a means of supernatural union*." "Christ" is "truly present through the agency of His servants to bless in the laying on of hands, and to *communicate through external means that supernatural life* of which His humanity is the source." After this, "the Holy Eucha-

* Wilberforce on Incarnation, p. 250. † Ib. p. 350.
‡ Ib. pp. 331–334. § Ib. p. 330.

rist" is "their *perpetual means of union* with His glorified humanity, *their soul's food*, the medium of the body's immortality."*

Lord's Supper.

The influence of the scheme last considered on the heart of its recipient is *soporific*. It tends to remove the necessity of repentance after baptism from all but gross offenders. The tendency of the one now under consideration is *to keep the conscience in distress*. It is commended by one of its exponents as retaining "something of the *bitterness* of the ancient medicine." And to the opposite system, which affords 'peace with God' to the self-condemned Christian through a continual cleansing by the blood of Christ, applied by faith, the objection is made, that it "stifles the strong emotions of terror and amazement which God has wrought upon the soul, and by an artificial wrought-up peace, checks the deep and searching agony, whereby God, as in a furnace, purifies the whole man, by the spirit of judgment and the spirit of burning."† What then is to be done with the Christian's sins after baptism?

Tendencies.

We are told that "we have no account in Scripture of any second remission, obliteration, extinction of all sin, such as is bestowed on us by the 'one baptism for the remission of sins.'"‡ "The fountain has been indeed opened to wash away sin and uncleanness, but we dare not promise them a second time the same easy access to it which they once had: that way is open but once: it were to abuse the power of the keys intrusted to us, again to admit them thus:

Sin after baptism.

* Wilberforce on Incarnation, p. 346. † Pusey's letter to Bishop of Oxford. ‡ Tracts for the times, No. lxviii. p. 54.

now there remains only 'the baptism of tears,' a baptism obtained, as the fathers said, with much fasting and with many prayers."* Nor even thus can they attain a sure peace with God: for we are in baptism "washed once for all in Christ's blood, but if we again sin, there remaineth no more such complete ablution in this life. We *must bear the scars of the sins* which we have contracted."† "There are but *two periods of absolute cleansing, baptism and the day of judgment.*"‡ The same writer, however, afterwards confessed that this "statement was imperfect, as making no mention of the healing and comforting power of absolution, or the pardoning grace of the holy eucharist."§ But after all, the most that can be thus obtained is "*a sort of restoration* of that life given . . . by virtue of (baptism); a restoration of *a certain portion* of their baptismal health. It is not *the* new birth simply; that is baptism: but it is a revival *in a measure* of that life; to be received gratefully, as a renewal of a portion of that former gift; to be exulted in, because it is life; but to be received and guarded with trembling, because it is the renewal of what had been forfeited; not to be boasted of, because it is but *a fragment* of an inheritance 'wasted in riotous living.'"‖

Details. Such is this system in the general. Let us scrutinize more closely a few of its leading features.

The righteousness which justifies. Primary among these is its view of the righteousness by which a sinner is to be justified In the language of one who was a forerunner

* Tracts for the times, No. lxviii. p. 59. † Tract lxviii. p. 63.
‡ Pusey's letter to Bishop of Oxford. § Letter to Abp. of Cant.
‖ Tract No. lxix. p. 207.

of this school in its present development, "our being righteous before God always and essentially implies a *substance* of righteousness *previously implanted* in us; and our reputative justification is the *strict and inseparable result of this previous efficient moral justification:*" "the reckoning us righteous *indispensably presupposes an inward reality of righteousness*, ON WHICH THE RECKONING IS FOUNDED."* Or in the words of a later writer, "In justification the whole course of sanctification is *anticipated, reckoned*, or *imputed* to us in its very beginning."† "Christ is our righteousness by dwelling in us by His spirit, justifies by entering into us, continues to justify us by remaining in us."‡ If any one should ask how this consists with the acknowledged *declarative and forensic* sense of the word justification, the reply is, "It is a pronouncing holy while it proceeds to make holy!"§ So that "*imputed righteousness is the coming in of actual righteousness.* They whom God's sovereign voice *pronounces* just, forthwith *become* just. He declares a fact, and makes it a fact by declaring it.(!) He imputes, not a name, but a *substantial word*, which, being engrafted in our hearts, is able to save our souls. God's word effects what it announces."‖ What shameful special pleading to get rid of acknowledged statements of the word of God! *The righteousness of justification is then in fact*, according to this scheme, *sanctification;* the two "are really one."¶ Accordingly, justification is on this scheme *progressive:*—"a state admitting of degrees according to the degree of sanctifi-

---

* A. Knox's Remains, vol. i. p. 306. † Newman on Justification, p. 79. ‡ Ib. p. 51. § Ib. p. 80. ‖ Ib. pp. 86, 87. ¶ Ib. p. 129.

cation."* "A state admitting of relapses and recoveries, but which is weakened by every relapse, injured by lesser, destroyed for the time by grievous sin; and after such sin, recovered with difficulty, in proportion to the greatness of the sin, and the degree of its wilfulness, and of the grace withstood."† On what quicksands must the trembling sinner build who embraces such a scheme!

Nature and office of justifying faith.

Let us next look at the nature and office of justifying faith according to this scheme. *Previous to baptism*, faith "is without availing power, without life in the sight of God, as regards our justification." "It comes," in baptism "to the fount of life to be made alive." "Its highest praise *before* baptism is that it *leads to it*, as its highest efficacy *afterwards* is that it *comes from it*:"‡ for "being the appointed representative of baptism, it derives its authority and virtue for what it represents. It is justifying because of baptism. . . . Baptism is the primary instrument, and *creates* faith to be what it is, and otherwise is not, giving it power and rank, and constituting it as its own successor. Each has its own office, baptism at the time, faith ever after."§ "Justification needs a perpetual instrument, such as faith can be, and baptism cannot be. Faith *secures* to the soul continually those gifts which baptism *primarily conveys*."‖ "It is a symbol of the nature and mode of our justification."¶ It is "*said* to justify, *not that it really justifies more than other graces*,"** but "as *including all other graces*

---

* Newman on Justification, p. 129. † Pusey's letter to Bishop of Oxford. ‡ Newman on Justification, p. 275. § Ib. p. 260. ‖ Ib. p. 276. ¶ Ib. p. 281. ** Ib. p. 346.

and works in it and under it."* "Justification by faith is justification by God's free grace in the gospel, as opposed to every thing out of the gospel."†

Virtue of the sacraments.

The nature of the sacraments, according to this scheme, has already been partially exhibited. Two more declarations will suffice to set the view clearly before us. In infant baptism the infant, we are told, is "the recipient of the greatest blessings which it can enter into the heart of man to conceive, even *the translation from the kingdom of Satan into the kingdom of Christ, and the transfiguration of the whole nature from a state of moral and spiritual debasement and helplessness, into one capable of performing the achievments of saints, and inheriting the glory of angels*."‡ Such is the view of baptism. The absolute and comparative virtue of the other sacrament is thus set forth: "As holy communion *conveys a more* AWFUL *presence of God* than holy baptism, so must it be the instrument of a higher justification."§

Such, then, is the system of sacramental grace. That it is altogether 'another gospel' from what has been set forth as 'the gospel of Christ,' who can fail to perceive? If we were ourselves disposed to soften down the opposition, and effect a compromise between the two, its own advocates would forbid the banns. We are peremptorily, but truly, told that "the sacramental and anti-sacramental systems are *two different religions*, and to rest our hopes of salvation on the one, is to say anathema to the other." "Allow the one, and the sacramental

---

* Newman on Justification, p. 346. † Pusey's views of Baptism, p. 22. ‡ Brit. Crit. No. lxvii. p. 75. § Newman on Justification, p. 169.

system is a groundless superstition; allow the other, and the anti-sacramental system is a presumptuous unbelief."*

SECTION V.

THE BEGINNING OF THESE ERRORS LAID BARE.

THESE are substantially the three systems held and set forth by members of our own Church; yet not in our own Church only, but, with unimportant variations, and changes of names, existing in all the Churches around us, and which have existed wherever the truths of divine revelation have been intrusted to the keeping of fallible and erring man. They are the growth, not of a time, nor of a Church system, but of human nature, at all times and under every system. Placed thus in contrast with each other, who, at all familiar with the Scriptures, can hesitate in the decision which of them it was that the apostles of our Lord, in the New Testament, 'testified as the Gospel of the grace of God?' But numbers who would not hesitate in a right choice between the 'Gospel of Christ' and these *full-blown* systems, are yet slow in detecting the first germination of unsound doctrine. Many a man has passed the boundary unawares, and unconsciously setting foot in bye-paths of error, has pressed along with honest logic, till he found himself in full possession and zealous maintenance of that from which he ever shrank, and which, up to the hour of the discovery, he always,

* Wilberforce on New Birth, pp. 214–217.

in name, most ardently opposed. But discovery is made when it is too late to retract. The spiritual instincts and sensibilities have kept silent correspondence with the doctrines progressively embraced; and when the former Evangelical awakes to discover that he holds *another system*, he is prevented from return by a second fact, which he does not discover, that he is himself *another man*. And there is, perhaps, for him no hope of a return, but by the reversed process of changing back the system by changing back the man. Many a melancholy change of views and decline of spiritual character to formalism and party zeal might have been prevented, had the boundary lines been kept clearly defined, and a sign-board, broad-lettered and legible to all, been set up at the very corner where human error first begins its seemingly slight divergence from the divine way of salvation. To find out this angle, and survey these diverging roads, is what we now propose to undertake.

There is a passage in Hooker's celebrated Sermon on Justification which will conduct us at once to the very root of the matter. "They teach, as we do, that all have sinned; that infants, which did never actually offend, have their natures defiled, destitute of justice, and averted from God. They teach, as we do, that God doth justify the soul of man alone, without any other coefficient cause of justice; that, in making men righteous, none do work efficiently with God but God. They teach, as we do, that although Christ as God be the efficient, as man the meritorious, cause of our justice, yet in us also there is something required. Christ hath merited to make us just; but as a medicine which is made for health doth not heal by being made, but by being applied, so by the merits of Christ there can be no justification without the application of his merits. Wherein, then, do we disagree? We disagree about *the nature and essence of the medicine whereby Christ cureth our disease;* about *the manner of applying it;* about *the number and power of the means* which God requireth in us for the effectual applying thereof to our soul's comfort."* The two fundamental questions, therefore, whose answers are the roots whence grow, by natural development, these different systems, are in the words of a living bishop, "1. What is *the righteousness* whereby we are to be justified or made acceptable before God? 2. What is *the mode or means* by which that righteousness is applied?" Their respective answers to the former of these questions will reveal the radical contrariety of these two systems to the 'Gospel of Christ.' Their answers to the latter will show us the point at which they first begin to diverge from it.

Test questions.

Gospel answer to the first.

The answer made by the Gospel to the former question may be thus stated, in the language of Archbishop Usher: "The gracious imputation of God the Father, accounting his Son's righteousness unto the sinner, and by that accounting making it his to all effects, as if he himself had performed it."† And this reply may be further unfolded in the words of Bishop Beveridge: "As Christ was made sin for us, not by the inhesion of our sins in him, but by the imputation of our sins to him, so we are made the righteousness of God in him, by the imputation of his righteousness to us, not by the inhesion of his righteousness

* Sermon on Justification, § 45. † Body of Divinity, p. 194.

in us. He was accounted as a sinner, and therefore punished, for us; we are accounted as righteous, and therefore glorified, in him. He was accounted as a sinner for us, and, therefore, he was condemned; we are accounted as righteous in him, and so we are justified." *

The answer of the legal system.

The answer to this question on the second scheme would be, *A personal righteousness accepted by God* for Christ's sake. "*Obedience to the moral law* . . brings fallen man into a state of acceptance with God, *by qualifying him* for the salvation which has been purchased."

The answer of the sacramental system.

The answer on the third scheme is, "Christians are justified by the communication of an inward, most sacred, and most mysterious gift. From the very time of baptism, they are temples of the Holy Ghost.' "*The Holy Spirit indwelling is the formal cause of justification.*" "The righteousness on which we are called righteous, or are justified, that in which justification results or consists," (we give the statement in its full mistiness,) "this justifying principle, though *within* us, as it must be, if it is to separate us from the world, yet is not *of* us, or *in* us, not any quality or act of our minds, not faith, not renovation, not obedience, not any thing cognizable by man, but a certain divine gift in which all these qualifications are included." It is, therefore, a righteousness *infused in baptism.*

With respect to these answers we say in the words of Bishop Hall, "*To be* IMPUTED *and to be* INHERENT *differs no less than God and man, Trent and heaven.*"

---

* On Art. XI.

But how shall we find the point where first branches off the track which leads its follower to this fundamentally contrary view of the nature of justifying righteousness? The answers to the second of the questions above stated will reveal it. For, inasmuch as these systems are the *working out of a native feeling of self-righteousness*, we shall find it just where the Gospel salvation *becomes a matter of personal application*; for there will the first wound be inflicted on the pride of the human heart. The view taken of the *nature and office of justifying faith* is the point of separation. The whole scheme, right or wrong, will be a development of what is held on this point. The true office of justifying faith is to be *the instrument* of our justification. "By faith we appropriate the merit of Christ. The *meritorious* cause of our justification is all in our Mediator. The *instrumental* cause is exclusively our faith. That *on account of which* we are justified is the righteousness of Christ. That *through means of which* we are justified is our faith in Christ. The vesture that covers our shame is of God; the *hand that puts it on* the part of man is on."* Moreover, it is the *only* instrument. "In that office faith stands alone. No sacrament, no ministry, no outward ordinance, no inward grace, stands with it, either to divide or make perfect its work."† In *nature* it is a *living principle*, "a faith which, while it essentially embraces the assent of the understanding, establishes its seat in the affections, and will," and "finds its pleasure in obedience,"‡ whose necessary

Point of separation, in the view of justifying faith.

Its true office.

Stands alone.

Its real nature.

*M'Ilvaine on Just., pp. 74, 75. †Ib., p. 76. ‡Ib., pp. 78, 79.

fruit is holiness. Yet "it is *not because* of these, its works, that it justifies." In the language of the homily before quoted, "It shutteth them out from the office of justifying." Nor does it justify as being itself a work, an obedience of a more spiritual character; "but simply as it is the empty hand whereby the beggared sinner takes, and relies on what Christ is, and has done for him, to the salvation of his soul."*

How it justifies.

It is here that these two false systems begin to separate from the Gospel. They both diverge from the same point and in the same way. The way for deviation is first prepared by denying that there is any *natural fitness and necessity* for the selection of faith as the instrument of justification, and the assertion, on the contrary, that its power to justify arises simply from divine appointment, and that it was selected simply because some *one* act or grace must necessarily be chosen to mark a sinner's transition from condemnation to acceptance; and why not faith as well as any other? But that there is such a *natural* fitness and necessity, which led to its appointment, the apostle Paul himself asserts, 'Therefore it is of faith, that it might be by grace.'† Faith, and faith only, can be the instrument of a salvation which is by free grace, because it not only disclaims and renounces, but is *absolutely inconsistent with* the idea of merit, and *in its own nature* indicates both the lost state of the sinner and the freeness and sovereignty of the grace which pardons and reclaims him. It is, in its very nature, the confession of unanswerable guilt and helpless ruin in the believing soul, and of a free, unmerited salva-

How the wall is thrown down.

* M'Ilvaine on Justification, p. 81.

† Rom. iv, 16.

tion only and sufficiently in Christ. It is the very act of flight out of condemned and perishing self into the arms of an all-sufficient and merciful Saviour. So long as this idea of the nature of faith is clearly understood and firmly held, the divine way of salvation is *hedged in* from all danger of mistake and wandering. The denial of this *throws down the fence and opens the gap* for departure from the truth. If faith is the instrument of justification simply because it has been so appointed by God, and *without any inherent necessity* for its selection, then it is just such an instrument as repentance or Love would have been, had they been selected. Then its efficacy for justification lies in the fact that it is *obedience to a command of God.* In other words, it justifies the sinner *as a work of his own*, as an *obedience to which* the promise of salvation has been annexed. This may seem to many a very slight deviation. In words it may be; but in the substance it is fundamental. It brings us at once over the dividing line between salvation by grace and salvation by works. The idea may be refined to the utmost by evangelical expressions, and denials of the presence of merit. But if it justifies simply because it is obedience to God's command, then faith is *the consideration for which* the salvation of the Gospel is granted to the sinner. Here, then, is *the first footstep into error.*

First step in error.

Another step.

At the next step faith ceases to be a simple, distinct act of the soul, and is viewed as the *pregnant principle* of holiness, justifying, now, not for what it is in itself, but for what it involves and will produce; not as being in itself a highly-refined, but as leading to a more palpable obedience. It is said to justify "as the root of all Christian graces," "the originating principle of love and every good work." A third step brings us to a change in faith itself. It is no longer a deeply spiritual grace, indicative of a renewed nature—no longer the faith of the heart, but simply of the understanding. It degenerates into *a mere naked assent* to the truths of Christianity, no longer justifying, but only *preparatory* to justification. The real cause of justification is viewed as something *subsequent to faith.*

A third step.

And here these two systems begin to diverge from each other. They separate on the question, what is this *subsequent means of justification* to which faith leads. The former runs into *justification by works of a moral character;* the latter into *justification by the sacraments:*—the former into justification by works done by man in his own strength, with such divine assistance as is common to all mankind; the latter into justification by an infused righteousness coming from the repository of the Church through grace given in baptism and the Lord's supper.

Separation of the two false schemes.

And here let us ask why it is that there should thus be two different systems, when both start at the same point, a denial of the self-renunciatory character of faith, and both originate in the same cause, the desire of man to have some part in his own justification; and why it is that one is adopted rather than the other. The true answer is, that one is the *religion of unawakened nature*, and the other of nature *awakened* but *in the dark.* The former is the religion of an unawakened sinner. By this is meant, not the religion of a man absorbed in this world and wholly forgetful of God. Such an one has no religion. But a man

Why there are two false schemes, and not one.

Religion of unawakened nature.

whose moral convictions uphold the great truths of religion, while he is unimpressed by any deep and abiding sense of his own corruption;—a man whose judgment teaches him the necessity and advantage of serving God, while his heart has no consciousness of his need as a sinner. Let a man be convinced on theoretical grounds of the duty of being religious, without having been aroused to feel that he himself is a lost sinner, and he naturally falls into this scheme of a legal Christianity. That scheme has, as we have seen, a contempt for all that is *experimental* in religion, by which is meant a present inward experience of the saving power of Christ—even denying anything of the sort to be possible. We are told by one of its advocates, that to "speak of Christ's power, faithfulness and love, of his ability to save, etc., from our own *experience*," "is no more possible than that we should speak of Christ's miraculous cures from our own experience." "Did man indeed NOW *experience* any of these blessings there would be an end of Christian faith: they would then walk, not by *faith* but by *feeling*." "Until we are actually saved, we cannot in any sense experience this salvation." It has, also, as we have already seen, no adequate sense of the evil and extent of sin, limiting the necessity of repentance to gross offenses, and lowering it in nature from a deeply spiritual exercise to merely "a gradual amendment of life and manners." Nor does it know any thing of that conflict of the flesh with the spirit, in the heart of a true child of God, which makes the real difficulty of a holy life. "For religion," we are told, "is easy and natural, pleasant and delightful, unless *we* have made it otherwise by contrary habits: and even then we may be reconciled to it without any of this unnatural dread or concern." Nor has it an idea of the direct, sanctifying influence of the Holy Spirit upon the heart. "What! *convert* to the Christian faith those who are already regenerated by baptism, who are already made, as our Church catechism declares, the children of grace!" "Conversion," "regeneration," the becoming "dead to sin," and "alive from the dead"—"mean nothing, i. e. *nothing to us, or to any one educated in a Christian country.*" Such is its language. And finally, it is a system in which a soul deeply exercised by a knowledge of its sins cannot abide. It knows no justification but by works:—no evidences of being justified but good works. But in proportion as the soul becomes awakened, it discovers its own sinfulness. Its redoubled efforts after holiness only reveal the strength of its corruption. The evil at first supposed to be slight and superficial, it finds to be deeply inwrought into the very constitution of its being. It soon has to fight, not with detached evil habits, but with whole armies of evil desires swarming forth at every temptation, from a fortress of which they were born possessors. The hope of thus overcoming sin and recommending itself to God is completely disappointed. It must either give up the attempt in despair, and settle down in reckless transgression, or, unless divinely guided to a salvation not dependent on itself, it will find out some system which promises an attainable expiation of its sin. Hence it is, that the legal scheme has always proved a soil in which the sacramental system takes easy root. It only needs an aroused conscience to carry a man from the one into the other.

The sacramental system is the religion of *nature awakened, but unenlightened*, the resort of Religion of awakened nature. "an *unsatisfied earnestness.*" It promises a remedy adequate to the extremity of the disease:—remission of all sins, regeneration and an infused righteousness in baptism; "a higher justification" in holy communion; "a baptism of tears," "obtained with much fasting and many prayers," and "the healing and comforting power of absolution," for sins committed after baptism. And it promises, and goes on to supply them with much more, as we shall presently see. It is the very system for a soul which delights in the luxury of self-torture, or which out of its prolonged anguish and agitation would fain derive a title to acceptance with God. And it possesses in addition the charms of a certain awfulness and mysticism, and of an imposing ceremonial.

Thus it is, that there must ever be, as there always have been, two false systems claiming each to be the way of life: the fears and austerities, "the deep and searching agony" of the one would be insupportable to the adherents of the other; the philosophic calmness, the absence of any expedients for the relief of deep distress in that will make it unsatisfying to the devotees of this. And from them both will he escape with delight, as on the wings of a dove, whose eyes have been opened to behold the merits of a crucified and interceding Saviour, as the one perfect righteousness wherein he may stand accepted with God. 'The law of the spirit of life in Christ Jesus will make him free from the law of sin and death!'

SECTION VI.

THE PROGRESSIVE DEVELOPMENT OF ERROR.

I.—THE LEGAL SYSTEM.

We are now to follow out these bye-ways that we may see whither they would lead us. The former of them we left at the point where faith becomes a mere acknowledgment of the truth of Christianity, and deeds of supposed moral worth are associated with it as "the coefficient conditions" of our justification. The value of human actions depends upon the standard to which they are brought, and the principles by which they are tested. There are two ways, therefore, of securing a favorable judgment for the works which man may perform in obedience to the law of God. One way is to impart such a *spiritual quality* to these actions as will increasingly, and at last, altogether accord with that 'spiritual' law. This is the way taken in that gospel which is the power and wisdom of God for the recovery of a lost world. For after having by the sacrifice of Christ held back the penal consequences of man's sinful deeds, it proceeds by the sanctifying influences of the Holy Ghost to make him 'a new creature in Christ Jesus,' infusing such a living principle into his actions, that he will at last once more become entirely conformed to the 'perfect,' 'spiritual,' and 'exceeding broad' commandments of God. This method the legal scheme rejects. The only other way of securing a favorable judgment is to alter the standard to suit the action, to *conform the law of God to the*

Bringing down the law to man's reach.

works on which it is to pass sentence. This is no easy matter, seeing 'the law of the Lord is perfect.' The most plausible way of doing it, however, is to represent it as the design of Christ's work under the gospel to bring the law down to men, rather than 'by a new and living way' to raise men up to the law. Accordingly there arises the notion that only "a sincere, not an unbroken, obedience is required in the gospel;" that "a great design of the covenant of grace is to remove the difficulty, and soften the rigor of the law of works;" and that "the new covenant admits of a defective obedience." But the holy and immutable character of the divine law, as designed to set forth the glory of its Author, stands in the way of such a representation: and the duties of the first table of the law, especially, are hard to be cramped down to a mere outward and formal service. This gives rise to the expedient of representing the law as given, not to manifest God's glory, but solely to secure man's happiness; and as the relative duties of the second table tend more visibly to this end than the more spiritual duties of the first, superior importance is attributed to them, and the others are undervalued. Thus we are told. "*For our sakes only* was the command given, 'Thou shalt have none other gods but me.'" "The happiness of men is *the end and the measure*, even of our duty to God." "The relative duties are of all the most indispensable;" "the essence of religion consists in a good life;" "preaching and praying, and all other external services, are necessary as far as they support this life," but "no further stress is to be laid upon them:" "too much is made of faith and devotion." The divine commandments are now cut down to the

Depression of the first table.

measure of man's ability. His nature corresponds to God's law. There is no longer that conflict between them, and that impossibility of doing right, of which the Gospel speaks. Man's nature, therefore, cannot be *fundamentally* depraved. What evil there is in him is the result of habit and education. Thus the doctrine of *original sin*, the inborn depravity of every descendant of Adam, is discarded from the system. In its place come eulogiums on the dignity of human nature. With the doctrine of man's native corruption must go also that of his necessary *renewal by the Holy Ghost*. The necessity for the latter lies wholly in the existence of the former. The evil of man's condition as a sinner is now very much mitigated. Instead of being absolutely ruined and lost, he is still in quite a respectable condition, and with a little assistance perfectly able to retrieve his credit. He therefore requires less in the way of mediation with God. Accordingly we are told that "Christ died more particularly to *make perfect* by his own sufferings *the obedience* of such as may have been almost inadvertent, or casual sinners." And therefore "faith in the merits of Christ *supplies the defects* of our obedience." Christ comes in to *make up* what the sinner cannot *quite* do by himself.

Original sin discarded.

Work of the Spirit rejected.

Christ dying to eke out man's obedience.

And here, I believe, we have reached the end, so far as ministers of our own Church are concerned. No laxity of interpretation or of conscience could cover a wider departure from her standards. The tether is stretched to its utmost tension. A further strain must snap it asunder.

But we have by no means reached the end of the

road. If Christ's death was not in the strictest sense a propitiatory sacrifice for sin, what could it have been but a most edifying *example* of piety in unjust suffering? There is no middle ground. No thinking mind can long remain poised between the two. The *reality* of an atonement having been already destroyed, even its name is now discarded. The central doctrine of the Gospel, atonement for sin by the death of Christ, is now cast out. The keystone of the arch is thrown down. But why then need He have been God manifest in the flesh? His *divinity is useless* in such a scheme. It only cumbers and perplexes the illogical mind that would still retain it. It involves and is involved in the doctrine of the atonement, and they must stand or fall together. The doctrine of the Trinity can be held no longer. The strong foundation of Christianity is uprooted. We have reached the level of Socinus. And we go down by degrees, driven by resistless logic, from the highest form of Arianism, where Christ is every thing but God, to the bald and dead scheme of those who see in him only a mere man. Whether the path end here, or whether there be a further tendency to the rejection, first of portions, and finally of the whole of the Book of Revelation, let the history of Unitarianism declare.

Atonement given up.

Christ's divinity discarded.

II. THE SACRAMENTAL SYSTEM.

The second of these bye-ways we left at the point where Faith is represented as bringing the sinner to baptism for his justification. The infusion of righteousness said to be made in baptism puts away sin, not only by a remission of its penalty, but by extinction of all past sin, both original and actual. But, in spite of this extinction, evil tendencies and desires still visibly remain in those who have been baptized. It becomes necessary, therefore, to deny that this forms any part of that original sin which is declared done away. But if it does not, then it existed in Adam before the fall, and was consistent with his native innocence. This, then, requires a new theory of original righteousness. It is found in the notion that after his creation, Adam received the gift of some supernatural grace in addition to his natural perfections. "Whereas we have gained under the Gospel what we lost in Adam, and justification is a reversing of our forfeiture, and a robe of righteousness is what Christ gives, *perchance a robe is what Adam lost.* If so, what is told us of what he lost, will explain what it is we gain. Now the peculiar gift which Adam lost certainly seems to have been a *supernatural* clothing. Christ clothes us in God's sight with *something over and above nature;* which Adam forfeited."

Original sin.

Original righteousness.

We have seen the difficulty experienced by the advocates of this scheme, in disposing of post-baptismal sins. "Now what," asks the bishop before referred to, "is the natural consequence of such a miserable, comfortless doctrine as this? A man who can never know whether his amount of inherent righteousness is sufficient, will always be ex-cogitating some device or other by which God may be more effectually propitiated and satisfied. A gloomy, or a poverty-stricken spirit resorts to those unbidden austerities and severe bodily macerations, by which it is hoped that sins may be fully expiated, and heaven meritoriously attained. In such righteousness there is

Expedients to get rid of sin after baptism.

something that seems tangible, measurable, appreciable. A man can count his penances, measure his pilgrimages, weigh his gifts, and thus keep account of his righteousness, and at last come to account himself sufficiently righteous to be at peace with God. Sinners of various descriptions will resort to various modes of establishing such a righteousness; the rich will purchase what they are not able to work out, by the prayers of priests, and the merit of saints, and the virtue of indulgences, to save themselves the pain of austerities. Thus will arise the monster of *supererogatory merit.* And so there grows out of the mere effort of the troubled conscience, to supply the awful uncertainty arising from a scheme of justification, which knows nothing better for righteousness than our own works and personal holiness, that whole retinue of vain devices for the making of a righteousness of our own, and easing the conscience with nostrums of man's quackery, by which the Church of Rome has been for so many centuries so defiled and degraded."* And again: "Justification is by infused righteousness. This infusion takes place in baptism. Baptism can not be repeated. But sin after baptism destroys the grace of baptism, that is the justifying efficacy of the infused righteousness. The light is quenched. The bright mirror is marred. What shall remedy the loss? There remains no sacrifice for the reinfusion of righteousness. The eucharist is only for its increase and brightening. The merits of Christ will not answer, because they are only applied for justification in baptism. Faith will not answer, for it is *subordinate to baptism*, and has been killed by sin after

* M'Ilvaine on Ox. Div. pp. 89, 90.

baptism. A *new sacrament*, such as that of *penance*, or else *a purgation between death and judgment*, is absolutely necessary to such a scheme."* And can we not see the felt necessity for such a purgation in the following language? "Who can tell, but in God's mercy, the time of waiting between death and Christ's coming, may be profitable to those who have been his true servants here, as a time of maturing that fruit of grace, but partly formed in them in this life; a school-time of contemplation, as this is of discipline, of active service? Such surely is the force of the Apostle's words, that He that hath begun a good work in you, will perform it *until* the day of Christ—not stopping at death, but carrying it unto the resurrection—as if the interval between death and his coming, was by no means to be omitted in the process of our preparation for heaven."†

Purgatory.

This impossibility of removing sins committed after baptism, makes the burden on the conscience too heavy to be borne. Some method must be devised of diminishing the load, if not by removing sin altogether, at least by preventing its too rapid accumulation. The notion entertained of original sin comes in to meet this necessity. The concupiscence of the heart, if not the result of a fallen nature, can not properly be called sin, and neither deserves the same condemnation, nor requires the same mode of removal as the sins of the life. Hence the distinction between *mortal and venial sins*, and all the practical abominations to which that distinction leads.

Mortal and venial sin.

* M'Ilvaine on Ox. Div. pp. 250, 251. † Newman's Paroch. Sermons pp. 411, 412.

Auricular confession.

We have seen the efficacy attributed to Priestly Absolution. But how is one entrusted with the awful power of the forgiveness of sins, to be able to exercise it with a due discrimination? Must there not be first a full knowledge of the case in hand? And so grows up *auricular confession*, a practice already encouraged, and attempted to be carried on both within our own Church and the mother Church of England.

The Holy Eucharist is supposed effectual to minister grace, because of the *actual presence of Christ therein.* This presence, however, is not a spiritual presence in the heart of the faithful recipient, nor is it a material presence of Christ's real body and blood under the form of bread and wine; but it is something between the two—something between a spiritual and a material presence! Must not a notion so radically unphilosophical develope into something further? The way for a development

Transubstantiation.

is thus prepared: "This body (Christ's human body) can not die again, nor can its material place be other than at God's right hand; yet must *this be the very body* which we present to the Father; for were it aught besides, our dependence would not be on that anointed first-fruit of man's nature, which, that it might be the instrument of mediation, was made personally one with God."* "So that what is done by His ministers below, is a constituent part of that general work which the one great High Priest performs in heaven: through the intervention of His heavenly Head, the earthly sacrificer truly exhibits to the Father that body of Christ, which is the one only sacrifice for

* Wilberforce on Incarnation, p. 285.

sins; each visible act has its efficacy of those invisible acts of which it is the earthly expression; and things done on earth are one with those done in heaven."* Here we have the ubiquity of Christ's material body, and an earthly sacrificer exhibiting that body in the Holy communion. What more is wanting for the doctrine of Transubstantiation?

Priestcraft.

And what words can sufficiently express the dignity of an order who are the creators and sacrificers of the body of Christ, the sole media of grace to men, and whose absolution is of such high consequence to the sinner? Extorting the very secrets of the heart upon the rack of the confessional, and holding over the head of the penitent, consciously degraded by the inquisition to which he has been subjected, all the terrors of eternal damnation, who could withstand their will? Here is the foundation of that priestly tyranny under which all Europe groaned for ages previous to the Reformation.

Doctrine of Reserve.

And now the preaching of the Gospel has become an unessential and antiquated part of the machinery for the conversion of the world. The doctrines of redemption are discovered to be too sacred a mystery to be exposed to vulgar gaze. They must be covered with a veil of awful reserve. Instead of being 'the power of God unto salvation to every one who will believe' them, they are 'the secret of the Lord' only to be unfolded after long perseverance and fidelity in the Christian race. "A sinner becomes a Christian under the preaching of 'natural piety,' 'of common honesty, repentance, judgment to come, fast-

* Wilberforce on Incarnation, p. 287.

ing, alms and prayer.' This sort of preaching will make him desire salvation, and therefore desire baptism, as that power of grace by which 'God saves us.' This *desire of baptism* is said to be the very essence of justifying faith. He comes and is baptized. Now he is a Christian, and without any knowledge of Christ. Truth is not taught him, but kept for him in the Church, behind the altar. It is his, because he is part of the Church. She gives him the benefit of its possession, without the necessity of his knowing what it is. It is enough that the Church knows. The more obedient he shall be to the Church, the more she will reward him with a knowledge of her secrets. By-and-by he may come 'fully to know that we are saved by faith in Christ only,' (in the sense of this system,) but his attaining eternal life has no connection with any such knowledge. All things belonging to his salvation are to be sought and found in, to be begun and finished by, the Church; through her priesthood, as her *hand* by which, and through her sacraments, as the *channels* through which, out of her own '*abiding*,' *inherent* treasure of grace, deposited in her as a storehouse at the beginning of the Gospel, she communicates regenerating and justifying grace to the sinner. She is, to the sinner, Christ. The language is not too strong for the head writers of this system. She is all the Christ to which they teach the sinner to look *directly* for grace."*

But how can such teaching be reconciled with the opposing declarations of the Holy Scriptures? And how is it to feign for itself divine origin and authority? Obviously there must be discovered for it some war-

---

* Bishop M'Ilvaine's Charge, 1843, pp. 19, 20.

Tradition a rule of faith.

rant other than that which the written word of God contains. It is found in the notion of *a word unwritten*, "another great gift equally from God" with the Bible. It is now discovered that Church tradition is "parallel to Scripture, not derived from it, and fixes the interpretation of disputed texts, not simply by the judgment of the Church, but by the authority of that Holy Spirit who inspired the oral teaching itself, of which such tradition is the record."* And now has this system a rule of faith suited to every emergency. This "tradition-doctrine can take in whatever is convenient for proof. If it need the aid of the Apocrypha, it embraces it. If it need the writings of the schoolmen, it puts them on a footing with the early fathers. The hardest canon to be settled is the canon of the books of authoritative tradition."† And what now is the result? In the words again of the revered bishop of Ohio: "Allow the authority of tradition as the rule, under any form, and then, since but a small part of men can judge for themselves of what is tradition, or what it teaches, and private judgment would be at least as much confounded amid the works of the fathers as the writings of the Apostles, you must have an *authoritative interpreter* of tradition to decide what are its Catholic sources, and what are the Catholic verities to be derived therefrom. But who shall authoritatively interpret the Church? She can not speak but by representatives. Where are they? General councils are no more. The ministry of the Church alone remains to be the *ecclesia docens*, the voice of the body of Christ interpreting the traditions which interpret the word of

* Keble's Primitive Tradition, p. 23. † M'Ilvaine's Charge, p. 12, Note.

God, which tells me what I must do to be saved. The authoritative rule of faith in this system, therefore, is really the word of the ministry of the Church as the teaching of the Spirit of God."* But who is to reconcile the discrepancies of the ministers of the Church?

Infallible head.

To whom are they to appeal in the conflicts of opinion that must arise in the individual survey of this vast and obscurely-bounded territory of written and unwritten tradition? How is there to be secured any uniformity of teaching by the ministers of the Church? Or is what is pronounced heresy by one, to be pronounced Catholic truth by another, while there is no appeal from either, and each is armed with the power of the keys to compel the assent of men to all that he sees fit to teach? There must be some *infallible center of unity*, if there is to be any stability in the faith on such a scheme. The anxious wayfarer, floundering in this bog of unsettled tradition, mired the deeper in every attempt to follow this *ignis fatuus* of an oracle in every pulpit, cries out for aid to reach some firm foundation for his faith. And here Rome opens wide her massive gates to the pilgrim's feet, and the voice of her Infallible Head bids him enter and be at peace. He halts and recoils at the suggestion. The lingering effects of early training, the force of long habit and association, hold him back. But how can he endure the yielding mire, the darkness, the buffetings of such tempestuous doubts and fears, while the ancient walls of Rome, glaring with artificial splendor, invite him to repose? The pressure of necessity is stronger than his horror of a *name*. He makes obei-

---

* M'Ilvaine's Charge, p. 11, Note.

sance to a Pope, and lies down to rest in the embrace of the mistress of abominations. He has only to believe and do as he is told, and she becomes responsible for his soul till the day of judgment.

If the logical necessity for the development of this system into Popery, if the multitudes who have traveled this road to Rome, are not enough to convince us of the necessary connection between the notion that faith justifies, not as a mere appropriation of Christ's righteousness, but by its meritorious character as an act of obedience, and full-blown Romanism, let Rome herself confirm our belief. When the divines of the Council of Trent were assembled, in consequence of the progress of the Reformation, to deliberate on the interests of the Church, it was said of Luther's attempt to overthrow indulgences and other gross corruptions of Rome, that "Justification by Faith only seemed to him a good means to effect this." "Therefore by a contrary way," (argued the council,) "he that will establish the body of the Catholic doctrine must overthrow this heresy of justification by faith only."

Testimony of Rome herself.

Thus have we seen the end of each of these bye-ways, which diverge in so seductive a region from the highway of salvation, cast up in Holy Scripture for God's redeemed. It is a distinct and interesting subjest of inquiry, but one upon which we can not now fully enter, how much *real agreement* there may be between systems apparently so diverse. The result of such investigation would be that, as the two break away from the Gospel at the same point,—the nature and office of justifying faith, as they move on under the same impulse,—the desire

Substantial identity in the two systems.

of man to have somewhat to do in his own acceptance with God, so it is in both substantially the same hope that is offered to the sinner, and the same view of man's nature and Christ's mediation upon which that hope finds its perilous foundation. As for the *ground of a sinner's hope of pardon*, it is in both a righteousness *within himself*. And the flimsy distinction which in the one case is set up of a righteousness that is *in* us, yet is not *of* us, we overturn at once by the short logic of Hooker: "If it is in us, then it is ours, as our souls are ours, though we have them of God." The *possibility of such a hope* to fallen man ariseth in both from an unsound and unscriptural view of human nature, denying man to be the inheritor of a depraved nature,—in the one system directly and openly,—in the other, virtually and really, by setting up a new view of man's original righteousness, founded on a subtle and unreal distinction between the 'image of God' and a grace of righteousness superadded; as if, (to use the illustration of an old writer,) one who had made a *round* body were afterwards to add to it *roundness* as a distinct quality. The Pelagianism of the one is avowed, that of the other is denied, and cloaked over by metaphysical subtleties. The real identity of the two is thus set forth by an English writer of the seventeenth century: "The difference between the Pelagians and Papists is not in respect of possibility or impossibility, but in respect of greater or less difficulty. For the Papists do not acknowledge that men by nature are dead in sin, and utterly deprived of the spiritual life: but that they are fickle and weak, and tied with the bands of sin, so that they can not fulfill the law of God, unless they be holpen and loosed by grace: but being holpen by grace, then the fulfilling of the commandment is easy to them. The Pelagians likewise confess, that by the grace of God, which they call *bonum naturæ*, or the power or possibility of nature, they were enabled; by the grace of God vouchsafed in His Word and Law, guided and directed; by the justifying grace of God freed from the bond of their sins; and by the sanctifying grace of God holpen with more ease to fulfill the commandments of God. So that the Papists, although they do not with the Pelagians *deny* original sin, or the necessity of saving grace: yet they do *extenuate* the original corruption, and so magnify the *strength* of nature, that they differ not much from them. And as touching the other difference; though the Papists hold that a man can not be without sin for any long time, though for some short time, (in which short time, if he shall say he hath no sin, he shall make St. John, and not himself a liar—1 John i: 8,) yet they say they may be without all sins excepting those which they call *venial;* which they do so extenuate, that indeed they make them no sins, as being no *anomies* or transgressions of the Law committed *against* the Law, or repugnant to charity, but only *besides* the Law; such as may well stand together with perfect, inherent righteousness. For they say he only is a righteous man in whom there is no sin, and yet that there is no man so righteous, as that he liveth without these venial ones. But if they be besides and not contrary to the Law, then they are neither commanded nor forbidden, and so no sins at all, but things indifferent."* Thus do these systems agree in the representation of

* Downame on Justification, pp. 503, 504.

human nature as yet capable of inherent righteousness, and in depriving the Law of God of that spirituality of requirement which is its chief glory.

Now what is the effect of these views in both systems on the doctrine of Christ's mediation? In the one case, we have seen the doctrine of redemption by the sacrifice of Christ upon the cross, openly stricken from its central position in the firmament of Christian truth. In the other case, the same doctrine is with "sacred reserve" carefully withheld from any "indelicate exposure" to popular apprehension. It is not necessary to be known that a sinner may be converted. It is not essential to the vigor of a Christian life. It is not essential to the final forgiveness of sins and admission into heaven. A man may live and die in the embrace of the Church, and by her be transmitted to heaven, without any real knowledge of Christ's death for the expiation of sin. Now what is the difference between the two? The 'one Mediator between God and man' is as effectually and really dethroned by this setting up of human mediators, as by the open rejection of his atonement for sin. Accordingly, Archbishop Usher long since declared, "it is *the point of His Priestly office which the Church of Rome strikes at;* that is, whether Christ hath reserved another righteousness for us, besides that which as a King, he works in our hearts; whether he hath wrought forgiveness of sins for us."* "We deny the grace of our Lord Jesus Christ, (says Hooker); we imbase, disannul, annihilate the benefit of his bitter passion, if we rest in those proud imaginations, that life everlasting is deservedly

---

* Usher's Sermons, No. xvi.

ours, that we merit it, and that we are worthy of it."

Thus is there a real affinity between these false systems of doctrines, apparently so unlike; and the *practical working* of the latter, when it has long had the upper hand in a community, is to drive men into the ultimate gulf of the former. There is in it a rejection of reason from matters of faith which must lead in turn to a rejection of faith, by a self-conscious and unsanctified reason. The uniform tendency of Romanism has been to produce infidelity in thinking men. Thus do these roads of man's invention converge at the last, and history presents us the spectacle of men who *have traveled to the end of Socinianism*, shaking hands with men who have *traveled to the end of Popery*, on the platform of infidelity.

SECTION VII.

CONCLUSION.

WE have now had a view of the two main systems of religion, which pass with multitudes for the Christianity of the New Testament, but which the Apostle Paul has condemned as 'another Gospel,' the device of those who 'would pervert the Gospel of Christ.' We have seen their beginning; we have traced them to their close. The subject as thus presented gives rise to some practical reflections with which we would bring this discussion to an end.

1. We may see from this survey of the diverse views actually held in our own Church at the present time, and of the ends to which they must lead, if those who

hold them are true to their own principles, the *impossibility of avoiding controversy*, even with the brethren of our own Church. It is impossible that these different systems should consent to live together in fraternal and equal communion. They are as opposite as light and darkness. The only way in which they could be held without collision, would be for the advocates of each to become wholly indifferent to truth and error. If there be the least vitality, if there be any earnestness of purpose or real conviction on either side, conflict must ensue. It is in vain for well-meaning men to entreat for peace. Even peace is less important than truth. And 'the wisdom which is from above must be *first pure*, then peaceable.' "There never was, and never will be, charity in softening down real distinctions; open hostilities are ever a shorter road to eventual peace than hollow and suspicious alliances."* This language of the leading journal of the sacramental party in England, should teach a lesson to those real friends of the Gospel, who are still desirous of maintaining such "hollow and suspicious alliances" as would result from the attempt to smooth over the serious diversities of doctrine, now held in the Episcopal Church. The result of this strong peace-spirit in years past, has been that error has been allowed to work almost unchecked, that many honest but undiscriminating minds have been beguiled into these false systems by their apparent coincidence with truth, and have been gradually forced both by outward and inward pressure along their development into antichristian doctrine. Especially, many a young and

---

* British Critic.

enthusiastic mind is now lost to the Church, or now stands pledged to a high development of error, who might have been rescued from danger, had there been more open and stirring discussion of the points here brought under review. The only way to prevent the continued increase of this mischief, is to 'put the battle in array' between truth and error; not with personal animosity of contending champions, but with the hand of love fraternally outstretched to rescue those whose principles we attack as subversive of the Gospel of Christ;—'in meekness instructing those that oppose themselves, if God peradventure would give them repentance to the acknowledgment of the truth; and that they may recover themselves out of the snare of the devil, who are led captive by him at his will.'

The beginning of error to be watched.

2. *The beginnings of error* are to be watched and guarded against, both in ourselves and others. No error can be looked upon as slight which concerns the question of our acceptance with God. We have seen how apparently slight is that first deviation from Gospel truth, which yet leads ultimately and of necessity either to Socinianism or Popery. 'The beginning of' error, as well as 'strife, is as when one letteth out water.' Let the false notion of justifying faith be once adopted, and there is no escape from the full-blown systems to which it leads; unless the mind be so sluggish that it can hold its principles forever in embryo, or unless the power of divine grace, keeping the soul in humble reliance on Christ, neutralizes the effect of its false theology, and represses its further increase. But what security can we have that this will always be the case in any individual? Onward pressure from without may drive the most

inactive mind to the legitimate conclusions of its premises, or cause a reflective and logical understanding to sweep along the opposing affections of a renewed heart, on the bosom of its own current. It is thus that the late movement which began in Oxford has carried on with it such numbers of clergy and laity. The seed was already there; the times only caused it to germinate. It may well be doubted, on the one hand, if a single one, save of the young who having since grown up under its influence, have imbibed it as a whole, has been entangled in this movement who had not the germ of the system already in possession: as it is matter of observation, on the other hand, how few of those who then held the position of what is called "old fashioned high churchmanship," have been able to stem the current which has borne their brethren to Puseyism, and some from thence to Rome.

Importance of clear views of justification.

3. Hence we see the importance of *a clear and discriminating view of the whole subject of a sinner's justification before God.* It may safely be affirmed that not one who fully understood this subject, experimentally as well as theoretically, has been carried from his moorings by the swell of this tidal movement to the Church of Rome. But how few, comparatively, there are who have this clear insight into this all-important question, and can discern the first appearance of deviation from the 'truth as it is in Jesus.' How many are unconsciously in error! And how many more so confused in their conceptions that they can not impart accurate instruction to others! And yet this is, as Luther calls it, "articulus stantis aut cadentis ecclesiæ. "The Church will stand or fall, according as she is founded wholly on the

rock of the Redeemer's righteousness, or partly upon any foundation which man's ingenuity can uprear in the quagmire of human corruption. How important that the clergy should clearly understand this central doctrine of the faith! How important that it should be fully and explicitly unfolded to their congregations, both from the pulpit and through the press! When our clergy see and set forth this doctrine in all purity and precision, we shall have no more congregations, nominally evangelical, ready to be led off into error by any preacher whose oratorical abilities may have commanded their admiration. When our people have learned to understand and value it, they will no longer be satisfied with the confused and inconsistent, if not wholly heterodox, teaching to which so many are now content to listen.

Danger of ambiguous language.

4. Another reflection to be derived from this discussion is, *the danger of ambiguous forms of speech, and the duty of avoiding them.* Much of human error upon all subjects has arisen from the use of language susceptible of two interpretations. It is especially so in the department of Theology: not only because the language of the science is transferred and accommodated from other topics; but because also the human heart is prone to error and corruption in religion, by reason of its fallen nature. Now on all subjects in Theology, but especially upon those relating to the operations of grace in the soul of man, there have long been in use forms of expression very loose and equivocal,—meant to convey a right sense, but capable of being taken in a wrong one. It is invariably under these that error first makes and hides its entrance. What was meant to be used in one sense

is afterwards used in another: and its original use, especially in ancient or authoritative standards, is appealed to for countenance and support of error. It is a solemn duty either to avoid the use of such language, or to accompany it with an explicit declaration of the sense in which it is used. An example of what is meant may be found in the word "regeneration." The ordinary acceptation of the term is now a spiritual new-birth of the soul. But there are those who think its use in the standards of the Church to have been wholly *external*, and that by its connection with baptism is meant merely a change of state, the acquirement of a covenant right to the *privileges* of the Church of Christ. Such an one may speak, and insist on the truth, of Baptismal Regeneration. But the chances are ten to one that he will be understood of a spiritual change of nature effected in that rite. A still more striking and dangerous instance is in the use of the word "condition," as descriptive of the relation of Faith or good works to Justification. The word has really *three* distinct significations. It may mean the *meritorious or availing cause* by which any thing is produced. In this sense the *righteousness of Christ* is the only "condition" of justification, and with respect to us it is *unconditional*. Or it may mean the *instrumental cause* or necessary *medium* of communication. In this sense *Faith* is the only "condition" of justification. Or it may mean simply a *necessary accompaniment*, that without whose presence something else never exists, a *sine qua non*. In this sense good works, all Christian graces, may be called "conditions" of justification: for no man can be justified, whose faith is not that living 'faith which worketh by love.' Now, to speak of good works as the "condition" of justification, while true in the *third* sense, may, and probably would, be understood in the second, in which it is *false;* and might even be taken in the first, in which it is *monstrous.* Other illustrations abound in current modes of expression respecting the efficacy of the sacraments, a priestly power and apostolic succession in the Christian ministry, and the authority of the Church: but this is not the place to attempt their enumeration. Let every one, then, beware that he is not himself imposed upon by some equivocal expression which he may hear or use, and that he is not guilty of thus misleading others also.

Symbols of error.

5. A similar caution, equally in place, is to *beware of practices which symbolize false doctrine.* Things in themselves indifferent often derive importance from the circumstances of their introduction, or the purposes they are designed to subserve. Thus questions of posture, and raiment, and genuflexions, and of the arrangement and decoration of churches, may cease to be matters of indifference, or of mere taste, and required to be considered in the very serious light of inlets of destructive error. Whether a communion table should be solid like an altar, or open like a table; whether it should be conspicuously elevated, and separated by steps from the residue of the chancel; whether the officiating minister should kneel in approaching it, and read the prayers with his face in that direction, and bow towards it at the name of Jesus, and deliver his sermon in a surplice, these and such like questions might at some times be treated with unconcern; but when they form a part of an evil system, when they are designed to be symbols of a human priesthood in

the ministry of the Gospel, and of a continuation in the Holy Communion of that sacrifice for sin made once for all by Christ, they are not only to be protested against when found in association with these errors, but to be feared as tending to introduce them. For we are but poor creatures of sense, affected in spite of ourselves by our daily habits and associations. We may be all sound at the beginning, but habitual use of error's appendages will be as dangerous as to put on the garments of one who has died of the plague. We may be insensible of any evil influence, we may still rejoice in reputed orthodoxy, but the functions of spiritual health will be seriously impaired, the system progressively disordered, until at last the infection will come with power, and hurry the soul into hopeless collapse. When infection is brooding in the atmosphere we breathe, more than ordinary care of vesture and habits is required; and things harmless at other seasons become pregnant with disease.

Tendency of the age to be resisted.

6. There is always a pressure on each individual by the movement of the collective mind, or in other words by the *tendency of the age*. As this tendency results from the common impulse of a society mainly unsanctified, it must always bear perilously on 'the faith once delivered to the saints.' Whatever truth and necessity there may be in the oscillations of public sentiment, reacting from some erroneous extreme, the mighty mass of united mind will always go as far the other way. It is always in extremes. And he who would hold fast the truth must get close to the central point of divine revelation, and plant his feet in firm opposition to the movement of the masses. Society is now reacting *from dead formalism*

to an overworking of the mere machinery of religion. Camp-meetings and magnificent temples, got-up revivals and daily communions, anxious benches and confessionals, are among the heterogeneous indications of the one tendency to a bustling externalism,—working alike by a mystical symbolism which impresses the overawed senses, and by a confused excitement which makes trophies of the victims of an overwrought nervous system; and having, by a removal of all real tests of a change of heart, the one effect of crowding multitudes of unconverted sinners into a membership of the visible Church. Such being the pressure of the times, it becomes us to be on our guard, and to withstand its influence; to seek a deeper spirituality both of sentiment and feeling in ourselves and others; to save truth from being superseded in its office of chief instrumentality for the conversion and sanctification of the soul, by either nervous excitements or impressive ceremonies of human manufacture; and to insist upon a faith which 'worketh by love,' 'purifieth the heart,' and 'overcometh the world,' as the indispensable evidence of any man's right to be called a child of God.

Danger of resisting errors on one side exclusively.

7. Let us be on our guard against being betrayed by too zealous an opposition to merely *one* species of error. There is a tendency in all minds to be driven by controversy farther off from what we are opposing. Now in a clear sea, with only one enemy, we can not get too far away from that one. But surrounded on all sides by error, compelled to hold the course of truth steady amidst all their concealed dangers, there is great hazard in being too much occupied with one class of opponents. And should that one happen to be of a less dangerous char-

acter, the risk of fatal shipwreck is increased. There are questions of order, and there are other questions of vital truth, to both of which the attention of the Church must be directed. There are irregularities of discipline on one side, and perversions of saving truth on the other. And it has happened to many in a controversy with the former, heated to an unnecessary degree by local excitement or educational prejudice, to be driven into the fellowship of those who were guilty of the latter. It is no easy matter to be on all sides well guarded. But let us not be guilty of the folly of placing the weakest battery and fewest guards where the most deadly enemies of the faith are stationed.

Growing knowledge of the fulness of Christ.

8. And finally, for the comfort of our own hearts, the stability of our own peace with God, for the cleansing of our consciences from those sins into which we are daily betrayed, let us learn and tread yet more and more the way of immediate access to the cross of Christ by faith. "The best things that we do (says Hooker) have somewhat in them to be pardoned. . . We see how far we are from the perfect righteousness of the law; the little fruit which we have in holiness, it is, God knoweth, corrupt and unsound: we put no confidence at all in it, we challenge nothing in the world for it, we dare not call God to a reckoning, as if we had him in our debt books: our continual suit to him is, and must be, to bear with our infirmities, to pardon our offences." And what is the only hope that can sustain us in this growing acquaintance with the sinfulness of our own nature? Let the wise and Christian Hooker still be our teacher: "Christ hath merited righteousness for as many as are found in him. In Him God findeth us, if we be faithful,

(i. e. believing); for by faith we are incorporated into Him. Then although in ourselves we be altogether sinful and unrighteous, yet even the man who in himself is impious, full of iniquity, full of sin; him being found in Christ through faith, and having his sin in hatred through repentance; him God beholdeth with a gracious eye, putteth away his sin by not imputing it, taketh quite away the punishment due thereunto by pardoning it; and accepteth him in Jesus Christ, as perfectly righteous as if he had fulfilled all that is commanded him in the law: shall I say more perfectly righteous than 'if he had himself fulfilled the whole law?' I must take heed what I say: but the Apostle saith, 'God made him which knew no sin to be sin for us; that we might be made the righteousness of God in him.' Such we are in the sight of God the Father, as is the very Son of God himself. Let it be counted folly, or fury, or frenzy or whatsoever. It is our wisdom and our comfort; we care for no knowledge in the world but this, that man hath sinned, and God hath suffered; that God hath made Himself the sin of men, and that men are made the righteousness of God."*

* Sermon on Justification, § 7, 6.

HISTORIC SKETCH

OF THE

BAPTISMAL QUESTION,

AS AGITATED IN THE

PROTESTANT EPISCOPAL CHURCH:

BY

A PRESBYTER OF THE SOUTH.

BALTIMORE:
PRINTED BY JOHN D. TOY.

1853.

PREFACE.

The endeavor of the writer has been to ascertain and set forth in a brief space the true history of opinion on the efficacy of baptism. Unless the statements here presented can be overthrown, (and the most searching investigation by all who love truth is solicited)—it must appear to be not only useless but dangerous to speculate too much upon the immediate spiritual effects of the ordinance, especially in the case of infants. That it is the duty of all to be baptized who are properly qualified, and that an abundant blessing attends upon the due observance of this ordinance, even in the case of infants, few, perhaps none among us, will dispute; but the manner and the method in which the blessing shall be imparted in each instance are among "the secret things which belong to God." Surely the modest temper of Ridley is to be commended, who, when writing to Bradford, on another difficult subject, says, that in regard to such points "he dared not speak farther, yea, almost none otherwise than the very text doth lead us by the hand." Yet it would seem that some in all ages have been confident and positive just in proportion as a subject is uncertain and hard to be understood; yea, they often carry their opinions beyond mere assertion, and are bold to denounce and even to persecute those who differ from them. Thus it has been on the question of the efficacy of baptism. The following pages will show how far from the line of Scripture and reason some have diverged, and may, by God's blessing, serve for the warning of others who are tempted to such speculations. It is a pleasing thought that among those who, under the general aspect of party names and action, are arrayed against each other in the Church, there are probably very many who on this and other controverted subjects differ more in appearance than in reality, and are far from intending to "go beyond the word of God to *say* less or more." Even where there is a difference of judgment in some respects there is often an entire agreement to condemn the extravagant notions of the nature and efficacy of baptism whether put forth in former or in recent times. It is in the hope of increasing the number and confirming the views of those who are determined to reject all ideas of baptism not clearly set forth in Scripture, or in strict analogy with the word of God, that this tract has been prepared. May the Lord use it as an humble instrument to call attention to his own instructive voice uttered through the history of the Church.

It may be proper to mention that several of the notes are by the hand of a friend.

HISTORIC SKETCH

OF THE

BAPTISMAL QUESTION.

PART I.

Opposing views of Baptism.

It is well known that in the Protestant Episcopal Church of England and America there is a wide difference of judgment as to the efficacy of baptism. Some hold that according to the plain teaching of Scripture and the Church, now, as in all time before, regeneration, the grace signified by the washing of baptism, always accompanies the due administration and reception of the ordinance, that is, unless impenitence and unbelief stand in the way. These cannot exist in infants, so that they must always be regenerated in baptism. As for adults, they too coming with due preparation, are in the proper sense to be considered as regenerate, not previously, but at the font. At that time a specific grace is communicated, different from what has been had before; they are now made the children of God by the participation of a new and heavenly nature. Others hold that baptism, rightly used, is indeed a means of grace, but only a means of increasing that which must be had before by every adult, who is a suitable candidate for the rite; that in such cases regeneration, the thing signified, has preceded; while, as it regards infants, they maintain that we have no certain knowledge of any immediate work wrought, unless it be their enrolment among the Lord's people, and that the application of "regenerate" to them is a mere judgment of charitable hope.

Both sides appeal to Scripture and think it sufficiently plain for them respectively. With that argument it is not now proposed to deal. That which is contemplated in these few pages is to consider the testimony which the stream of history brings with it as it sweeps along from the early ages of the Church. To that testimony, as establishing the doctrine of the Scriptures, both sides in this controversy will not equally defer; but each would be well pleased to have it appear to be in their favor. Certainly it is not likely that on any great topic of Christianity the judgment of the Church as handed down could be always erroneous. Perhaps no one would say that if the Scripture seems to be on one side and tradition on another, we must not forsake the latter, however unanimous; but in any matter whether settled in the plain letter of Scripture or not, all would wish to know the judgment more especially of the early Church, and if they can show that the judgment is with them it is considered as a large addition to their satisfaction.

Wall's History of Baptism.

Now happily no great amount of reading is necessary to test the appeal to the testimony and judgment of the fathers. Dr. Wall has with great industry collected the principal passages from those ancient authors bearing upon the subject of infant baptism. Without much labor therefore we may ascertain their sense upon this matter so far as infants are concerned, and reasonably infer their opinions in the case of adults.

Jewish notions.

Before giving the language of Christian authors, it may be well to refer to the Jewish writers on the subject of the baptism which was practised upon the admission of persons proselyted from the heathen. They were accustomed to say of such a one that he was like "a child new born." It is much more likely that the Saviour adopted the customary phraseology than that the Jews borrowed it from him or his disciples. The bitter prejudices of the Jews would prevent them from any thing of the sort: whereas, we know, that it was altogether consistent with the genius of our Lord's teaching to borrow from Judaism whatever could be turned to account in setting forth the brighter truth and higher grace of his kingdom. With the Jews the term "new born" was no doubt used in a figurative sense to signify the change by which the proselyte was incorporated with Israel and brought into covenant with God. But even then there were not wanting persons of a fanciful turn of mind who could not understand the metaphor. The new birth was "literalized," and it was by them supposed allowable for a baptized proselyte to marry any of his nearest kindred—yea, if he married his mother he did not sin.* His new birth was considered as effecting a change in his natural as well as in his spiritual relations.

Caution.

The fathers expressly apply John 3: 5, to baptism though it cannot be inferred from this that they understood it in the sense for which some of late contend. It would seem that they deduced from it not so much a doctrine relating to the internal effects of baptism toward the renewal of man's nature, as the doctrine of the cleansing from the *guilt* of sin, the taking away the imputation of original and actual transgression. It will be seen that regeneration with them is employed synonymously with baptism, and that the purpose of the ordinance is rather the application of the blood of Christ to the removal of guilt than the application of the spirit to begin in a proper sense the sanctification of the soul. And if the Holy Ghost is mentioned it will be found to be mainly as applying to the individual in some unexplained manner the pardon of sin.†

* Wall, vol. 1, p. 31.

† It is important to bear this in mind. Thus Cyprian (quoted by Jewel, vol. 3, p. 463,) says, "The remission of sin whether it be given by baptism or by any other sacrament is indeed of the Holy Ghost." When therefore in the fathers we read of the Holy Spirit as imparted, we must ask—in what sense?

Barnabas.

Barnabas seems to be the first Christian writer after the apostles who speaks of baptism. Mingled with much fanciful application of Scripture, is the following, which admits of a very good interpretation, though when the magical efficacy of the mere application of the water in the name of the Trinity is believed, it becomes very dangerous to use such terms.—"We go down into the water full of sins and pollutions, but come up again bringing forth fruit, having in our hearts the fear and hope which is in Jesus, by the Spirit."*—*Epist. Barnab. II.*

Hermas.

Hermas in the Shepherd Vis. 3: 3, makes the Church in vision teach an inquirer that our "life is saved and shall be saved by water." This we may take as parallel to St. Peter's words "baptism doth now save us," though whenever such a form of speech is used among those who are liable to misunderstand it, there should be added something equivalent to this: "not the washing away the filth of the flesh, but the answer of a good conscience toward God." In the third book of the Shepherd, entitled the Similitudes, this ancient writer, still in the form of a vision, is describing the growth of the Church under the idea of a tower. He says most emphatically it will avail nothing to take up the name of the Son of God unless we receive of the same spirit which dwelt in him, and that "the whole tower is of the same color as the rock, and made as it were one stone," 9: 13. It is to be feared that in what follows there peers forth the sentiment of a necessity and efficacy in baptism quite unknown to the writings of the apostles. He is speaking of the building of those who lived before Christ into the tower so as to form a portion of it. They are not considered as being of the one body by reason of the faith which constituted them the children of Abraham, or the circumcision which outwardly separated them from the world. "They therefore being dead were nevertheless sealed with the seal of the Son of God, and so entered in the kingdom of God. For before a

* Apostolical Fathers.

man receives the name of the Son of God he is ordained to death, but when he receives that seal he is freed from death and assigned unto life. Now that seal is the water of baptism." And who administered the rite to the departed? "The apostles and teachers preached to them who were dead before and gave this seal to them."—*Simil.* 9: 16. In our judgment of such a passage we ought indeed to remember the professedly allegorical character of the book, but we can readily perceive how injurious such language must have been in a writing so extensively read and of such high authority, that some of the fathers elevated it almost to a level with the canonical Scriptures.*

Justin Martyr.

In the celebrated passage of Justin Martyr, in which he speaks of the manner of admitting converts into the church, we read: "They who are persuaded and do believe that those things which are taught by us are true, and do promise to live according to them, are directed first to pray and ask of God, with fasting, the forgiveness of their former sins. Then we bring them to some place where there is water and they are regenerated by the same way of regeneration by which we are regenerated, for they are washed with water in the name, &c."† Now what is there here to be regretted, unless it be the seeming appropriation of regeneration to baptism as the ordinary signification of the word. There is no proof that Justin attributed anything to the ordinance but a sealing of the forgiveness which had been sought by "prayer and fasting."

This use of the term regeneration arose from the general understanding of the fathers, of John, 3: 5, as referring directly to baptism and as teaching the absolute *necessity* of that ordinance to salvation. Hence St. Ambrose says: "There is no regeneration without water." St. Augustine calls the persons by whose means infants are baptized, "those by whom they are regenerated." St. Jerome applies the term to the baptism of our Lord by John. From this application

* Apostolical Fathers.—Wake's Prelim. Disc. 10. † Wall, 1: 68.

of the word therefore, plainly nothing can be inferred as to the proper effects of the ordinance in adults or in infants. For the ideas of the fathers upon that subject we must look to their more complete statements.

Tertullian. Tertullian is thought to have been unfavorable to the baptism of infants unless in case of extreme sickness, and even of adults, he says, "they that understand the weight of baptism will rather dread the receiving than the delaying of it. An entire faith is secure of salvation."* Yet he, like the more orthodox, takes the words of our Saviour as teaching the necessity of baptism to salvation, and sets himself seriously to work to show how it was possible for the apostles to be saved notwithstanding their want of that ordinance.

Origen. Origen is a writer whose testimony on infant baptism comes to us in part through translations, laboring under some suspicion of having been accommodated to the controversies of a subsequent age. Jerome attributes to him the doctrine that infants were baptized for the forgiveness of sins committed in a former state. This, if it shews the speculative character of his mind, and the unscriptural tone of his writings, makes known also that in his view the regeneration of baptism was a washing away of guilt. "I will mention a thing which causes frequent inquiry among the brethren—infants are baptized for the forgiveness of sins." This seems to be the conceded point in the controversy! Now comes the matter of inquiry—"of what sins? Or when have they sinned? . . . . . . It is for that reason, because by the sacrament of baptism the pollution of our birth is taken away."† The one idea present to his mind is the taking away of the imputation of transgression. In none of the passages quoted from him by Wall is there any clear reference to any thing else.

Cyprian. When we reach the times of Cyprian, (A. D. 250,) the testimonies to the existence of infant baptism as an institution of the Church greatly

* Wall, 1: 94. † Wall, 1: 104, 5.

multiply. With these there is mingled the same error which we have already noticed, the idea of the absolute necessity of the ordinance to salvation. Cyprian and sixty-six bishops in council with him, wrote to Fidus, a brother bishop, who thought that infants ought not to be baptized within a few days of their birth as was the custom. They write: "Whereas our Lord, in his gospel says, the Son of man came not to destroy men's souls, but to save them; as far as lies in us, no soul if possible is to be lost."* Such was their reason for hastening baptism. In this letter is found a passage seemingly opposed to the idea that in baptism it was chiefly forgiveness of original sin of which they thought in connection with infants, but upon careful examination it will be found to say no more. He says, "the Scripture gives us to understand the equality of the divine gift in all, whether infants or grown-up persons." He speaks with disapprobation of the idea that "the grace which is given to baptized persons is greater or less according to the age of those who receive it; whereas, the Holy Spirit is given, not by different measures but with fatherly affection and kindness equal to all." By the gift of the Spirit it is most likely that he means nothing more than the sealing of pardon by the Holy Ghost, which in whatever way it be represented as taking place in infants, is no more difficult to be understood than some other ideas which have been advanced by the fathers and others. This view is confirmed by what follows toward the close. "If then the greatest offenders, and they that have grievously sinned against God before, [alluding to adults,] have when they afterward come to believe, forgiveness of their sins, and no person is kept off from baptism and the grace, how much less reason is there to refuse an infant . . . . . who comes for this reason more easily to receive *forgiveness of sins*, because, &c."† Here both in the adult and infant the same effect is contemplated—the removal of imputed guilt, and not the renewal of nature. And here it may be at once ac-

* Wall, 1: 129. † Wall, 1: 130—2.

knowledged that in some of the fathers, as in later writings of the Church, the distinction between these two things has not always been kept in view. The work of Christ for us in cleansing from guilt by his blood, and the work of Christ in us by his Spirit in taking away the corruption of sin are too often mingled together, to the confusion of author and reader.

Gregory Nazianzen. One hundred years after Cyprian, brings us to the times of Gregory Nazianzen who, in a sermon on baptism, calls it "the gift, the grace, the anointing, the laver of regeneration, the amending of our make or formation, the seal," all which expressions admit of a very good interpretation. He makes a distinction between the effects in infants and adults. To the former, baptism is "a seal," to the latter, it is "a restoring of the image which they had lost." He says the force and effect of baptism is "a covenant with God of a new and holy life." "Hast thou an infant child? Let not wickedness have the advantage of time; let him be sanctified from his infancy; let him be dedicated from his cradle to (or by) the spirit. Thou as a faint-hearted mother art afraid of giving him the seal because of the weakness of nature. Hannah, before Samuel was born, devoted him to God and as soon as he was born consecrated him and brought him," &c. Now here there is nothing more than the dedication of the child, with a hope of the divine blessing in answer to prayer. He seems to be the first Christian writer who expresses an opinion concerning the future state of those who without their own fault die unbaptized. He supposes that they "will neither be glorified nor punished by the just Judge as being without the seal."* He illustrates his idea in a way which will not be satisfactory to many. "If you would condemn for murder a man who has not murdered, merely because he has a mind to, then let him go with you for a baptized person, who had a mind to it, but had it not. But if that be absurd I do not see how this can be reasonable."† Now here there is

* Wall, 1: 175. † Wall, 1: 175.

an instance of that very kind of confusion which occasions so much embarrassment on the subject of baptism. Surely it is not absurd to call a man a murderer who has a mind to murder. "He that hateth his brother is a murderer" before God and will be so considered and treated at the last. But before a human tribunal such a character can not be convicted, for God only "trieth the reins and the heart." Our standing before God and our standing before man ought never to be confounded. He that is not baptized is certainly not a member of that visible society which God has established on earth, but it is going too far to assert that such an one may not be a member of that blessed company on whom God looks with favor. It is worthy of remark, Nazianzen recommends that unless there was danger of death children should not be baptized until three years old, or thereabout, when they may be "capable of hearing and answering the holy words."*

Basil.

Basil was a cotemporary of Nazianzen. He interprets John, 3: 5, in the same way as if it taught only the necessity of baptism to salvation. In reading his fervid exhortation to the catechumens to offer themselves for baptism, one is reminded of the indiscreet addresses with which in our own day persons have been urged to come to the "altar" or "anxious seat." The minister would be much shocked at the intimation that he is putting the outward act of approaching the designated place in the stead of the inward approach of the heart in penitence and love to Jesus. Unconsciously he has in his own mind identified the two things and often leads others into the same error to their great disadvantage. So Basil notwithstanding the wide distinction in his own thoughts between repentance and faith as necessary qualifications for baptism and the ritual action itself does use language which might easily be misunderstood. He bids his hearers to anticipate the lamentations of those who deferred baptism until too late. "Fool that

* Wall, 1: 177.

I was! Why did not I put off this heavy load of sin? Oh woful purpose of mine! for the short pleasure of sin to suffer eternal torments. I might have been one of those who shine in glory." He adds, "These and such like complaints you will make if you depart hence before you be baptized."*

Ambrose.

Of the extravagant estimate of baptism, we have an illustration in Ambrose who sees a type of that ordinance where no modern, however far-sighted, could have suspected it, and which it would require a new revelation to confirm. He says, that the returning of the waters of Jordan toward their spring head, which was caused by Elias when he divided the river, "signified the sacrament of the laver of salvation which was afterwards to be instituted, by which infants are reformed from wickedness to the primitive state of their nature."† On this, Wall remarks, he means that infants were thereby freed from original guilt. That Wall is right appears in the words which follow. Ambrose had been speaking of circumcision. "No time ought to be void of the remedy because none is void of *guilt*." He makes a transition to baptism. "All must be circumcised by *the forgiveness of sin* . . . . no person comes to the kingdom of heaven but by the sacrament of baptism." Both circumcision and baptism were, with a view to the removal of guilt. Quoting John, 3 : 5, he says "you see he excepts no person, not an infant, not one that is hindered by any necessity."‡ If they should by any possibility escape punishment, he professes uncertainty whether they could get to heaven. He rather inclined to the Greek doctrine of a middle state.

Chrysostom.

In Chrysostom it can easily be shown how cautiously the oratorical language of the fathers is to be interpreted, and what injustice would be done to them and to the truth always to insist upon a literal interpretation. When he would set forth the blessings of baptism he contrasts it with

* Wall, 1 : 214. † Wall, 1 : 221. ‡ Wall, 1, 223.

circumcision and says, "it procures us a thousand benefits and fills us with the grace of the spirit," whereas in circumcision there was no other advantage than that by this sign, the Israelites were "known and distinguished from other nations."* He says circumcision "signified nothing to the soul," but he gives a reason for it, which those who are fond of diminishing the honor of circumcision that they may exalt baptism, will be slow to receive. His reason is conveyed in the form of a question. "For a new born child that knows not what is done to him, nor has any sense, what profit for his soul can he receive thereby."† This reasoning, however, is as good against the efficacy of baptism as of that of circumcision, or rather, it is inconclusive in both cases. This father has an eloquent passage in which in reply to those who maintained that "the heavenly grace of baptism consists only in forgiveness of sins," he sums up all the spiritual benefits which attend forgiveness. He had in view the case of adults, but he adds, "for this cause we baptize infants also, though they are not defiled with sin, that there may be superadded to them saintship, righteousness, adoption, inheritance, a brotherhood with Christ and to be made members of him,"‡ which may be understood as an oratorical expansion of the Scriptural statement that "of such is the kingdom of heaven."

Augustine.

We come now to Augustine who proposes the very question which would elicit his views. "What good the sacrament of Christ's baptism does to infants? Whereas, after they have received it they often die before they are able to understand any thing of it. As to which matter it is piously and truly believed that the faith of those by whom the child is offered to be consecrated, profits the child."|| It is to be remarked here how he connects the blessing with the faith of those who bring the child. What the blessing is he does not here define. The following passages are deserving of

*Wall, 1: 228. †Wall 1: 229. ‡Wall, 1: 232. ||Wall, 1: 245.

marked attention. "As the thief who by necessity went without baptism was saved, because by his piety he had it spiritually, so where baptism is had, though the party [an infant] by necessity go without that [faith] which the thief had, yet is he saved. Which the whole body of the Church holds, as delivered to them in the case of little infants baptized. . . . We may make a true estimate how much the sacrament of baptism avails infants by the circumcision which God's former people received. For Abraham was justified before he received that, as Cornelius was endued with the Holy Ghost before he was baptized, and yet the Apostle says of Abraham that he received the sign of circumcision, a seal of the righteousness of the faith by which he had in heart believed, and it had been counted to him for righteousness. Why then was he commanded to circumcise all his male infants. . . when they could not yet believe . . . . but for this reason, because the sacrament itself, is of itself of great import? . . . And as in Isaac . . . the seal of the righteousness of faith went before and the righteousness itself . . . . came after, so in infants baptized, the sacrament of regeneration goes before and . . . conversion of the heart, the mystery whereof went before in the body, comes after."* What can be more satisfactory as to Augustine's ideas of the benefits of baptism to infants than this illustration from the case of circumcision! The reader will observe these are not words uttered incautiously on another subject, but a formal reply to the very question which ought to have elicited all his views on the efficacy of baptism.

The epistle of Augustine to Boniface, in reply to certain questions in relation to infant baptism, contains some very important observations. His correspondent suggested the difficulty that some did not bring their infants with any view to spiritual good, but with a superstitious idea that their bodily health would be benefitted. The reply of Augustine is not that the

* Wall, 1: 244—5.

spiritual blessing would be communicated because in such cases no "bar" was interposed, but because the infants were offered not so much by the hands of those who brought them as "by the whole congregation of saints and faithful men .... by whose holy and united charity they are assisted toward the communication of the Holy Spirit."*

Another question proposed by Boniface was in reference to the promises which are made for the child, a custom then fully established. He had a difficulty in understanding how they could be made, considering our ignorance of the future character and conduct of the child. In giving a reply, Augustine enters on the subject of the use of metaphorical language. "When Good Friday is nigh, we say to-morrow or next day is our Lord's passion. .... So on the Lord's day we say, this day our Lord arose. ... Why is there no body so silly as to say we lie when we speak so, but for this reason, because we give names to those days from the representation they make us of those on which the things were indeed done, so as that is called the very day which is not, but answers to it in the revolution of time. ... Sacraments would not be sacraments if they had not a resemblance of those things whereof they are sacraments, and from this resemblance they commonly have the names of the things themselves. As therefore the sacrament of Christ's body is after a certain fashion Christ's body. . . So the sacrament of faith is faith. ... So when an infant that has not yet the faculty of faith is said to believe, he is said to have faith because of the sacrament of faith, and to turn to God because of the sacrament of conversion, because that answer belongs to the celebration of the sacrament." In other words, as the sacrament of baptism belongs to infants as well as adults, and the ordinance in its own nature is the same in the two cases, we must suppose the same answers in the former, that are really made in the latter. The ordinance is based on conditions. Receiving in the

* Wall, i: 263.

gospel a command to baptize infants, to give them "the sacrament of faith and conversion," we must attribute to them that which they really have not, nor in so saying, ought any one to say, we depart from the truth. That this is a fair exposition of Augustine's meaning, is plain from what follows. "An infant, though he be not constituted one of the faithful by that faith which exists in the will of believers, yet he is by the sacrament of that faith."—Speaking of the effect of the ordinance, he says, if the child "departs this life before the use of reason, he will by this christian remedy of the sacrament itself (the charity of the Church recommending him) be made free from that condemnation, which by one man entered into the world." * Not one word is said of any immediate work wrought in all baptized infants, any transformation of nature once for all then taking place in them. He plainly speaks of the washing away of original sin.

Several passages are quoted from Augustine, in which he speaks of "the Holy Spirit as dwelling in baptized infants," but such a general statement is very different from those objectionable theories which afterwards came to prevail, and to which we will refer by and by.

Wall's interpretation.

Wall gives the following as his understanding of Augustine; "that God by his spirit does at baptism seal and apply to the infant the promises of the covenant of which he is capable, viz: adoption, &c. On which account the infant is said to be regenerated by the spirit; not that God does by any miracle at that time illuminate or convert the mind of the child. And for original sin . . . . . God by his covenant does abolish the guilt of it . . . . and consigns by promise such grace as shall afterward . . . be sufficient." † If this representation of the sentiments of Augustine be correct, he must be spared the imputation of giving countenance to the idea that it

* Wall, 1: 269-272. † Wall, 1 281.

invariably confers the mighty gift of the new creation in Christ.

Acknowledged error of Augustine.

That he was in error in relation to baptism, few perhaps will deny, his mistake was however of quite a different kind.—Following the interpretation which had been early given to our Lord's words, "Except a man be born of water and of the spirit," &c. he thought and strenuously maintained that the salvation of an infant was absolutely impossible without baptism; it was however, because he supposed that ordinance was in their case, the only effectual application of Christ's blood to the removal of the *guilt* of sin. Nor was he satisfied with the notion that for such there was an intermediate place. He could find nothing of such a state in the Scriptures, and therefore he consistently followed out his doctrine to the belief that all unbaptized infants must be consigned to hell, although indeed he supposed their punishment would be comparatively light.

Not his error only.

Nor was this idea of the necessity of baptism confined to Augustine and his followers. It was conceded by the Pelagians and by the semi-Pelagians after them, though the former thought the only effect of the want of it would be to keep the infant out of heaven, in some less privileged condition. Wall thus states the difference between the followers of Augustine and the semi-Pelagians. The former "held that God by his mere gratuitous pleasure does ordain that such and such infants shall come to have baptism and so be saved," but the latter said, "that such as God foresaw would have been faithful Christians if they had lived, he by his providence procured to be baptized." *

Extreme doctrine modified.

It is interesting to observe in the history of opinion on this subject of the efficacy of baptism, how early the necessity was felt of modifying the extreme view gathered from the misinterpretation of our Lord's words. Very soon the case of some was presented to notice with regard to whose salvation,

* Wall, 1: 479.

even though without having had the washing of baptism, no rational doubt could be entertained. It was the case of persons suffering martyrdom immediately after their conversion. Every feeling in the heart of the Christian rose up against the thought that such could be lost. Reason so far asserted her prerogative against received opinion and erroneous interpretation of the words of the Saviour. Yet it was not a perfect triumph which reason achieved. All she could secure was a compromise expressed in the phraseology that such persons were "baptized in their own blood." Thus did the prejudice of the absolute necessity of baptism maintain itself. Really the staining of the body with blood, though it be in the cause of Christ, is not the sacramental washing which he instituted, and in effect the substitution of the former for the latter, was to confess that this ordinance of Christ was not absolutely essential to salvation.

Unbaptized Adults.

The fathers did not overlook the question of the probable condition of others beside the martyrs who were prepared for baptism, but died without it. Nazianzen and other Greek fathers favored the idea of a middle state for them. Ambrose is doubtful when speaking generally; yet when a particular case was brought before him he expresses confidence in the person's safety. Augustine was of the same opinion, arguing from the case of the thief; yet afterward, in his Retractions, he says this instance is not certainly to the point; for, possibly, the thief had *been baptized before!*

A case proposed.

The idea of the necessity of baptism to salvation, appears in all its difficulty in a circumstance which took place in the early part of the sixth century. At Carthage, a Christian master had instructed a slave brought from the interior of Africa. The man had, according to custom, made the usual renunciations and promises some days before that fixed for his baptism. Meanwhile, he fell sick, and into an insensible condition. In that state he was baptized, some one making the answers, as in the case of an infant. The opinion of Fulgentius, a bishop, was asked, in reference to the hope which might be entertained in such a case. A deacon writes, "I entreat your opinion, whether his want of speech will be no hindrance to his obtaining eternal salvation." The answer of Fulgentius was favorable to the servant's safety, but the ground of the hope is singular enough. The sum of it was, that our Lord requires of adults both faith and baptism, and this man had both. "He had his senses when he professed, and he yet had life when he was baptized."* He afterwards grants, that without baptism in that insensible state, the man could not have been saved.

Opinion of Fulgentius.

Unbaptized Infants.

It is one of the strongest facts connected with this subject, that these ancient writers judged more hardly of infants than of adults dying unbaptized. As we have seen, the Greeks were disposed to think more favorably of their case than the Latins, and invented the notion of a middle place. Augustine did not agree in this. After expressing the idea that the thief might be no exception to the general rule, for that he might be considered as one baptized in his own blood, or perhaps he had been baptized before, he concludes, that whatever be thought of his case, "no one ought thence to promise to unbaptized infants, a place of rest and happiness of any sort."† This sounds very severe, yet he contrived an escape from much that is horrible in the idea, by imagining that though such infants must be consigned to hell, their state might on the whole be better than if they had not been born.‡

Fulgentius (the same, it is believed, who was before mentioned,) is said to have gone beyond Augustine in his judgment of this matter, and hence acquired the unenviable appellation "*durus infantum pater*," the father who is so hard to infants.

Pope Gregory, a hundred years later, (A. D. 600,) expresses himself to the same effect; "they undergo eternal torments." And such in substance was the

* 1: 521. † Wall, 1: 487. ‡ Wall, 2: 203.

prevailing opinion of the doctors in the Church for several hundred years. Bernard says, "infants, since by reason of their age, they cannot have faith, nor the conversion of the heart to God, consequently can have no salvation if they die without baptism."*

Opinion changed.

About the eleventh century, there was a great change of judgment in the West, and the opinion of the Eastern Church became general, that original sin deserved only a negative, not a positive punishment,—and that in consequence, infants only suffer the loss of the vision of God. This was confirmed by a decree of Pope Innocent A. D. 1100. Hence the Greek notion of the *limbus infantum* became prevalent. The schoolmen were much perplexed to get over the authority of Augustine, who was supposed to say in one place, (though the writing was afterward proved not to be his,) that such infants "are tormented with eternal fire." But ingenuity soon overcame this difficulty. Alexander de Ales invented a distinction to this effect. "To be punished with fire may be taken in two ways—either on account of the heat of it, or the darkness of it. They that have actual sins, will be punished with the heat; *others only with the darkness*." Thus unbaptized infants were supposed to be afflicted only with the obscurity occasioned by the smoke of the torments of hell.

Wall tells us he had been at some pains to find out the earliest maintainers of the probability of the salvation of unbaptized infants. It appears that a young man named Vincentius, in Augustine's time, advocated this view, but such an outcry was raised against him by that father that he was glad to recant, probably finding none to sustain him. After that no more is

Hincmar.

heard of this view until the time of Hincmar (A. D. 860.) He ventured to express a good hope of some dying without baptism, in consequence of the rashness and obstinacy of a bishop, who had excommunicated all the clergy of his diocese, so

* Wall, 2: 198.

that there were none to perform any of the public offices of religion. Some of the schoolmen thought well of the case of still-born children. "Such an infant being subject to no action of man, but of God only; he may have ways of saving it for aught we know."* If, however, the children were born alive—if they lived but a moment and died without baptism, their case was hopeless. Wickliffe employs the following language, shewing both the force of the current of common opinion, and the contrary force of sentiment and feeling within him. "When an infant of believers is brought into the Church to be baptized, and the water or some other requisite be wanting, and the people's pious intention continuing, if he dies meantime naturally by the will of God, it seems hard to define positively the damnation of such an infant, ... Where then is the merciful liberality of Christ?" &c. The Hussites of Bohemia, and the Lollands in England, who were both followers of Wickliffe's doctrine, had the same charitable hope, and perhaps carried it farther than he; and among those who to the last maintained a good standing in the Roman Church, were some who leaned the same way. The Council of Florence (A. D. 1339,) determined that all who die in original sin, (that is unbaptized,) go to hell. But they had adopted the idea of the limbus infantum, where there are no torments. This continues to be the general belief of Romanists, though it is not considered a dogma of the Church strictly so called.†

Wickliffe.

*Wall, 2: 212.

†The Theological Faculty of Paris, at or before the Reformation, gravely used the following language: "A difficult question is discussed by the doctors, whether an infant in danger of death, and no water be at hand, ought rather to be thrown into a well than to be commended to God in expectation of the event. This would be homicide and worthy of death, *unless* it could be said, that baptism is necessary to salvation." Wall, vol. 1: chap. 15.

PART II.

Reformation. Thus we are brought to the times of the Reformation. The Protestants found nothing in the Bible to countenance the idea of a middle state; we accordingly meet with nothing of it in their writings, except to condemn it. They generally, with Augustine, adopted the severer judgment of the desert of original sin. The Augsburg Confession (Art. 2) says, "that it causes eternal death to all those who are not born again by baptism and the Holy Ghost." It also declares concerning baptism (Art. 9) that it is "a necessary ordinance." But the nature of the necessity is not defined, and it would be absurd to interpret such language, so as to deny the charitable doctrine before held in regard to adults baptized with blood and with the spirit, though not with water. In reference to the case of children dying unbaptized, no opinion is to be inferred from such general statements. The 13th Art. of the same Confession says that sacraments "demand faith, and then only are they rightly used when they are received in faith." In strict accordance with this definition, Luther maintained that in infants brought to baptism, there was what might be called faith; "a certain beginning of faith exists in infants:"* and again, "we bring a child .... to be baptized in this hope and persuasion, that it certainly believes."† Here again, we see the result to which we are led by a misapplication of words intended for adults to infants. That the former must believe in order to salvation, is plain. But how absurd to speak of infants as having faith in any intelligible sense!

(Margin notes: Augsburg Confession. — Luther's notion.)

* Goode on Baptism, 175. † Same, 170.

Zuinglius. Zuinglius is charged with holding, that the sacraments are bare signs, though he is by others vindicated from the imputation. Whatever the truth may be in his case, those who followed him in his branch of the Reformation, were careful to deny the charge, when brought against themselves. Thus Calvin. Calvin (Institutes, B. 4, ch. 15, sec. 1,) says, "those who have imagined that baptism is nothing more than a mark or sign .... have not considered the principal thing, which is, that we ought to receive it with this promise—"He that believeth and is baptized, shall be saved." He writes (B. 4, ch. 16, sec. 21,) "if any of those who are the objects of the Divine election, after having received the sign of regeneration, depart out of this life before they have attained years of discretion, the Lord renovates them by the power of his Spirit. . . . If they happen to live to an age at which they are capable of being instructed in the true signification of baptism, they will hence be the more inflamed to the pursuit of that renovation with the token of which they were favored in their earliest infancy, that it might be the object of their constant attention."

Bullinger. Bullinger, of Zurich, did not follow Calvin in his extreme statements on the subject of the divine decrees. His opinions are specially interesting, in conseqence of the high place which his name and writings had in the estimation of the English Reformers from Cranmer on. He seems to have avoided the application of the doctrine of election to infants. His general views may be gathered from the following extract found in his Decades, a volume of Sermons which the Archbishops and Bishops in 1586 ordered junior ministers to study—" They are sacramental and figurative speeches when we read and hear that the bread is the Body of Christ; . . . also, that they are purged from their sins, and regenerated into a new life, which are baptized unto the name of Christ, and that baptism is the washing away of all our sins.—After this manner speaketh the Scripture, and this form of speech kept the old doctors of the Church, which for so doing, none that is wise doth dispraise, neither can we discommend any man which speaketh after this manner, so that he also abide in the same sincerity wherein it is manifest those holy men of God did walk. . . . . They used the words significantively, sacramentally, mystically and figuratively."

It is the glory of the Church of England that, at the Reformation, she neither despised the aids furnished by the labors of the Continental Reformers, nor did she servilely copy their model of doctrine and discipline. In several most important points, under the guidance of divine Providence, she made improvements upon the forms they presented. The ruling mind in all these changes is allowed to have been that of Cranmer. His earlier writings are sometimes quoted by controversialists to sustain interpretations of the formularies, in which at a later period, he had the chief hand. This is evidently unfair. He himself confesses that he had been "many years in divers errors—being brought up from youth in them;" and that only "by little and little, he put away his former ignorance."* We are interested only in knowing what his views were at the time when the formularies and articles of the Church were framed. Not that we are bound to his particular meaning; that were unreasonable indeed. Certainly, the true doctrine of the Church is to be looked for in her words, as at the time understood and intended to be understood by those who compiled her formularies.

Cranmer.

On the subject of baptism it is likely that Cranmer agreed in sentiment with the rest who were engaged with him. At least we hear of no disagreement on that topic; and yet there are extant the words of some of the leading divines of the Church of that day quite inconsistent with the idea of the invariable efficacy of baptism to the proper regeneration of the infant. In 1552, the second of the two Liturgies of Edward VI. was brought into use. In that the expressions in the

* Works, 1 vol. p. 134—Parker, Soc. Ed.

baptismal office and the catechism which are the occasion of stumbling to many, are found. The year following we have another Catechism "for all school-masters to teach" sent forth with an injunction from the King, commanding the general use of it in schools. He says it had been committed to the diligent examination of certain bishops and other learned men, and he enjoins the teaching it "immediately after the other brief Catechism," meaning no doubt that sent forth with the Common Prayer. In the enlarged Catechism thus put forth, there is not a word of that view of baptism which is founded on a literal interpretation of the former. In reference to the sacraments, there is nothing which those who hold the opinion contrary to that just alluded to, object. Appended to the Catechism were the articles agreed on in Convocation the year previous, which are essentially the same as those now in existence. How little thought was had of fixing upon the Church the doctrine so vehemently contended for by some in these days, with regard to the renovation of all infants in baptism, appears from the language of the articles generally, and especially from the conclusion of one of them. Instead of the final sentence of *Art.* XXVII. as it now stands, it read "*The custom* of the Church to christen young children is to be commended and in any wise to be retained in the Church." It is likely that by this use of the word "custom" nothing more was meant than that infant baptism was not *expressly* commanded in Scripture, but only to be *inferred* as a duty; yet the language is worthy of notice. Nothing like it would be employed by those in our day who hold the extreme opinions in reference to the ordinance. The words afterward substituted for those above quoted and which are certainly a stronger declaration of the duty, are very moderate and seem not at all consistent with the ultra ideas on the subject.

King Edward's Catechism.

In reference to the understanding of the baptismal office of our Church in the time of Edward VI. much light is thrown by the circumstance that it had the minute revision of Bucer and Martyr, whose well known opinions render it impossible they could have approved of it, as they did, if they had understood it to assert the certain regeneration of all baptized infants. It is not necessary to affirm that there was minute conformity of view between these eminent men and Cranmer, though the contrary cannot be proved. They, as freely as he, used the customary language in regard to baptism, and no more can be inferred from that circumstance in his case than in theirs. Certain it is that Cranmer, knowing their views by their writings and by conference, placed them, the one at Cambridge and the other at Oxford to teach divinity, and that his confidence in them was continued in the case of Bucer until his death, and in the case of the other, until Cranmer sealed his own testimony at the stake. It is certain moreover that Cranmer addressed letters, which are extant, to Melancthon, Bullinger and Calvin, asking them, "forasmuch as their adversaries were holding their councils of Trent to confirm their errors," to unite in devising measures that "in England or elsewhere there might be convoked a synod in which provision might be made for the purity of ecclesiastical doctrine and especially for an agreement upon the sacramentarian controversy."* Ignorance of the sentiments of the persons to whom he wrote is not to be supposed.

Bucer and Martyr.

Cranmer's invitation to Continental Reformers.

If then in Cranmer's life the extreme ideas as to the effects of baptism could not have been intended, much less is it to be supposed the sense of the leading men in the Church at the restoration of the Liturgy in the time of Elizabeth. It is often suggested that the tendency to an assimulation of view with the Continental Reformers began during Mary's reign, the time when so many of the leading divines of England were exiles, and so hospitably received at Frankfort, at Strasburg, at Zurich and

Common error.

* Cranmer's letter to Bullinger.

Geneva. No doubt the tendency was much confirmed by that circumstance, but as we have seen, it began long before by the introduction into England of the religious literature and of certain distinguished divines of the continent. Whatever modification may have been effected in the opinions of the English Reformers by communion with foreign Churches, yet it is the language and opinions of those very men, it is their understanding of the formularies of the Church of England, which is mainly to be considered in determining what the sense of those formularies is, for by them the work of the Reformation was completed. Now whatever persons may think or say of the difficulty of interpreting the language of the offices in any other than as teaching the regeneration in its highest sense of every child baptized, that could not be the understanding of these men whose sentiments are so fully known. They may have differed among themselves as to the way in which the language was to be explained; some *may* have held the absolute regeneration of all infants, but (if so) they were few in number, and so secondary in position that they cannot be identified.

Jewel.

There is one man at this stage of the Church of England, who may be considered as a representative of his brethren. He has spoken copiously and almost with authority for the rest. It was Jewel. He had been an exile, for some years a resident at Zurich, and to the end of his days a correspondent and friend of Bullinger. To Peter Martyr, then resident at that place and holding entire agreement with the leading divines of that Church Jewel writes in 1562, the year of the final settlement of the Articles "as to matters of doctrine we have pared every thing away to the very quick and do not differ from your doctrine (vestra, the doctrine of the Swiss,) by a nail's breadth."* These are the words of one who had the chief hand in whatever was then done. In the same

Agreement in doctrine with the Swiss.

*Burnet, vol. 4: p. 567.

year he published his apology for the Church of England. In that work he says of baptism, "it is a sacrament of the remission of sins and of that washing which we have in the blood of Christ." Not one word of the new creation of nature as thereby effected. Had he believed that, he could not have remained silent concerning it in such a writing, or at least if he had held it, he could not have honestly professed entire accordance with such of the Reformers as expressly repudiated it. Yet from Jewel himself, quotations are made to shew that he was of a different mind from them on this point. These passages are principally taken from his treatise on the Sacraments not published until some years after his death, and its title sets forth that it is a compilation by another hand, "gathered out of certain sermons, preached at Salisbury;" so that the treatise is of very questionable authorship. In that we find such language as this, "For this cause are infants baptized, because they are born in sin and cannot become spiritual but by this new birth of water and of the spirit."* This sentence, taken by itself, would mean all that the most ultra can desire. But however incautious the language was, the meaning of the writer was more moderate as is evident from other parts of this very production. "The sacrament maketh not a Christian but is a seal and assurance of the grace of God unless they make themselves unworthy thereof. . . . God hath his purpose in us and our children. Before we were born, when we had done neither good nor evil, he hath mercy and compassion on us. Judgment appertaineth unto God. He knoweth who are his."† When however, we turn to writings which were prepared by his own hand for publication, there is much more clearness. In them he says, "the conjunction and incorporation" into Christ "is first begun and wrought by *faith*. . . Afterward the same incorporation is *assured unto* us and *increased* in baptism."‡

* Works, 1104. Parker Soc. Ed.
† Same, p. 1107, 8.
‡ Same, vol. 1. p. 140.

And in his defence of the Apology, replying to his Popish adversaries who suggested that in the passage above quoted from the Apology, he had spoken but "slenderly" of the sacrament of baptism, he lets us understand his theory upon the subject. He intimates his dissent from the doctrines of several of the fathers, Augustine and others, who at times expressed themselves as if the faith of the parents and sponsors was the ground of the efficacy of infant baptism. "Thus they write: how truly I will not say; but their words be plain. The prophet sayeth, 'The just man shall live [not by the faith of his parents, but] by his own faith.'"* In reply to the objection, that infants believe nothing—he produces the words of Augustine, where, in a certain place, he says that infants "believe by the hearts and mouths of those who profess" in their name. It would seem therefore, that Jewel embraced the view distinctly brought out by others,† that to the efficacy of the ordinance there must be in the infant, faith, or the seed of faith. Baptism did not produce this, but supposed its existence. In this view the ordinance is as truly conditional as in the case of adults.

Reformers all held the same language on baptism.

Those who desire satisfaction as to the actual sentiments of the Reformers on this subject, ought to read the work of the Rev. W. Goode. He shews conclusively that the same mode of speaking was used by the continental and English Reformers, and that in the writings of both, there is a wide distinction between their general popular statements of the doctrine of the sacraments, and those more exact definitions which they sometimes gave. Perhaps they were not always consistent

* P. 462.

† So Hooper—"Thus be the infants examined concerning repentance and faith before they be baptized with water, at the contemplation of which faith, God purgeth the soul. Then is the exterior sign added, not to purge the heart but to *confirm, manifest and open* unto the world that this child is God's." Early Writings, p. 74. The relation of baptism to the spiritual state of children is thus expressed by Becon, "Through baptism the congregation of God receiveth the infant into the church of Christ, which was received *before* through the grace of his promise." Catechism, p. 220.

with themselves; more frequently the inconsistency is only in appearance, and arises from the omission of limitations and conditions which they did not and could not always express. Doubtless many statements would not have appeared, or would have been more carefully guarded, if the writers could have foreseen the use which has been made of their language. Yet on a comparison of one thing with another in the writings of the Reformers it has been shown, that if the extreme doctrine had been ruled to be the doctrine of the Church, such men as Latimer, Hooper, Bradford, Philpot, Coverdale, Becon must have been ruled out of it. The first of these in his conference with Ridley makes the following observations on the language of the ancient Fathers, with regard to the interpretation of which they had so much difficulty with the Romanists, and the observations apply in some measure to the writings of the Reformers. "In all ages the devil hath stirred up some light-heads to esteem the sacraments but lightly, as to be empty and bare signs, whom the Fathers have resisted so fiercely, that in their fervor they seem in sound of words to run too far the other way and to give too much to the sacraments. And therefore they are to be read warily and with judgment. But our papists (an [if] they seem a little sounding to their purpose) they will outface, brace and brag all men:—it must needs be as they will have it. Therefore, there is no remedy . . . . but patience." * Thus the Reformers had to contend not only with one here and there among themselves, who undervalued the sacrament of baptism, but there was the sect of anabaptists, against whose contempt of the baptizing of infants they had to bear testimony. This, and the charges of the papists, that the Reformers had no proper value for the sacraments because they did not attribute so much to them as they, and differed so widely in their understanding of the manner of Christ's presence in the supper, no doubt had its effects on the general state-

Latimer on the interpretation of the Fathers.

* Ridley's Works, 114.

ments of which so much is made. The writer has often been reminded of another remark of Latimer in reading some of the extracts of English divines by the Tractarians. "The Fathers have both herbs and weeds; and papists commonly gather the weeds and leave the herbs." *

From the more moderate views of the subject of the divine decrees which appears in the Articles and in the writings of the Reformers generally, there was plainly an advance into the regions of decided Calvinism on the part of the succeeding divines of the Church of England. Whitgift, whose opinions are well known, was divinity professor at Cambridge from 1566, four years after the Articles were framed; and from that time until 1604, he was prominent in the Church, the last twenty-one years being Archbishop of Canterbury. During this period we read in the pages of English authors of the application of the doctrine of predestination to infants, and some of them spoken of as elect in contradistinction to others. At that time the name of Calvin was universally held in esteem, and his authority hardly disputed. Yet during all this while we hear of no difficulty in the use of the baptismal service. The Puritans were active with pen and tongue, raising up all kinds of objections to the Church of England. How it is that among the points stated by them and remarked upon by Hooker in his fifth Book, no mention is made of an objection so formidable (as would appear in the eyes of extreme Calvinists) that the Church taught the invariable regeneration of all infants baptized? The only way of accounting for it is, that the language of the baptismal office was then understood by friends and enemies of the Church in the hypothetical sense, or in some other way not necessarily involving the idea of the certain regeneration in the Scriptural meaning of all the baptized.

Advance of Calvinism.

Puritans make no objections to baptismal service.

Though Hooker notices no difficulty of this kind, it is likely that *his* language on

Hooker.

* Ridley's Works, 114.

the sacraments, and especially on baptism, was the foundation of difficulty to others. Thus we find his sentiments contrasted with that of preceding divines and with the Articles by the authors of the Christian Letter.* They asked for explanation of language which has to this day perplexed persons of whatever school in theology, such as, where he says that baptism is "the first apparent beginning of life, a seal perhaps of the grace of election" and "predestination brought not life without the grace of external vocation wherein baptism is implied." The immortal Hooker has some how acquired the name "judicious," but those who quote him so largely on the sacraments, would no doubt, think him much more worthy of the designation if he had not written as he has on the subject of the "Church mystical" as well as of the variable nature of the government of the Church "visible," to say nothing of his doctrine relating to "justification."

Davenant.

Bishop Davenant held, that the justification, regeneration and adoption which belongs to baptized infants, is not identically the same which belongs to adults: but "a Christian infant who is regenerated in baptism acquires another regeneration, when, as an adult, he gives credence to the Gospel." With him the regeneration of the infant consisted in "the remission of original sin."†

His successor in the divinity chair at Cambridge, Dr. Ward, who entered on his duties about the year 1621, seems to have been one of the first in the Protestant Church of England to adopt and maintain the doctrine of the schoolmen, that sacraments always work their proper effects in one who interposes no bar, and applying it to the case of infants, he like Davenant, held that all baptized infants were regenerate; but even he carried his idea of regeneration in their case no further than to the remission of original sin.‡

Revival of School doctrine.

* To be found in Hanbury's edition of Hooker.

† Goode, 311.

‡ Wilberforce's Reply to Goode, Appendix.

This doctrine of the Schools, "sacramenta semper auferre suum effectum non ponenti obicem"—when about the same time brought forward in controversy by Thomson, was characterized by Bishop Abbot, (brother of the Archbishop of Canterbury,) as that "papistical sayings of the scholastics, which is the foundation of the opus operatum doctrine," and he holds it up to condemnation as contrary to the Protestant doctrine, that "the efficacy of sacraments depends solely on faith." Mr. Wilberforce, in his work on Infant Baptism, in reply to Goode, seems very indignant at this representation, but without sufficient reason; for to say that a sacrament is efficacious for the work wrought, is certainly very similar to saying that it is effectual to the good of the soul, if no hindrance nor positive obstruction be interposed. It is of no importance to explain, that the efficacy is attributed not to the outward act of giving or receiving, but to the grace of God which accompanies. This is said by the Romanist for what the Council of Trent puts its seal to, denominating it the opus operatum, and both when sifted, are liable to the rebuke of Jewel, pronounced in reference to the latter. "Verily, to ascribe any felicity or remission of sin, which is the work of the Holy Ghost, unto any manner of outward action whatsoever, is a superstitious, a gross, and a Jewish error."* What Jewel and the rest of the Reformers thought of the schoolmen—the inventors of these terms, and in whose writings some have hoped to find an elucidation of the meaning of the formularies of the Church—may be learned from an expression or two. "These words opus operatum, &c. . . . . have lately been devised by certain new scholastic doctors of Mr. Harding's own side." So continually they are spoken of as being of the contrary part, and if ever the Reformers quote any thing from them approvingly, it is as so much taken out of the mouths of adversaries.

Yet this very doctrine so like, if not the identical doctrine of Rome, was introduced and became one of

* Jewel, 1: 757.

the elements of English theology; that is, it is found to a greater or less extent, mixed up with matter of a better kind in the writings of many divines down to the present day. The enemies of Calvinism laid hold of it as a weapon wherewith to inflict a fatal wound upon the authority of that system. For if all infants are regenerate in baptism, then it is plain that the doctrine of perseverance will not bear the test of observation—since so many thus regenerated, fall away and perish. This was urged by Montagu, the friend of Archbishop Laud. To him Bishop Carlton replied, that Augustine's explanation was sufficient for the purpose. Such were regenerate, "only sacramento tenus."—Montagu said it was not a mere judgment of charity which pronounced baptized children regenerate, "because we are taught by our service book earnestly to believe that Christ hath favorably received these infants," &c. To this Carlton makes the spirited answer, "all this we receive and make no doubt of: but when we have said all, we must come to this—that all this is nothing but the charity of the Church; and what more can you make of it?" Such replies made by Davenant and Ward also, as defenders of the same scheme of doctrine, did not arrest the downward tendency of Calvinism. For various causes it declined; but the opposite view of the sacraments did not long maintain the supremacy. Such men as Burnet arose, who, while falling considerably behind the Reformers in clearness of evangelical statement, were most decidedly averse to the view of the sacraments entertained by the Laudean school. To which side Burnet thought the maxim above alluded to belonged, is evident from his statement on the sacraments. "The one (extreme) is of the Church of Rome, that teaches that as some sacraments imprint a character upon the soul, which they define to be a physical quality, that is supernatural and spiritual, so they do all carry along with them such a divine virtue, that by the very receiv-

Baptismal regeneration employed as an extinguisher of Calvinism.

Decline of Calvinism.

But Baptismal Regeneration not established

ing them, (the opus operatum,) it is conveyed to the souls of those to whom they are applied, unless they themselves put *a bar in the way of it* by some mortal sin."* Speaking of the office of infant baptism, he says, "it carries on the *supposition* of an internal regeneration, and in that helpless state, the infant is offered up and dedicated to God; and provided, that when he comes to age, he takes those vows on himself, then he shall find the full effects of baptism; and if he dies in that state of incapacity, he being dedicated to God, is certainly accepted of by him." A statement in regard to the safety of baptized infants, which if extended to all heathens as well as Christians, would in these days be objected to by few. Even those whose Confessions speak of elect infants, will no doubt be found to come very near the confidence here expressed, perhaps under the notion, that all infants dying before reason as such, are among the elect.

Wall and Waterland.

From Burnet's time the moderate view prevailed in the Church of England. There were those who, like Wall and Waterland, in the early part of the last century, thought that the term regeneration ought to be restricted to whatever spiritual effects may be supposed to be connected with baptism; but when their words are weighed, they seem to have had no more belief in the invariable, internal, efficacy of the ordinance than others. Wall's statement has been given already. Waterland, speaking of the baptism of infants says, "they become consecrated in solemn form to Father, Son, and Holy Ghost,—pardon, mercy, and other covenant privileges are made over to them, and the Holy Spirit translates them out of their *state* of nature, (to which a curse belongs,) to a *state* of grace, favor and blessing; *this is their regeneration.*" This, he says is what is meant when in our public offices we pray that the infant may be "washed and sanctified with the Holy Ghost," and all similar expressions. Then he adds, "it may reasonably be *presumed*, that from the time of their new birth of

* Burnet on the Articles.

water and the Spirit, (which at the moment is a renewal of their *state* to Godward,) the renewing of the heart may come gradually on with their first dawnings of reason," &c.* If this were all that is meant in the language used on the subject of baptismal regeneration, there would be little to awaken concern. But we are brought to apprehend something very serious when we examine the statements of this learned divine more narrowly. He distinguishes between regeneration and renovation. "Those first addresses or influential visits of the Holy Spirit turning and preparing the heart of man, are the preparative renewings, the first and lowest degrees of renovation. Afterward, in baptism, the same Spirit fixes as it were his dwelling or residential abode, renewing the heart in greater measure, and if his motions are still more and more complied with after baptismal regeneration, the renewing grows and improves through the whole course of the spiritual life."† Now, here is a view of the whole of the Spirit's work for man, according to the ideas of Waterland. At what step of this course did he look upon the person as by the Spirit brought to the beginning of that holiness, without which no man shall see the Lord?

Certainly, it would not be maintained, that "the first addresses" of the Spirit in the heart bring a man into that privileged state. In a Treatise on Regeneration, nothing is said to satisfy an inquirer on the question, in what consists that new birth which is necessary to "see the Kingdom of God." All the satisfaction we get is, that if we are baptized then, we have been regenerated. Either this is very heterodox, or else it is very unsatisfactory.

* Treatise on Regeneration, p. 19. † On Regeneration, p. 12.

PART III.

AFTER this there was nothing marked in the history of opinion on this subject until about the year 1815, when Dr. Mant furnished the Christian Knowledge Society with two "Tracts, intended to convey correct notions of Regeneration and Conversion." The views thus put forth are seemingly much the same as those of Waterland, but not presented in so cautious a manner. Dr. Mant says, from the time of baptism, "we have a new *principle* put into us—the *spirit* of grace—which besides our soul and body, is a *principle of action.*" Surely, there is here something more than a "renewal of state," which Waterland says must not be confounded with "renewal of mind."* He seems to have been the first to speak of the opposite opinion as "heresy." He even said the denial of his doctrine was, "in some sense, to do despite to the Spirit of grace." Dr. Mant.

Upon the Society's list of books and tracts, were nearly fifty containing statements on the subject of baptism, which could only be understood upon the supposition of the separability of the outward sign and the inward grace; while it was found that only two of all their numerous publications contained the doctrine of Dr. Mant.† It was not to be expected that a new Tract containing such decidedly antagonistic views would be allowed to come forth without replies. Accordingly, he was answered by Mr. John Scott and Mr. Biddulph who took somewhat differing views, the former interpreting the service in the hypothetical sense, and the latter adopting the distinction which we have seen expressly made And his opponents.

* On Regeneration, p. 26.

† See Christian Observer for 1816.

long before, of regeneration in its proper sense, and regeneration *sacramento tenus*. Subsequently, Mr. Budd and Mr. Faber entered into the controversy, and the subject was ably reviewed in the Christian Observer. All these writers understood Dr. Mant in the same sense, namely, as teaching that regeneration always takes place in baptism, and that adults as well as infants partake of the proper grace of the sacrament; "a death unto sin and a new birth unto righteousness." They complained of a want of distinctness in some of his statements, and an apparent contradiction in others, but all agreed that this objectionable view was presented in his Tracts. Great was the surprise of all these writers to find it denied by those who followed on the same side with Dr. Mant, that any one maintained the general proposition which has so often been stated. They complained of a misrepresentation of their views, while their opponents very properly rejoined, that every one would naturally draw such an objectionable doctrine from the pages of Dr. Mant, whose Tracts had been circulated with extraordinary zeal, so as to involve many beside himself in the charge of holding very heterodox, or very uncertain notions upon this important subject.

Bishop Rider.

Bishop Rider, in his primary charge published the same year, expressed his opinion on the subject in question in the following words: "I would wish generally to restrict the term (regeneration) to the baptismal privileges; and considering them as comprehending not only an external admission into the visible Church—not only a covenanted title to the pardon and grace of the Gospel, but even a degree of spiritual aid vouchsafed and ready to offer itself to our acceptance or rejection at the dawn of reason,—I would recommend," &c. This view met with the concurrence of many who were very far from holding any radically objectionable doctrine. But the question is not about the allowableness of applying the term in that inferior sense, it is as to whether we shall give up a word to this exclusive meaning, which in

Scripture is connected absolutely with the possession of spiritual and holy character, and the enjoyment of the highest blessings. "We know that whosoever is born of God, sinneth not: but he that is begotten of God, keepeth himself, and that wicked one toucheth him not."—1 Jno. 5: 18. Certainly, one merely with "aid vouchsafed and ready to offer itself," is not in the sense of this passage, "born and begotten of God."

Oxford Tracts.

After the controversy now alluded to subsided, the next era in the history of the doctrine is the publication of the Oxford Tracts, in which, and in the writings of a kindred spirit which have followed, there are views not before known to English theology since the Reformation; and to this day we are left in doubt whether these ideas have been dug up from mediæval theology, or imported from the foggy region of German speculation, or are the genuine products of the minds of Dr. Pusey and his followers. He writes thus: "One may then define regeneration to be that act whereby God takes us out of our relation to Adam, and makes us *actual* members of His Son. . . . . This is our new birth of God, of water and the Spirit, . . . herein also are we justified, or both accounted and made righteous, since we are made members of Him who is alone righteous, freed from past sin, . . have a new principle of life . . . imparted to us, since having been made members of Christ, we have a portion of His life, or of Him, who is our life."* Now observe this definition, and what can be made of it? Who will pretend that he understands it? From this definition the author plunges into a depth of learning, scriptural, patristic, mediæval, modern, to prove his point. And when we ask what the point is—what that blessing is which always accompanies the due ministration of the ordinance—what is this being made "actual members of Christ," on which our being, "accounted and made righteous," depends?—The only reply we get from Dr. P. is, that we are "incorporated into Christ;"—"we are sons of God be-

Dr. Pusey.

* Pusey on Baptism, 24.

cause He in whom and of whom we are made, is the Son of God, not by any figure or likeness, but actually, parts of the second Adam, as we were by nature of the first."* Elsewhere, Dr. Pusey says, "no change of heart or the affections, no repentance, however radical, no faith, no life, no love, come up to the idea of this birth from above: it takes them all in, and comprehends them all, and is itself more than all."†

From this master of dark sentences we turn to books since published, bearing the honored name of Wilberforce. That name will be long associated in the minds of Christians, with the title of the excellent volume now more than fifty years old, The Practical View of Christianity. Would that it could be said, the same clear and scriptural views were presented in the volumes now to be referred to.

R. J. Wilberforce.

Taking up the theory of Dr. Pusey, the Rev. R. J. Wilberforce has made two attempts to render it intelligible. With what success the reader may judge from the following. "Adam was the type in which humanity was originally made—our Lord the fresh type on which was remodelled the nature of mankind."‡ To Adam "there was superadded to his natural qualities some supernatural gift."|| That gift was God's "image."§ "The guiding light of original humanity . . . was a special and supernatural indwelling of the great Author of all knowledge."¶ This divine light was lost through sin. "The peculiar gift of the Holy Ghost, which is bestowed in the gospel is, that through union with the Son of God, we may regain the perfect image of the Creator."** This union is with "the humanity of Christ."†† "Through the union of Godhead and manhood in his single person, there was infused into that humanity which he shared with us, such grace as sufficed for the whole generation of his kindred. . . . . The union of mankind with Christ is . . . a real union whereby all renewed

* Pusey on Baptism, p. 44. † Ibid, p. 43. ‡ On the Incarnation, p. 59. || P. 62. § p. 64. ¶ p. 66. ** p. 67. †† p. 225.

men are joined to the second, as they were by nature to the first Adam."* As there is "a transmission of the nature of our common ancestor which causes us to be what we are"—so there is "a spiritual presence of the *manhood* of Christ by union with which we become what it is given us to be."† Of baptism he says, "Then men are joined by heavenly agency to Christ, that the life of their souls may from that day forth, have its development."‡ "There must be a gift antecedent to our efforts. This gift is that first union with Christ, wherein all communication of graces from him to us depends. Out of this beginning arises the whole system of the Christian life.—And this heavenly impulse is expressly declared in Scripture to be extended to us in baptism."|| "The enslaved will of man was first restored to freedom . . . in Christ. It is only through union with "him that we can escape bondage. A new birth is needed to the first actings of the will."§

In the second volume Archdeacon W. endeavors again to explain the system. If we cannot understand his previous ideas on account of their diffusion over so many pages he gives us an opportunity of making the attempt in the following definition.—"What is regeneration? It is the effect of that gift of grace which the Father of all mercies was pleased to embody in the manhood of the incarnate Son, that thereby humanity at large might be reconstructed, and which in him and by him is received by those happy members of the family of man to whom the gospel comes and by whom it is not rejected through unbelief or impenitence."¶ Reader! do you now understand? Is it made clear to your comprehension what regeneration is? A certain gift for man is treasured up in the manhood of Christ. What the gift is he does not explain. We know what the ultimate purpose of it is. It is to restore man to a perfect state. But what is the gift so much spoken of? As to this

* P. 229. † p. 230. ‡ p. 330. || p. 332. § p. 338.
¶ Doctrine of Holy Baptism, p. 39.

we are left quite in the dark; but then to add to our perplexity the writer in this *definition* tells us that regeneration is the *effect* of that gift. What the effect is we are left to conjecture. A page or two after this definition we have another description. "When this work is wrought in individual men, what is effected is not the complete and instant change of their whole nature, but only the infusion of a divine seed of a higher humanity, by which their spiritual progress is commenced. Such a gift does not exclude the action of man's own responsibility. It is but to place man in a higher state of trial, by the infusion of a principle above nature."*

It is not the purpose of this essay to enter at large into the subjects directly or indirectly presented in the volumes from which these extracts are made. The writer would only make a remark or two to assist in understanding the theory, so far as it has any thing intelligible to an ordinary mind. Regeneration, according to this doctrine, being a participation of Christ's, "man's nature"—is something peculiar to the Gospel. It was not known before. The pious patriarchs were therefore not regenerated.—If that be so, we may well ask what reason there was in our Lord's reproving question to Nicodemus, "Art thou a master in Israel, and knowest not these things?" As it regards children, it is well known that the theory maintains their universal regeneration in baptism. In adults, repentance and faith are supposed to be requisite to the efficacy of baptism, but they are not properly Gospel graces; they are gifts preparatory to the great gift of incorporation into Christ. They are different in kind as well as degree, from that repentance and faith which are found in baptized persons. A baptized adult, it would seem, is supposed to receive the gift of *union with Christ*, no matter what may be his state of mind, though the due effects of the gift are not communicated until he repents and believes. To such an adult as a baptized person, all those Scriptures

New theory of Baptism.

* P. 44.

apply, "born again," "raised to newness of life," "new creatures," though in fact he is "in the gall of bitterness and the bond of iniquity." To say nothing of the vast variety of Scriptures, which by the magical touch of this theory, lose all their signification, as hitherto understood, what are we to say of the duty of ministers toward adults coming to baptism. Why surely it must be wise to baptize them all without much inquiry, since they will certainly be partakers of Christ's humanity, and by that means, be better fitted to exercise repentance and faith, and so obtain all the blessings of pardon and life. They will then have the antecedent gift of which so much is said, and which is absolutely essential to their future progress.

Sewell.

In Sewell's Christian Morals, we have an exhibition of the modern view, in popular application. Looking at the doctrine as it lies in the writings of Pusey and Wilberforce, it might be considered as comparatively a harmless speculation, which would never get beyond the study of the recluse or the dusty pages of unread books. In Sewell, it is presented for the common belief and practice. "By the rite of baptism, the Church places the recipient in an entirely new position, ... restores him at once to a state of security and goodness, instead of urging him to save himself by some subsequent efforts. . . . . The very things which a heathen moralist would most desire—such as the mortification of the flesh, the death unto sin, the creation of a new spirit within us, the enlightenment of the mind, the cleansing of the conscience, the forgiveness of sins, and restoration to the favor of God and union with his nature—all these are described in the Bible as effected by baptism already. And the subsequent struggle (for struggle it must be,) is to defend what we have received, to secure ourselves from falling from the high estate in which we have been placed."* "Disbelieve all that you can—deny all

* P. 210, Eng. Ed.

meaning in outward forms—reject the mystery as impossible, or as leading to practical evil—still you cannot escape from the historical fact, that for eighteen hundred years the rite of baptism has been transmitted through the Church as the supposed means of conveying to man, some real deep, incalculable blessing, which *without it man cannot attain*."* He makes a baptized inquirer ask, "Where is the evidence that the power of evil in me really is destroyed?—that my sins really are forgiven—that God really is imparted to me by the waters of baptism?" He answers: "To give this proof does not belong properly to the ethical teacher. It is rather the business of the theologian, or perhaps of ecclesiastical history."† To the objection, that the results as seen by us daily, do not correspond with the anticipations raised by such a view of the efficacy of baptism, the reply is, "This is the common stumbling block." But think for a moment: are you not mistaking the promise? No where is it made unconditially."‡ This is the first mention of any condition. Thirty pages after the first quotation, (pages taken up with illustrations of the efficacy of the ordinance,) this is the first intimation of any thing of the kind, and then it is dismissed, not again to be introduced, unless in the most general manner for fifty pages after. On the subject of the conditional nature of the blessing imparted in baptism, he introduces three illustrations; but all based upon his favorite idea, that the gift has been imparted, and all man has to do is to preserve it. Not one word is said of any condition *preparatory* to baptism. The conditions have relation only to the *preservation* of the benefit. You would suppose that there were no professions of repentance and faith—that these were not a necessary part of the covenant of baptism, as our Church and the Church in all ages, has insisted, even in the case of infants. What shall we say to such language as this concerning the power

Church almost divine.

claimed by the Church—"a power which places it almost on a level with God himself,

* P. 218. † p. 238. ‡ p. 241.

the power of forgiving sins, by wiping them out in baptism, of transferring souls from hell to heaven, without admitting a doubt of it, as when 'baptized infants, it is said, dying before committing actual sin, are undoubtedly saved'—the power of bringing down the Spirit of God from heaven, and incorporating it in the persons of frail and fleshly men." . . . . "If such an authority has never been given, then the Church, in every one of its most solemn acts, is guilty of the most frightful blasphemy that man can conceive." * Again, he speaks of "the miracle wrought in us by baptismal regeneration."† What shall we say of those who could not have baptism, on whom this miracle could not be wrought. "Were no men good before the coming of our Lord? . . . Take the case of Abraham, of David, of Socrates. . . . . I answer, the question is not whether they acted virtuously, &c., but whether their virtue emanated wholly from an internal self-acting spring within them, without which . . . . they were the creatures of circumstances. And it is, I think, to circumstances created and combined by a merciful Providence, ... we must attribute, as Plato did, all the natural goodness of man before the Christian era. The real and internal power was still wanting."‡ This is said of Abraham and David, the covenant people of God, as well as of Socrates. What must we think if those who in the New Testament, are so often held up for our imitation and example, were after all men without the peculiar power of divine grace offered in the gospel? They were the mere slaves of external circumstances—sometimes good, sometimes evil. "External power cannot change the heart: and therefore, the Church gives more; it puts into the heart a new principle, or rather a new being; or rather, if we may so dare to speak, God himself by imparting to it the Holy Spirit, and uniting it to the body of Christ. It is from this Holy Spirit that all the real power and spontaneity of man proceeds."§ Under this system it

The Patriarchs without internal grace.

* P. 247. † p. 251. ‡ p. 247. § pp. 279, 280.

is difficult to conceive how a human being can ever be brought into the state which the Church and the Scripture contemplate as a sufficient preparation for baptism. Without that ordinance, he has nothing of that union with God through Christ, on which his capacity for religion consists. He must be baptized, that he may repent and believe in a godly manner. Hence, the Romish missionaries do wisely to baptize all who ask it, yea and those who ask it not. Are there any Protestant ministers who carry out the theory in the same manner?

Concerning the progress of opinion in our own Church on the subject of this essay, it may be proper to add a few words. There were two alterations made by the General Convention at the adoption of our Liturgy which are worthy of notice. The one is the omission of the rubric which is subjoined to the baptismal service of the English Church. It reads as follows: "It is certain by God's word that children which are baptized, dying before they commit actual sin are undoubtedly saved." Of this much use has been made in the recent controversy to prove that the doctrine of the invariable efficacy of baptism is the doctrine of the English Church. It seems to have been too generally overlooked that the rubric is of late origin, it is not found in the book of Elizabeth and cannot be brought in to explain the meaning of the language of the Reformers whose sense, and not that of the Laudean divines, is to be regarded as authoritative. But even if in the English Church they could be supposed to be trammelled by this rubric, our fathers of the American Church have wisely liberated us and restored the office to its original state.

Another change bearing on this subject was made in the first rubric in the Burial Service, where in the English form its use is prohibited to "all that die unbaptized" including infants. Wall justifies this upon the ground that the use of that service for such an infant would be "to determine the point and acknowledge him for a Christian brother." If so, then our

Church recognises the Christian membership even of unbaptized infants, for she forbids the employment of that form of burial only in the case of *adults* dying without baptism. It is remarkable that in this instance also our own forms are brought nearer to what they were originally.*

Bishop White, (who states that the first rubric alluded to was omitted, because it seemed "to countenance the notion that unbaptized infants are not saved,") held that infants are by baptism brought into "a state of grace,"† apparently in the sense of Waterland. Bishop Seabury expressed the strongest confidence in the future happiness of infants dying without baptism, and seems to have looked for the full baptismal blessing only in answer to faith and prayer.‡ Dr. Jarvis, quoted by Bishop Brownell in his book on the Common Prayer, pronounces the question whether the Holy Spirit always accompanies the outward act of baptism one of the unprofitable ones which the Apostle cautions us to avoid, "knowing that they do gender strifes." Bishop Hobart urged the appropriation of the word regeneration to baptism, but with him baptism was "a change of spiritual *state*,"§ or "spiritual condition" "a translation into a state in which our salvation is rendered possible," to be distinguished from a change of heart, without clearly teaching any thing beyond this as to the *immediate* effects. But he went so far as to pronounce that those children who die unbaptized, though not deprived of every degree of future felicity, yet fail to attain to that "super-eminent bliss reserved for those who pass into

*The Reformers were far from regarding the infants of Christians as aliens from the Christian commonwealth until baptized. Jewel in the Apology, (ch. xi. Divis. 3) says, "they pertain unto the people of God," and *infers* thence the duty of baptizing them. Becon argues at some length on the subject and concludes, "Now if the infants of Christians be pure and holy and the sons of God, shall any man . . . . take that [baptism] from them which God hath appointed and ordained for his sons." It was therefore in perfect consistency with their general views that they gave Christian burial to unbaptized infants.

†Lectures, p. 13. ‡Sermons, vol. 1. p. 121, 123.

§Sermons, vol. 2: 455, 472, 488.

the kingdom of glory through the kingdom of grace on earth."

More important than any thing else perhaps as indicating the sense of our divines in this country is the *unanimous* action of the House of Bishops in 1826, on a resolution proposing a change in the prayer at confirmation, commencing "Almighty and everlasting God, who hast vouchsafed," &c. While they proposed to add "in baptism" to the word "regenerate," so that the regeneration always in their view took place at that time, yet in explanation of what they meant by it, they appended the words, "*thus giving them a title* to all the blessings of the covenant." This, together with the other changes, was proposed by Bishop Hobart.

How far some in our Church in the present day are disposed to go beyond him who a few years ago was thought to go the farthest in such matters, is evident from what was preached on a great occasion last year in London by one of the so-called representatives of our communion. In his jubilee sermon, Bishop McCoskry says, in baptism "every child is made a new creature in Christ Jesus," whereas Bishop Hobart only says (in Catechism No. 3 of the Protestant Episcopal Union) baptized infants "*must become* new creatures." In explanation of this and similar scriptural expressions he says of the baptized, "by the power of the Holy Spirit their hearts and lives must be conformed to the doctrines of Christ;" whereas Bishop M. confines the new creation to baptism. All the spiritual influences which result in genuine conversion of heart leave the individual short of "the mighty change which makes the new creature in Christ." This it will be seen is in exact accordance with the modern view put forth by the new school of English theology.

In healthful contrast with all such teaching, is that contained in one of the most important works ever sent forth by any of our divines, the book entitled, Mysteries Opened. In that work Dr. Stone analyses with great power the erroneous theory of Dr. Pusey and his school, on the subject of baptism, and exposes its contrariety to the word of God. Like several other valuable books put forth by the opponents of the innovators in the English and American Church it remains unanswered, as indeed, in its main positions, it is unanswerable.

PART IV.

GENERAL VIEW OF THE WHOLE.

Thus have we reached the termination of our sketch of the history of opinion on the efficacy of baptism. As we have seen the ancient fathers very early began to apply the term regeneration to that ordinance, and to speak of all the baptized as "regenerate." But that this was done in any one consistent sense throughout, does not appear. In many of the passages quoted, it may very plausibly, if not certainly, be maintained that they, like the moderns, used this phraseology sometimes in a merely sacramental manner; at other times with a nearer approach to its Scriptural signification in reference to the great spiritual change, the commencement of true holiness of heart and life; but the predominant idea to be gathered from these quotations which have been made is, that in baptism there was an application of the blood of Christ to the washing away of the guilt of sin, accompanied with a measure of the Spirit of God. What that precise gift was, over and above an introduction to a covenanted title to salvation does not appear. It would seem that satisfied with the general promise of the Holy Ghost, they speculated little upon this subject. Their error was of a different kind, that of supposing that the virtue of Christ's atonement was so tied to the sacrament that except in certain extraordinary cases there was no remission without baptism. With almost one voice they pronounced unfavorably upon the case of children dying without baptism, because of the imputation of original sin, which it was supposed could not otherwise be removed. Those who profess to be governed

Original error.

Supposed necessity of baptism.

by the unanimous consent of antiquity, to be consistent, must embrace this view of the state of infants dying unbaptized.—In substance, this was the common opinion until the Reformation. And what was the effect of it? It led no doubt to much preaching and much anxiety about baptism. But did it lead to that due and reverent administration of it which we gather from the Scriptures to be our duty?* So far from it, we find it was deferred by parents on behalf of their children, and by adults when brought to some knowledge of Christianity, under the idea that in that ordinance, there was to be had a cleansing from sin, such as could not be hoped for in any other way; and they wished by all means to pass out of the world with the supposed immediate and peculiar benefit of the purifying water, as if the blood of Jesus Christ could not always cleanse from sin. It furthermore led to the administration of baptism by women to children at their birth, whenever there seemed to be the slightest danger of death.—Indeed, if there be any universally acknowledged error in the baptismal offices of the English Church as left unchanged, even in the time of Elizabeth, it was that relating to such use of the sacred rite. The rubric in the office of private baptism, as it stood down to the times of James I. merely prescribed, "let them that be present call upon God, ... and then one of them shall name the child and dip him," &c. Wheatly says, "when they came to have clearer notions of the sacraments, and perceived how absurd it was to confine the mercies of God to outward means,"† they made a change; though the allowance of the custom may have resulted not from the conviction of the governors of the Church of the absolute necessity of baptism; it may be understood as a mere temporary concession to public sentiment. Yet, however, we may

Effects of this mistake.

* Bingham, the learned antiquarian of the Church, states, that St. Ambrose assigns as a reason why this doctrine about the necessity of baptism for the salvation of infants was earnestly pressed, "that parents might not be so negligent in bringing their children to baptism."—Book 10, ch. 2. How dangerous is it by such means to add weight to the authority of divine precepts!

† On the Common Prayer, in loco.

interpret the action of the leaders in this case, it shows that the exaltation of the sacraments to a higher position than that given them in Scripture, does in fact frustrate their due observance as institutions of the gospel.

After the Reformation, we have seen the gradual introduction of the Romish view, that sacraments always work their effects unless a bar of positive unbelief opposes;—so different from the universal statement of the Reformers, that they were means of grace to *worthy* receivers,—a view of their nature which led some of them to contemplate infants as having a species of faith, and all of them to insist, that baptism was a covenant transaction, in which the answers were always *impliedly*,* if not expressly made on behalf of the child. Connected with this Romish principle, (in fact, the opus operatum, however disguised,) was the denial of the propriety of the application of the term regeneration to any other change than that effected by baptism; but there the matter seemed to rest until the time of Bishop Tomline, Dr. Mant, and others. From that day to this, speculation has been busy to find out some specific gift, which is always communicated in baptism, unless frustrated by unbelief. It could not be denied, that repentance and faith are necessary in adults to the due reception of the ordinance, nor that these were graces of the Spirit.† In dealing with this case, the advocates of the theory of baptismal regeneration have always had great difficulty, at one time granting what at another they

Doctrine of Reformers.

Speculation busy.

Difficulties.

* This is a sufficient answer to the argument from the office of Private Baptism, as urged by Mr. Wilberforce and others.

† Mr. Alexander Campbell, the leader of a considerable sect of Baptists in our Western Country, holds an opinion in common with Romanists and Puseyites on the efficacy of baptism, which he has sometimes endeavored to fasten on our Prayer-book. He maintains, that the Holy Ghost is so connected with baptism, that no man receives it in order to regeneration, until he is baptized. An historical faith, which may be had without the Holy Ghost, is all that is necessary for baptism. At the time of baptism, the Holy Spirit descends and changes this historical or dead faith, into a living and saving faith. This accords with Dr. Pusey's declaration, "that faith before baptism is not faith." Of course, Dr. Pusey, as well as Mr. Campbell, refer to adults coming to baptism.

deny, involving themselves in confusion, from which they can manage to escape only by getting off their ground as to the proper use of the words regeneration, &c. If by this word, they mean the beginning of a genuine holy character, they have to confess that this has already taken place in every adult duly prepared for baptism, that the new principle has been implanted before. They have, therefore, generally avoided the discussion of the subject in this light, and confined themselves to the case of infants,—with the more plausibility, inasmuch as it is chiefly with those baptized in infancy we have to do. Now we may well complain of this as an unfair advantage, and that for two reasons—first, that in Scripture, it is the case of adults that seems to be chiefly contemplated in connection with this subject. "He that *believeth* and is baptized," &c. Any theory which will not bear the test of application to it, must be erroneous. Secondly, the case of infants is in Scripture left very much to inference. What God may work in them we know not. That they are capable of all that is needful to prepare them for heaven we know; but what the work of the Spirit in their case may be, who can tell? If they live, we are sure that without the operation of the same Spirit, they cannot have any thing truly good, and how early, and by what methods the Holy Ghost may act upon them, we are quite ignorant. We are here entirely without the possibility of any rational conclusions. Men may assert what they will of effects wrought upon infants, we cannot disprove their assertions; but this is not necessary on our part—it is for them first to give us some rational ground of conviction.

Avoidance of the proper test.

In this state of uncertainty, as to what was to be maintained as being the *specific* gift of baptism in adults and infants, Dr. Pusey seems to have been the first to bring out the idea, that it was union with Christ—not with Christ spiritually by faith—not with the society of his professing people, nor yet with the society of his true people, (his

Result of the labors of speculation.

body mystical according to Hooker,)—but with his human nature. This he denominated "incorporation into Christ." Others have worked upon this idea, until at last Mr. Wilberforce has presented it to us in all its proportions. Regeneration is "Christ taking up his dwelling in man," and that not spiritually, by grace and power—that with him is only a figurative indwelling. He says *really* and to him, the only reality in this matter is a participation in Christ's humanity, his man's nature, as we are really partakers of Adam's nature by natural descent.* Now suppose this can be understood in any good sense, consistent with the spiritual and heavenly character of the Gospel dispensation, let it be vindicated from all that seems to be in it of what is gross and carnal—we ask two questions with regard to it.

What acquisition has been made.

First, what is there in this view more within the grasp of the human mind than the ordinary Protestant idea, that Christ Jesus, our ascended and glorified Redeemer, is spiritually present with us?—spiritually the food and life of the souls of believers? What more do we want than in the exercise of faith to contemplate Jesus as not only in heaven, but as really with us to apply to our souls by the Spirit, all that is needed for health and life.

If to be understood what is there to support it.

Secondly on what does this theory rest for support? To what word of God does it appeal? Mr. W. has a chapter in his second work headed "Testimony of Scripture, as to the time and manner in which regeneration is bestowed." The first reference is to Jno. 3 : 5. The second to Tit. 3: 5. To these are added such as Gal. 3: 27, Rom. 6 : 3, 4, Col. 2 : 12. From the position which he gives to the first two, it is plain he

* Wall quotes a Romish author as saying, that men of learning are most subject to error, and he illustrates it by some strange fancies of the learned persons himself. Wall adds as a reason of the fact alluded to, (so far as it is a fact,) that "vulgar people having no assistance from learning or philosophy, having nothing but common sense to trust to; so they generally keep close to that." He goes on to say it was not plain common sense people who fell into the error of transubstantiation.

assents to Dr. Pusey's confession that they are the chief pillars of the doctrine, if it be one of the Bible. Hear the Dr:—mentioning the first two references above made, he says: "These then are the only passages of the Holy Scriptures in which the first origin of regeneration (so to speak) is marked out, and the circumstances under which it takes place *at all hinted at*."—Now mark the words which follow. "Surely this ought to any careful Christian to be of great moment and instead of longing, as the habit of some is, for more evidence, he will thank God that the evidence is so clear, that all Christians of old times confidently relied upon it and transmitted it to us." How much we are to make of such assertions concerning the judgment of "the Christians of old times," the readers of the preceding pages may judge. Let it be observed and pondered that even Dr. Pusey in the passages referred to can only see the invariable connection of baptism and regeneration *hinted at*. There are many places of Scripture in which to the popular ear, that connection seems much more decidedly set forth, as for instance, "Arise and be baptized and wash away thy sins." "By one Spirit we are all baptized into one body."—But the leaders of opinion on that side when addressing those who look for something more than words are ashamed to put them forward as their chief reliance. In all the Bible there is nothing so relied upon as those two passages, "except a man be born of water and the Spirit he cannot enter into the Kingdom of God," and "according to his mercy he saved us by the washing of regeneration and renewing of the Holy Ghost." It is for every one to say as in the sight of God, whether these are sufficient to support the doctrine, and that one, which when really embraced must modify almost the whole circle of Christian belief and practice.

Appeal to moderate men.

The writer is fully persuaded that there are many now as there have been in time past who hold a certain doctrine of baptismal regeneration to whom such views as those presented in the later writers on that side must be altogether abhorrent, when clearly understood. To them he would appeal and ask, whether of such a fanciful union with Christ all those precious Scriptures are to be interpreted which speak of "Christ's dwelling in us" and we "in him," of our "being buried and raised with him," of our "being made one with him." Let it be observed that all these and similar expressions are by this theory understood of that union with Christ in baptism which may or may not be followed by holiness. If we can think of a regenerated man without faith or love as some suppose, can we conceive of one as having "a death unto sin and a new birth unto righteousness" without being really righteous. Surely the tendency, aye, the immediate result of all such handling of the word of God must be to make it of none effect, to empty it so far as man is concerned, of all that is life-giving and divine. It is to draw us off from the pure and spiritual religion of the Gospel and send us back to the ceremonial service of Judaism,—it may be to something not half so good.

The new theory aggressive.

I have already intimated that this obscure doctrine has left the shades of the recluse and been presented even in a book of Christian Morals designed for popular use. It is served up in volumes of fiction and is set before children in books of Sunday School instruction. In how many pulpits it is taught in our country and England who can tell? It is I suppose much the same carnal view which has taken possession of the minds of some of the bishops of the mother Church. If they have not yet adopted all its later developments yet the old doctrine has some how acquired a wondrous tendency toward activity. Baptismal regeneration has become a test at Episcopal examinations. A few years ago when the Bishop of Exeter examined Mr. Gorham previous to his entering on his new preferment, the Bishop zealous as he was in the maintenance of his views, was not so firm in his adherence to what he pronounced to be the doctrine of the Church, but that he would have let Mr. G. pass if the latter had only promised not to make the matter public. Now while the pen traces these lines, news is brought from England that the Bishop of Ripon refuses orders to a young man unexceptionable in all respects save that he would not assent to the inseparability of the sign and the thing signified in baptism;—while a few weeks ago the papers announced the same stand taken by another Bishop in a distant Colony of England. Judging from the past it is not unlikely that something of the same kind may soon be enacted in our country.

As one contemplates the threatening aspect of this spirit in these days the feeling of scorn which is first excited by the manifestation of such narrowness of mind and bigotry of feeling, quickly gives place to indignation that such characters should have found their way into Episcopal seats once graced by Cranmer, Latimer, Ridley, Hooper, Jewel, to say nothing of those in subsequent times who, if they did not come up to the spirit of the Reformers, yet manifested in their administration of their dioceses something of their freedom of view. Thank God that in our own Church if we have had some bishops who have not been satisfied with the perfectly Protestant character of her institutions we have had such names as White and Griswold upon our lists, men of differing views in some material respects, and yet uniting in strong condemnation of every tendency toward Romish doctrine and the Romish spirit.

Successors of the Reformers.

Before the party which contemplates the enforcement of the dogma of the invariable connection of the grace of baptism with the administration itself, can be successful in their designs they will have a great work to do. Surely they have not considered it. If those who hold the contrary of the above proposition are not to be admitted into the ranks of the ministry those ministers who hold with them in their views in our own country and abroad, have no right to remain where they are. If they were to be put forth how many would be left? Nay there will

A difficult work.

have to be a work akin to that performed by the Romanists in Queen Mary's day, when they dug up the bodies of some who had been active in the English reformation and executed sentence on them, so far as it was yet in their power. Thus the modern movers in the baptismal controversy will have to sit in judgment not only on the living but the dead, and consign the names of some of the most learned and holy to a place outside the Church. All that has been written by such men as Jewel, Hall, Usher, Tillotson, Burnet and a host of others must be given to oblivion. Surely in this view of the movement it seems superbly ridiculous.

Mischievous effects.

Though such be its character we cannot but take up a lamentation for the mischiefs immediate and remote it is likely to inflict. To say nothing of the annoyance to many good men who are to be harassed at every step of their progress into the ministry, and afterward, how much does such an intolerant course on the part of bishops and others favor the designs of those who entertain unfriendly feelings toward the Church, and understandingly or not, would see her prostrate in the dust. But above all what injury is done to souls when in a promiscuous assembly it is preached that all who have been baptized have already been made children of God, are regenerate and that they must only be zealous to improve a gift long since imparted; and the contrary doctrine that men are to presume themselves unregenerate until the new nature manifests itself in the fruits of holiness, is not to be tolerated. The former view, qualified as it may be, cannot fail to be acceptable to all who would hide their sins from their own eyes; and whatever eloquence and learning may be used in recommending it will prove as music to compose the soul already prone to slumber for a lasting and a fatal sleep.

END.

THE

HIGH-CHURCH THEORY

OF

BAPTISM.

PHILADELPHIA:
T. K. & P. G. COLLINS.
STEREOTYPED BY L. JOHNSON & CO.
1853.

THE

HIGH-CHURCH THEORY OF BAPTISM.

FOUR Sermons by the Rev. George Stanley Faber, "On the doctrine of Regeneration according to Scripture and the Church of England," have recently been republished by the Messrs. Biddle of Philadelphia.

The object of Mr. Faber in these discourses is to define the position of the Church of England on the great doctrine in question, and to refute the argument of Dr., afterward Bishop Mant, in favour of the *inseparability* of baptism and spiritual regeneration.

Dr. Mant's tracts were first issued in the year 1815, by the "Society for the Promotion of Christian Knowledge." The view taken of this doctrine in these tracts was so extreme, so inconsistent with the former publications of this Society, as to produce a long and very animated discussion, which brought forth many of the ablest writers of the Church of England. In the year 1816, Mr. Faber entered into this controversy, and published his celebrated sermons. His able and intelligible argument was so convincing to the great body of the English church, that the friends of Dr. Mant were compelled to abandon their ground and publicly renounce their favorite theory. Dr. Mant *himself*, however, never denied that he taught the doctrine which it was the aim of Mr. Faber's argument to counteract, and which his (Dr. Mant's) opponents attributed to him.* This took place in the year 1816. In 1853, these sermons were republished in this country, for the purpose of doing the same work in America which they so effectually performed in England. This has been to a great extent accomplished. The un-

---

* Even the case of Simon Magus, Dr. Mant insisted upon, as did Dr. Pusey after him, as a necessary case of regeneration—followed by an immediate falling into sin.

prejudiced readers of Mr. Faber's argument are convinced of the unscriptural character of the opinion that baptism and regeneration are inseparable; but certain newspapers, belonging to the ultra church party, now deny that it is actually held by any in the church.

The REGISTER, a church paper in Philadelphia, the CHURCH JOURNAL in New York, and the GOSPEL MESSENGER of Western New York, make use of almost the same language which was adopted by the friends of Bishop Mant in 1816.

The editor of the former appears to be much distressed that Mr. Faber's sermons should have been disturbed at this late day, and says they "are aimed against a theory of baptism which, if we "could believe that any one actually held it, we should be among "the first to condemn."*

The Gospel Messenger replies to Mr. Faber's argument by calling it very hard names,—"gross unfairness," "outrageous misrepresentations," "wholesale slanders," &c. And the Church Journal says, "Faber adopts a definition of regeneration which sound "churchmen have never been willing to receive." That *sound* churchmen have never been willing to receive it there cannot be

---

* We commend the following language, from the Register, to those who distinguish between a desire to know the truth, and a determination to maintain opinions at the expense of even propriety. The prototype of this language may be found in the Irish Romanist journals and speeches, when the "Irish Church Missions" sent their "feathered seeds" in the same manner to the homes of the papists. May God grant this "seed" the like abundant harvest!

"They [Mr. Faber's sermons] have been sent to us,—but by whom we cannot "say, for they are re-issued under no responsible name,—'free, gratis, and for "nothing.' We learn on inquiry, that most of our clerical friends have been "equally favoured; so that in all probability similar 'feathered seeds' are now on "the wings of every wind, destined (if thirty-seven years have not exhausted "their vitality) to swell the harvest of strife in many quarters of the Union.

"Now the first question that arises, with regard to such gratuities, is, where "do they come from? Who sends them,—who edits them,—who stands responsible for them,—above all, who pays for their free circulation? By what right "or title, and at whose instigation, do they thus invade the quiet of a private "house? It is seldom we receive such presents of any thing useful. Apothecaries do not give us their drugs, grocers do not favour us with gratuitous tea "or sugar. If we receive a package from a bookseller, we expect as a matter "of course to find some token that we have ordered it, or at least that it is something worth ordering; or if there is any thing unwelcome or mischievous within, "we know where the blame lies, and where is the remedy. In the case of a certain sort of pamphlet, however, we have no such protection. Whether we "want them or not, they find their way to our doors. The postman, who brings "us a letter from a friend, presents us with one of these missives. The servant "girl, when she sweeps the steps, finds another thrust under the door. Believing as we do, that bad divinity is, from its lightness and cheapness, more easily "circulated, and goes abroad further than good, we cannot but regard the gratuitous distribution of loosely written tracts as a most portentous evil."

the shadow of a doubt; but that churchmen of the Puseyite school advocate it, and that High-Churchmen intentionally or ignorantly give it their influence, the following pages will fully prove.

These extreme views of baptism, certain parties in the church have been industriously inculcating for many years past. Inculcating them in the pulpit, in the newspaper and periodical press, in novels, tales, and tracts, in the Sunday-school and in Sunday-school literature,—in fact in every possible manner they have taught that spiritual regeneration is the consequence of the administration of baptism.

This has been their darling theory; this has been their favorite doctrine; this has been their starting-point in religion; their all and in all; and upon this their whole system of theology rests. But this doctrine, like others of the same kind, will not bear the light of day, it cannot stand the test of God's holy word, and the consequence is—now that Mr. Faber has again driven them to their legitimate position, and they have reason to fear the effect of his argument upon the minds of practical, common-sense men—that they deny ever having been the advocates of such a system. Mr. Faber is ridiculed. He is accused of "erecting a man of straw and "then knocking it down." He is charged with "caricaturing the "doctrine of baptism." His sermons are stigmatized as "a bitter "controversial pamphlet," and his arguments are compared to "Canada thistles, which are noxious weeds and grow apace." Any one at all acquainted with the life and character of Mr. Faber, must be struck with the perfect absurdity of a position which maintains Mr. F. to have been so ignorant of the subject in controversy as not to know the nature of the error he was combating. He *perfectly understood* Bishop Mant's views. His sermons were aimed at those views. The aim was perfect, and the shot told. The republication of these sermons was directed at the same opinions now and for a long time past pressed upon the Church by Tractarians, and too hastily admitted by High-Churchmen; and judging from the excitement of their newspapers, it is very evident that the advocates of these semi-Romish sentiments are touched upon a vital spot! Is it the essential character of error thus to prevaricate and shift its ground? Or has the vague semi-transcendentalism of the great apostles of this school, Pusey and Wilberforce, obscured the judgment and weakened the conscience of their followers until they know not what they believe, or are not bold or honest enough to examine?

The object of these pages is to prove that Mr. Faber's argument is not a "caricature;" that Dr. Mant in 1815, and the Tractarian party, and their sympathizers in the Church of England and in this country for the last few years have been assiduously engaged in inculcating the doctrine, that spiritual regeneration invariably accompanies the baptism of every infant, and also of every adult, where the recipient places no wilful bar. In some instances, the ground being taken, that spiritual regeneration invariably accompanies the administration of baptism even in adults.

This is the position which has been advocated by a large portion of the High-Churchmen in this country and in England, and against these opinions the Evangelical portion of the Church have ever contended, because they view them as the seeds, nay, as the very plants which produce the fruits of Puseyism and Romanism.

These have been the views of that large class of clergymen and candidates for Holy Orders, both in this country and in England, who, having failed in their efforts to *unprotestantize* the Episcopal Church, have at last taken refuge under the wings of the "Holy Mother" of Rome. These have been the views of your Newmans, your Mannings, your Wilberforces, &c. &c., in England, and, in this country, of your Walworths,* your Berrians,* your Majors, your McMasters,* your Pollards, your Huntingtons, your Stoughtons, your Dr. Allens, your Dr. Forbes, and last, though not least, your Bishop Ives, the first Protestant Bishop who ever openly renounced the Protestant Church. In all these cases and in several others this doctrine of the new birth in the article of Baptism has been the starting-point in that sliding-scale which has landed them in the withering and deadly embrace of POPERY.†

---

* Candidates for Holy Orders.

† It is a remarkable and pregnant fact that these perverts had been known to hold the most extreme views, and to be strongly impregnated with Romish doctrine, for a long period prior to their leaving the Church, and yet many Bishops and clergymen defended their soundness in the faith to the very moment of their secession. Bishop Ives and Drs. Allen and Forbes were sustained by High-Churchmen until their admission to the Church of Rome was publicly announced. The friends of Bishop Ives indignantly repelled the charge of his perversion, and

The advocates of this view of baptism have always been afraid of arguments which would drive them to their legitimate position. Hence their great anxiety concerning the circulation of Mr. Faber's sermons. They fear lest this able exposition should shake the faith of some of the clergy in the sacramental theory of religion, and open the eyes of reflecting laymen to its fallacious and dangerous character.

The Tractarian, and so far forth the High-Church system of theology, is purely a sacramental system. It trains up our children and youth, it teaches our young men and maidens that in BAPTISM the great work of the soul's regeneration is effected. It repudiates those mental and spiritual emotions, that anxiety and sorrow which in a greater or less degree, according to God's providence, always accompany the new birth of the soul. It would lead us to the belief that if baptism is properly administered, the subject of it placing no mental bar to its efficacy, if it is followed

---

pronounced the whole thing a falsehood and a slander, until articles from the European prints placed it beyond a contingency.

It is not a little mortifying to "sound churchmen" that these Romanizers are thus upheld and countenanced by so large a portion of our clergy; and when they are charged with heretical views, to find so many censuring those who sound the alarm.

Who does not remember the letter of Bishop Doane, endorsing Newman, which appeared in a Burlington paper a few days before the authentic account of his defection reached this country?

Who does not remember the abuse which was heaped upon Bishop McIlvaine of Ohio for his solemn warning against the dangerous principles of Tractarianism in his unanswerable work on "Oxford Divinity?"

Who does not remember the storm which burst upon the Rev. Drs. Smith and Anthon when they so boldly protested against the ordination of Mr. Arthur Carey of the New York Seminary? And what has been the sequel to the event which brought upon those clergymen such abuse from nearly all the High-Churchmen of the land?

In Mr. Carey's class there were twenty-one students: Gordon Huntington and Ferdinand C. White gone to Rome! In the middle class, twenty-six students: E. P. Wadhams and H. B. J. McMasters, gone to Rome! In the junior class, nineteen students: William Everett and N. C. Stoughton gone to Rome!

We also find the names of Clarence Walworth, H. McVickar, and Chandler Berrian on the seminary catalogue, the former now a Romish priest.

Mr. McVickar was tried by the faculty for theological error (Romanism) and sentenced. He at once withdrew from the seminary and shortly after was *ordained deacon* by BISHOP MCCOSKRY. Mr. McV. is since deceased.

Mr. Berrian has now supervision of several Roman Catholic Sunday schools, in the city of New York, and is preparing for orders, it is said, in that church.

Mr. McMasters was to have been ordained with Mr. Carey, but it was decided by the faculty that his examination should not take place, and that he should remain in the seminary another year. He is now the editor of the Freeman's Journal, a Roman Catholic newspaper in New York, and has stated that Mr. Carey's views were similar to his own before Mr. C.'s ordination, and that their views were Roman.

Bishop Onderdonk was the ordaining Bishop—where is he? Bishop Ives, who read the litany, and fully sustained Bishop O.—where is he? Who believes that the end is yet?

by confirmation, and the reception of the Lord's Supper, if there is a proper regard for the external demands of the Church, and withal a moral life, the great work in the soul of the sinner has been commenced, and is properly progressing; the result of which must inevitably be a mere outward religion, and must fill our churches with a class of members who have the form of godliness, but know nothing of the power thereof in their hearts and souls.

This theory has been the root of that long controversy which has so sadly disturbed the peace of our Church. It is because these views have been so pressed, so insisted upon, so made the test of churchmanship, the test of loyalty to her formularies, the test of fitness for ordination to the ministry, that the friends of evangelical truth have been compelled to resist their farther progress, and exert themselves to awaken the Church to a sense of danger, and to arouse her to a sense of duty.

The supporters of these views have gloried in their success in winning over to their opinions some Bishops and some clergymen.

It is true they have not laboured in vain. Many who once loved and taught the truth as it is in Jesus, and preached his simple Gospel to dying sinners, are eager defenders of Sacramentarianism, and bow down soul and body before its semi-Romish forms and doctrines. But while they have thus won some to erroneous churchmanship, have they not nursed Ives, and Forbes, and the rest of the decided and undecided Romanists? They have sown the wind—they are now reaping the whirlwind; and upon them, the advocates of this theory, must the blame of our troubles be laid. Ye ministers in the church of God—ye successors of the martyrs for the Reformation—ye upon whose souls lies the awful oath taken before the throne of Heaven to "banish and "drive away from the church all doctrines contrary to God's word," and to be examples and patterns to the flock of Christ—when a BISHOP of the Protestant Episcopal Church, when Presbyters and Deacons and candidates for Holy Orders, when laymen, for whose souls' blood the ministers of Christ will have to answer, have left our Church and taken refuge in the false doctrine and corrupt practices of Rome, walking in the very steps in which *you are now* walking,—is it not time to review your ground? to ask yourselves if your premises are not false?

The bolder of the Tractarians are the open advocates of this system, while *all* High-Churchmen (we submit to them, so far as they act with and countenance the others by their sympathy or defence) are abettors of it; their influence *does* go to build up this theology, and even when they have no sympathy with the extreme views of their party, they sustain and uphold the very men who are the troublers of our Church, they encourage and countenance those who have gone and are going to Rome, and who have brought all this odium and disgrace upon our Protestant Episcopal Church. Our blessed Lord has expressly said, "He that is not *with* me is "against me, and he that gathereth not with me scattereth."

The pamphlet now offered is designed to show, to the mind open to conviction, that, notwithstanding the contrary assertion of party leaders, and party newspapers, the doctrine, that regeneration, in its scriptural and proper sense, necessarily takes place in and by baptism,—the existence of a moral change in the soul by the administration of that ordinance *is* entertained, taught, and defended by Bishops and other ministers of the Church of England, and the Protestant Episcopal Church in America; and that this doctrine is far more boldly and strongly insisted upon now than thirty-seven years ago, when Mr. Faber overwhelmed its advocates with confusion.

In presenting the evidence to prove that Tractarians and many High-Churchmen believe and teach the inseparability of spiritual regeneration and the outward ordinance of baptism, we begin with quotations from the tracts of Bishop Mant, which gave rise to the discussion which first brought out Mr. Faber's four sermons.

Bishop Mant says of baptism: "*Supernatural grace* is conferred "thereby." "Baptism is a new birth by which we enter into the "new world, the new creation, the blessings and spiritualities of "the kingdom." "From this time forward we have a *new prin*"*ciple* put into us, the spirit of grace, which, besides our soul and "body, is a principle of action."

"The doctrine of regeneration by baptism is most clearly assert"ed by her, (the Church of England;) she supposes not merely "all real Christians are regenerate by God's Holy Spirit, by which "I understand all those who live a Christian life; but that *those* "*also* are so regenerated to whom baptism is rightly administered, "notwithstanding by their future conduct they may forfeit the "privileges of their new birth."

"Denying the doctrine of baptismal regeneration is a heresy."

"If the work of regeneration is not effected by baptism, it is "almost impossible for any sober man to say when and by what "means it is."

"For the express purpose of regeneration, not only is his (the "Holy Spirit's) operation necessary, but it must also (humanly "speaking) be administered through *the mediation of water.*"

"To deny the regenerating effect of baptism is, in some sense, "to *do despite to the spirit of grace.*" "To the Romans he (St. "Paul) employs the same figure, describing baptism as a burial; "adding withal a particular which confirms an opinion presently "to be insisted on, *that no other than baptismal regeneration is* "*possible in this world.*"

"*Sanctification and purity, unspotted and unblemished holiness,* "are attributed to the Church of Christ as the effect of the wash- "ing of water."

"Does not the language of the apostle warrant the argument "that we are born anew in baptism, and *in baptism exclusively.*"

"To deny the regenerating influence of baptism, is to deny its "sacramental character."

"Neither it nor any other passage of St. John, nor any other "text of Scripture appears to me to authorize the doctrine of a "second, or of any other, distinct from baptismal, regeneration."

From these extracts it is evident that Bishop Mant held just the views which Mr. Faber attributes to him. They prove that in his (Bishop Mant's) estimation, regeneration, or the new birth, is conveyed by baptism, and by baptism exclusively; that every person duly baptized is actually born of God, has a new principle of life infused, even the spirit of grace, purity, and holiness, that no other new birth is possible in this world, that none who have been baptized ever are, or can be, in an unregenerate state; and that no baptized person ought to be exhorted to pray for regeneration, nor be taught that it is necessary, or even possible.

The position that no other than baptismal regeneration is possible in this world is again enforced by one of those who immediately succeeded Bishop Mant in this controversy. Says Dr. Bethell, the Dean of Chichester, in his Apology* addressed to Mr. Faber on the subject of the four sermons: "As to those persons "who, after having been baptized in a state of hypocrisy and wilful "sin, afterward became true penitents and believers, I for my "part, entertain no doubt of their forgiveness and salvation. *But* "*by what* PHYSICAL PROCESS they are brought into a state of salva- "tion and acceptance with God, whether by the infusion or resuscita- "tion of the incorruptible seed, or by what other mysterious "mean, I neither know nor do I wish to inquire. It is a case "not mentioned in the covenant, nor supposed, nor provided for "in the Church of God."

The reader will perceive that so absolutely inseparable are baptism and regeneration, that even when wilful sin and hypocrisy have nullified the work of baptism, if the man ever becomes a penitent afterward, he can only be saved by the revivification of the baptismal water dropped upon him when a hypocrite.

Let us now look into the Tracts for the Times, No. 67, written by Dr. Pusey, and we shall see how little changed is the later statement of this doctine: "Nicodemus asked; how can these things "be? and most of our questions about baptismal regeneration are "Nicodemus questions. We know it in its author, God; in its "*instrument, baptism;* in its end, salvation, union with Christ, "sonship to God, resurrection from the dead, and the life of the "world to come. We only know it not where it does not concern "us to know it, in the mode of its operation. But this is just "what man would know, so he passes over all those glorious privi- "leges * * * he would fain know how baptism can be the same "to the infant and to the adult *convert.* Yet the gift *is* the same "* * * to both it is nourishment and life. * * * One may then "define [this] regeneration to be that act whereby God takes us out "of our relation to Adam, and makes us actual members of his "Son, and so his sons, as being members of His Ever Blessed "Son; and if sons, then heirs of God through Christ. This is our "new birth, an actual birth of God, of water, and of the Spirit, as "we were actually born of our natural parents; herein then also "we are justified, or both accounted and *made* righteous, since we

* Page 5.

"are made members of Him who is alone righteous; freed from "past sin, whether original or actual; have a new principle of life "imparted to us. * * * The view then here held of baptism, fol- "lowing the ancient church and our own, is that we be engrafted "into Christ, and thereby receive a principle of life."* Again: "First, whereas confessedly regeneration is in Scripture connected "with baptism, there is *nothing in Scripture to sever it* therefrom. "The evidence all goes one way. * * * But, secondly, not only "is there nothing in Scripture to sever regeneration from baptism, "but baptism is spoken of as the *source of our spiritual birth, as* "*no other cause is,* save God. * * * * In baptism two different "causes are combined, one God himself, and the other a creature "which he has thought fit to hallow for this end. * * * Our "birth, when its direct means are spoken of, is attributed to the "baptism of water and of the Spirit, and to that only. * * * "Our life in Christ is throughout represented as commencing "when we are by baptism made members of Christ, and children "of God. * * * A commencement of life in Christ after baptism, "a death unto sin and a new birth unto righteousness, at any "other period than at that one first introduction into God's cove- "nant, is as little consonant with the general representations of "Holy Scripture, as a commencement of physical life long after "our natural birth is with the order of His providence."†

Again, speaking of St. Paul: "It is commonly thought that he, "having been miraculously converted, was regenerated, justified "by faith, pardoned, had received the Holy Ghost before he was "baptized: not so, however, Holy Scripture, if we consider it at- "tentively; before his baptism he appears to have been neither "pardoned, regenerated, justified, nor enlightened. * * * But, if "even to St. Paul, for whose conversion our Saviour himself "vouchsafed to become visible to human sight, regeneration and "the other gifts of the Holy Spirit were not imparted without the "appointed sacrament of grace, why should this be expected or "looked for by others.‡ If baptism be the cleansing and quick- "ening of the dead soul, they (the ministers) do work miracles."§

"We are saved by faith *bringing* us to baptism, and *by baptism*

* Page 24. † Tracts for the Times, No. 67, p. 24, 25, &c.
‡ Tracts for the Times, vol. ii. p. 179. § Tract 85.

"God saves us." "We are by baptism brought into a state of "salvation, or justification."

'There are but two periods of *absolute* cleansing, baptism and "the day of judgment." "As the child is created and nourished "in and by the womb of the mother, so is the new soul begotten "and nourished in the waters of baptism."*

The practical working of the two systems of teaching is utterly different, and this cannot be more clearly set forth than by Dr. Pusey himself, in his comments on an incident in the life of the missionary Williams.

"A mother sent to the missionary in great agony, on her death-"bed, on account of the infanticides of which she had been guilty "when a heathen. 'I began to reason with her,' said he, 'and "urged the consideration that she had done this when a heathen, "and during the times of ignorance which God winked at; but "this afforded her no consolation. I then directed her to the "faithful saying which is worthy of all acceptation, that Christ "Jesus came into the world to save sinners. This imparted a "little comfort, and after visiting her frequently, and directing "her thoughts to that blood which cleanseth from all sin, I suc-"ceeded, by the blessing of God, in tranquillizing her troubled "spirit, and she died about eight days after my first interview, "animated with the hope that her sins, though many, were for-"given her. And what but the gospel could have brought such "consolation?'" This mode of treatment of such a case must commend itself to the experience of every truly Christian mind and heart. But Dr. Pusey repudiates the direction of this faithful missionary to look to the blood which cleanseth from all sin, and says, "Consolation is not the main object of the gospel. Yet the "Gospel would have brought much more consolation had this "teacher known it all, and could have told her of the one baptism "for the remission of sins; that she had been washed, had been "cleansed; and so could have declared authoritatively, without "altering our Lord's own words: 'Thy sins are forgiven.'"†

Without further comment, it will be seen then that God's work in the soul, according to Dr. Pusey, is the result of baptism; that

* Pusey's Letter, p. 54, &c.; Tract 67, p. 49, &c.

† Note to Tracts for Times.

baptism is never to be severed from regeneration; and that pardon, sanctification, redemption, and the gifts of the Holy Spirit are as much the consequences of baptism as the ordinary functions of natural life are the consequences of our natural birth, and hence they are inseparable.

The present Bishop of Exeter is one of the champions of the doctrine of regeneration in baptism. His letter to the Archbishop of Canterbury fully sets forth his opinion. The principal subject of this letter is a condemnation of the judgment of the Privy Council in the Gorham case. From the charges made by the bishop against Mr. G. and the court who decided for him, we select the following, as showing the mind of Bishop Philpotts. Thus, on page 43, he condemns in Mr. Gorham that he "separates "regeneration wholly from baptism;" and again, on page 45, "Mr. "G. separated entirely the inward and spiritual grace from the "sacrament, inasmuch as he stated 'regeneration' to have pre-"ceded baptism."

What the views of Mr. Gorham were may be seen in the following extract from the Sentence of the Judicial Committee, who tried the case; and if our readers will remember that *against* these views the whole fire of the Bishop of Exeter's indignation has been ever since poured out, they will see that in his opinion regeneration and baptism are one.

The view of Mr. G., according to the Sentence, is that baptism is a sacrament generally necessary to salvation, but that the grace of regeneration does not so necessarily accompany the act of baptism that regeneration invariably takes place in baptism. * * * That without reference to the qualifications of the recipient, it is not in itself an *effectual* sign of grace. That infants baptized and dying before actual sin are certainly saved; but that in no case is regeneration in baptism unconditional.

Agreeably to the spirit which dictated the earnest *objection* made to these views, we find *direct* statements of the bishop. Thus, in an address to candidates for confirmation in the English Churchman, he says—"If any of you have the least doubt as to the com-"pleteness of the gift bestowed in baptism, or that it places you "in any other state than that of *actual salvation*, I entreat and "beseech you, if any such there be, at once, rather to leave the

"Church than to receive the holy ordinance of confirmation under "such circumstances."

Again, *Pastoral Letter*, &c.—"By some supernatural and mys-"terious operation we, our bodies and souls, are in baptism united "to the body and soul of Christ; and, thereby, to the Godhead; "and the Holy Spirit it is by which we have this union—an "union which makes us to be as truly of the lineage of the second "Adam, as we are naturally in the lineage of the first Adam. "This is our new birth, the being born of the Spirit."

Again, the bishop is commenting upon a sermon in which were the words "at the *font* it was that we put on Christ and were re-"generated, or made new creatures in Him; then the old world of "sin and wrath passed away; then all things became new in our "new birth to grace and reconciliation." Of these extraordinary expressions, the bishop says he had rarely read a sermon which puts forth plain *apostolic teaching* in a more *sober or guarded* tone. In the same letter he asks if the doctrine of the atonement "is "more truly the doctrine of the gospel than the efficacy of the "blessed sacrament (baptism) which, by Christ's own ordinance, is "the one only way in which He first confers the benefit of the "atonement."

In these sentences nothing can be more clear than the Bishop of Exeter's view. It is plainly that it is God's ordinance that the *moral* change of regeneration is effected in the soul by baptism, hence that the work is *done in the act* of baptism.

The Bishop of London, in a charge to his clergy in 1842, speaking of baptism, says, "The doctrine of our Church as to the "Christian's spiritual life has always appeared to me to be this: "*justification* begins in *baptism*, when the children of wrath are "regenerated by water and the Holy Ghost, and are made children "of God. Remission of sins is expressly declared to be *then* "given, and the remission of sins implies justification in the "proper sense of the term." In baptism "a new principle is in-"fused, a man is regenerate."*

The present Bishop of Ripon has recently refused to ordain the Rev. Mr. Hayward to the priesthood, because he was not prepared to assent to this new Puseyite test of fitness for the ministry.

* Bishop of London's Three Sermons.

His examining chaplain was directed to furnish Mr. H. the following propositions:—

"Are you prepared to teach as the doctrine of the Church,

"1. That regeneration is the grace specially conferred in and "by baptism, and that the term is not applicable to any grace be-"stowed before or after baptism?

"2. That regeneration is in such a manner attached to baptism, that "it is withheld from no person baptized according to the due order of "the Church, unless in the case of wilful impenitence and unbelief?

"3. That infants being incapable of wilful impenitence and un-"belief, * * * every infant baptized *is in and by baptism* regenerate?"

"I never can but lament," is the Bishop's remark, "his (Mr. "Hayward's) failure in seeing that the Church of England mani-"festly applies the term *regeneration* to a grace * * * which she "in faith believes attaches to *all who are duly baptized.*"

Let us pass on to Mr. Sewell, one of the more moderate of English writers of this class. The following brief extract is from his work on Christian morals:—

"The very thing a heathen moralist would most desire, such as "the mortification of the flesh, the death unto sin, the creation of "a new spirit within us, the enlightenment of the mind, the ad-"mission into a noble, spiritual polity, the cleansing of the con-"science, the forgiveness of sins and restoration to the favour of "God, or union with his nature—all these are described in the "Bible as effected by baptism already. It is something past and "done, and the subsequent struggle, for struggle there must be, is "to defend what we have received, to recover ourselves from fall-"ing from the high estate in which we have been placed."

Mr. Gresley, the author of "Bernard Leslie," an English clergyman of some notoriety as a Tractarian writer, says that baptismal regeneration "is the beginning of the life of God in the soul," "is the planting in the heart the seed of Divine grace." "God "does then and there implant the *principle of faith* in the child's "heart. * * * The church takes each child in her arms, and "by the use of Christ's holy ordinances *she* confers on him a new "nature by water and by the Spirit." Mr. Gresley in another place says "that *every thing is given in baptism.*"*

* P. 133, 155, &c.

"Baptismal regeneration * * * is in fact the starting-point "in the Christian's course. *It is the beginning of the life of God "in his soul.* It is the *implanting in the heart of the seed of Di- "vine grace,* thenceforth to be cherished and confirmed. It is the "grafting the redeemed soul into the stock of Christ."*

"The denier of baptismal regeneration, looks on confirmation in "the light of conversion—a favourable time for the commence- "ment of a religious life; which with the true churchman *was* "commenced at the time when, in the sacrament of baptism, the "*Heavenly Spirit* first lighted like a dove on the regenerated "babe."†

These are the views of a man who is one of the most popular of the Tractarian writers, and whose books are recommended by the great body of High-Churchmen in this country.

A writer of the same school in the Christian Remembrancer, who advocates the inseparability of baptism and regeneration, speaks thus of impenitent adults:—"Not only in the language of "charity, but of FACT, of even an *impenitent* adult coming to "baptism, it may with truth be said, as the Church of England "says, that he is 'born again,' and 'grafted into the body of "Christ's church,' that he is 'regenerate.'" And to palliate the offensiveness of such a statement, it is added, that "such regenera- "tion and salvation are given only *conceptionally,*" and "the pre- "sence of sin closes instantly round the baptismal seed, and ren- "ders it unfruitful, and prevents his sins being actually forgiven." So that the man is maintained to be truly born again, and regene- rate, though his sins are not forgiven him; and the almost blasphe- mous assertion is made, that even a wicked hypocrite, coming to bap- tism is *necessarily* a recipient of Divine grace!

In Wilberforce on the Incarnation, the question is asked, "How "can God's image be created anew in the soul?" It is said, "If "man had never fallen, it had been sufficient to inherit it; fallen "as he is, there must be the gift of a new life." "This new life has "its commencement in the fact of the incarnation." "Out of this "beginning arises the whole system of this Christian life, and this "heavenly influence is extended to us in *baptism.* The basis of "our spiritual growth is laid in it. The soul's regeneration, like

* P. 13. † Real Danger of the Church of England.

"the body's growth, is a protracted process, which the whole life "is not too long to complete. But what gives to baptism its es- "pecial character, is that in that holy rite this process (of regenera- "tion) is begun, for then are men joined by a heavenly agency to "Christ, that the life of their souls may from that day have its "development."*

Again, the British Critic declares that in infant baptism, the infant is "the recipient of the greatest blessings which it can en- "ter into the heart of man to conceive, even the translation from "the kingdom of Satan into the kingdom of Christ, and the "transfiguration of the whole nature from a state of moral and "spiritual debasement and helplessness, into one capable of per- "forming the achievements of saints, and inheriting the glory of "angels."†

What is thus set forth by the leading writers is re-echoed in a thousand forms by others of less note. For instance, in a tract called "A Voice from the Font," the author speaks of the baptismal font as "bearing water, which, when duly consecrated by "prayer, '*washes away sin*, not the face only,'" "by which they "(the baptized) are divested of the imperfections of the *old*, and "sanctified by the purifications of the *new* Adam, and are *spiri- "tually* born again." "I repeat it, and would have you, my good "friend, repeat it again and again, that every child of man is born "in the corruption of human nature; and that that nature cannot "be purified, nor that corruption cleansed away, but by the laver "of regeneration—*the waters of baptism*. And as all are, by one "Spirit, thus brought into one body by this sacrament, so all ad- "mitted by baptism into this society of Christians, are grafted into "the Church, the catholic Church. Their previous sins being now "remitted, they are *adopted as sons of God by the Holy Ghost*, "and their faith confirmed, and being in communion with him in "his holiness, they are sanctified." This, in the estimation of this writer, is the "*necessary result of baptism*."‡ Surely the fact that these men teach the inseparability of baptism and spiritual regeneration cannot for a moment be questioned.

Having set forth in these brief extracts from the writings of several bishops and clergymen, the views of the party which they

---

* Incarnation, p. 330, 333. † No. 67, p. 75. ‡ P. 7, 8, 81, &c.

represent in the Church of England, on the subject of baptismal regeneration, may we not appeal to every candid mind to bear us out in our assertion that all these writers *do* hold the identity of baptism and spiritual regeneration; that in baptism the Holy Ghost is poured into the heart of the baptized; that the regeneration of the soul by the Spirit of God must be dated from the moment of baptism, and a moral change in the nature of the baptized belongs to the *article* of baptism.

Let us now examine the testimony of the bishops and clergy of our own American Church.

During the summer of 1852, the Right Rev. Bishop McCoskry, of Michigan, and the Right Rev. Bishop De Lancey, of Western New York, visited England to attend the closing exercises of the Jubilee of the "Society for the Propagation of the Gospel in Foreign Parts." Bishop McCoskry was invited to preach the anniversary sermon in St. Paul's Cathedral. In this sermon the bishop's trumpet utters no uncertain sound on the great subject of baptismal regeneration. He unequivocally declares that by baptism the child *invariably* receives the gift of the Holy Ghost; that, *without any exception*, every child in baptism is regenerated, born anew of the Holy Ghost; and, in consequence of this act of outward baptism, is in a state of salvation. But we will let this advocate of the doctrine of the inseparability of baptism and regeneration speak for himself. We quote his own language.

Bishop McCoskry says—God "has given his own Son to be "the head of a new family on the earth, the descendants of which "are bound together by stronger ties than blood. They are, in the "higher sense, brethren. They are connected through the Son of "God. It becomes an important matter to inquire, in what man-"ner are we admitted into this family, and thus made brethren? "*It is by baptism.* This is the initiatory rite. No amount of "personal holiness, (if it can be ever acquired out of this family,) "or inward experiences, or raptures, can make us members of the "Church of Christ. We must enter through the door which its "Divine Head has opened, and we must enter by receiving from "those whom He has constituted as his earthly representatives the "right to enter; and this right, we have observed, is baptism. In "this ordinance *every* child is made a *new creature in Christ Jesus.*

"They are born again, born of water and the Spirit. And," for this great, this mighty, this heavenly work, the Bishop says, "there "are no qualifications required; and to guard against failures, the "Spirit of God is given to *every* child in *baptism, without any* ex-"ception, not only to begin, but to carry on and complete the "great work of their salvation. The relationship thus created will "remain. It can never be shaken off in this world: however un-"worthy the members of this family may become, they will still "remain the children of God.

"In adults the terms are different. There is actual sin in con-"nection with the sad inheritance of a fallen nature. Hence, there "must be previous qualifications; and these are repentance, faith, "and obedience, or in other words, conversion. But this is not "regeneration, or the new birth."

In the estimation of the Bishop of Michigan, a compliance with the Divine direction, the exercise of repentance of sin, and faith in the Lord Jesus Christ, a true and genuine conversion to God, do not effect that great vital change which avails to the sinner for the pardon of his sins and reconciliation with God. The exercise of a living faith in Christ *does not* justify. He that believeth shall *not* be saved. All these Divine requisitions, in the estimation of Bishop McCoskry, amount to nothing, as far as the pardon, reconciliation, justification of the penitent and believing sinner is concerned; they only prepare the way, and believers "are thus *made* "*ready* to be born." The great work, the mighty change, the new creation in the soul, the change from death unto life, the new birth, "CAN ONLY BE ACCOMPLISHED IN HOLY BAPTISM;" that is, when the hands of a priest shall sprinkle the baptismal water upon the brow of an adult, he is born of the Spirit, he is regenerate, he is made a child of God; not made so by the exercise of repentance and faith in Christ, but the regeneration of the soul is so inseparably connected with baptism that, until the act of baptism takes place, he is yet in his sins; but the instant that act is performed, the soul is regenerate by the Spirit of God; and is regenerate in consequence, not of the former preparation, but of the very article of baptism itself.

Whatever refinements, let it be observed, may be used to show that baptism, in this theory, does not invariably produce regeneration, cannot, in view of such passages as these, weigh against this unquestionable inference. Regeneration is here made inherent in the *ordinance,* and not in any thing else. If it belongs thus inherently to the ordinance, it *must* be, in the nature of things, inseparable from it.

Bishop Whittingham, in a charge delivered in 1843, says, "The "Divine commission of the ministry, in apostolical succession, as "the authorized dispenser of *justifying* and *sanctifying* grace in the "sacraments of *regeneration* [baptism] and of the communion of "the body and blood of Christ, has been the uninterrupted doc-"trine of the church."

Here the sacrament of regeneration, or baptism, is made the *authorized* dispenser of *justification* and *sanctification.* If it is the authorized dispenser, it must be the *only* dispenser; and hence, wherever this authorized dispenser [baptism] is used, there must follow the justification of the sinner before God.

Bishop Doane, in a charge delivered in 1842, states, "Man is a "sinner. * * * He must be born again. This, as the Saviour "says, must be of water and of the Spirit. He is regenerated, the "church declares, in holy baptism. Now he has washed away his "sins in the fountain opened on the cross." That is, in and by baptism he was washed in the fountain of the cross. "This is the "new or spiritual birth. Whether it be the infant of an hour, "brought in the faith of parents and sponsors, or whether it be "the man of threescore years and ten, converted and become a "little child, the laver of the new birth is the font of baptism. "* * * It may be the captain of the king of Syria's host; or it may "be the heir of that vast empire in whose circuit the compass of "the earth is spanned; still he must wash, or he cannot be clean. "It may be Saul, with hands imbued with Christian blood, or that "dear child which Jesus took and set before him as a pattern for "apostles, still it is baptism that must save him."

Again, in his fifth charge, (pages 8–17,) in speaking of the relation of the believer to Christ, "the oneness of believers with their "Lord," he says, "the incorporation with this living, growing, "grace-enlivened body," [not the Church, but Christ,] "is in holy "baptism:"—and on page 25, "now between the body and the Spirit "the sacraments do mediate. A child is born. What is it? a "foul and worthless thing, conceived and born in misery and sin, "the heir of wrath and shame. It is baptized, and it becomes the "nursling of grace and heir of glory, a member of Christ, an heir "of God, and an inheritor of the Kingdom of Heaven. It has "been born of the Spirit. The sacrament of baptism has been "made to it the medium of heavenly grace. Not by virtue of the "water; not by the power of the administrator; not by the merit "of the recipient; but of grace all—all of God: as He appointed, "and because of his appointment."

The qualifications here do not affect the main statement, which is, that by "God's appointment" a *moral regeneration* takes place in the article of baptism. A few lines below it is said, the infection of a sinful nature does remain "even in these regene-"rated" persons, (quoting from Article IX.;) this infection is remedied in the Lord's Supper; and hence, and from the proof texts adduced, which have no limitation in the Scripture as to age, it must do this work in adults as well as in children.

The Episcopal Sunday School Union has also brought forward these extreme views of baptism in many of its more recent publications.

In "Bevan's Catechism," the question is asked, "What persons "are authorized to reconcile sinners to God? *Ans.* The ministers "of Christ." "Does the Church require grown persons to per-"form repentance and faith before they are baptized, or only pro-"fess them? *Ans.* To profess them." "Does the Church require "infants to perform these things before they are baptized, or only "profess them? *Ans.* To profess them."* Thus making no difference between children and adults as to previous requirements.

In the "Manual of Oral Instruction upon the Bible," (page 8,) the question is asked, "When is the Christian justified? *Ans.* "The infant is justified at his baptism: it is the first step in the "Christian life." "Very young children are ready to do wrong; "but when they are *baptized*, then they are made clean from sin, "that is from wickedness."† A mother loses a child, and "They comforted her, and said her little girl had gone to a safe place, "and that, as she had taken her to Church to be baptized, she "might feel sure her little girl belonged to Christ's Church, and

* Pages 50, 106.

† Juvenile Rep. vol. i. p. 72.

"would go to heaven." "He knew that if he had died as a "young baby, he would have been safe, too, for he too had been "*baptized*."*

Again, in the Juvenile Repository, 1844, page 113, the children are taught that *unbaptized* children are not entitled to say the Lord's prayer. "Do you remember that we have no right to say "the Lord's prayer until we are baptized? When we have been "made part of Christ's Church by *baptism*, then we are made the "children of God; then we have a right to call God our Father." If this be so, then a Christian mother, whose unbelieving husband will not consent to their children's baptism, is debarred the unspeakably precious privilege of teaching her offspring the beautiful words of our blessed Lord, OUR Father who art in heaven, &c.; nay, she cannot teach her children to pray at all. They have not been baptized—they cannot in any wise pray to the Father in Heaven. A *dreadful* and UNSCRIPTURAL doctrine. Oh, the guilt of those who would thus shut up the kingdom of heaven to those who, from a variety of causes, have never received the blessed gift of Christian baptism!

The "Protestant Episcopal Tract Society" have issued several tracts which teach the very doctrine now denied to be held.

In Tract 163, Augustine's bishop recommends him to read the prophet Isaiah. "This was in preparation for his baptism, as the "church in this our day baptizes all grown-up converts who have "never been born again in this sacrament of grace. This was the "cleansing, health-giving, and healing sacrament for which he had "longed; and with what sacred feelings of awe in God's presence "did he present himself to be washed in that fount of water 'which "springeth up into everlasting life;' the waters of God's grace, "the *stream of salvation, conveying remission of sins*, giving us "*new life*, imparting to the faithful recipient a new and regenerate "life."

In Tract 125, we read, "I might have told you that only by "baptism are we admitted into Christ's flock on earth; that in "baptism the good Shepherd 'gathers the lambs with his arm, and "carries them in his bosom;' that by baptism are we adopted into "his covenant, incorporated into his Church; made, in short,

* Child's Mag. vol. 34, p. 200.

"'members of Christ, children of God, and inheritors of the king-"dom of heaven;' that in *baptism all our sins are pardoned*, and "the *Holy Spirit bestowed*."

Tract 171 is a very remarkable production; containing more unadulterated error than any other work of its size ever issued by this society.

"Regeneration is the inward and spiritual grace of baptism, and "so, *as a matter of course, accompanies* the due reception of that "sacrament—accompanies it, *i. e.* whensoever no obstruction hin-"ders its operation."

The *obstruction* here referred to, is wilful opposition to its reception. If there is a willing mind, the inward and spiritual grace, as a matter of course, *invariably* accompanies the outward act, and unites the recipient to the manhood of Christ. "It therefore ad-"mits each individual *man* to this new heavenly manhood. As "Christ took the nature of that man, and died to save him, only "his *own obstinate rejection* of the boon can hinder his obtaining "it." So that all who are willing to receive the ordinance of baptism are *necessarily* united to Christ—born again—regenerate by the Holy Ghost; for "in baptism there is conferred on him a "spiritual constitution, with spiritual faculties and powers which "he could never have inherited by his first birth, and *whereby* he "can *apprehend heavenly truth*, and *discern, obey, and love the* "*spiritual law*."

"It is frequently asserted, in opposition to the doctrine of bap-"tismal regeneration, that the meaning and design of baptism is "simply to admit into the visible Church. * * Because baptism was "ordained by way of admission into the visible Church, have we "any right to say that it was ordained for no purpose besides? "But let us take the statement as it stands. Baptism is admission "into the visible Church of Christ. What does that mean? I "maintain it means admission into *all spiritual blessings whatso-"ever*, that it means nothing short of that comprehensive benefit "we call REGENERATION."

"Baptism is to be considered as conveying to us the Holy Ghost. "The baptized person is born into the covenant of grace, and, by "the terms of that covenant, has a right to the indwelling and aid "of the blessed Spirit. Consequently, whether or not he will put "them to use, he receives in baptism powers which by nature he "could not have. Born carnal, he has now a spiritual constitu-"tion, with spiritual faculties—faculties which he could never have "inherited by his first birth, and whereby he can apprehend heaven-"ly truth, and discern, obey, and love the spiritual law." "And I "take this opportunity of observing, that this covenanted" [*i. e.* baptismal] "presence of the Spirit in each baptized *man*, is the *only* "presence of the Spirit of which we at all know in any man."

This, the reader will bear in mind, is not a view of the child's baptism, but that of the adult.

"Infants are regenerated in the very fact of being made mem-"bers of the visible church. Born far from God, they are now "brought very nigh unto him. Born exiles, they are now taken "into the everlasting covenant. Born children of wrath, they "hereby are 'made children of grace.' Born to an inheritance of "sin and sorrow, and darkness and death, they now enter on an "inheritance of *holiness* and *happiness*, and *light* and *life everlast-"ing*. So truly is the *day of their baptism*, the day to them of a "*new and better birth*,—a birth not unto the world, the flesh, and "the devil, *but unto God*." But should this baptized infant grow up in sin, and, "in spite of baptismal grace, have long lived merely "to this world, he is yet, on being aroused to a sense of this, to "believe that the covenant of baptism is still on him, and that he "has but to resume his baptismal attitude to be replenished with "baptismal grace. Nothing is more perverse than to urge the re-"volutions we see in certain persons, at some definite period of "their after-lives, from the service of sin and the world to that of "Christ and of God, as an argument against baptismal regenera-"tion. Rather are they wonderful manifestations of its power, "such as we had no right to expect. We see that, even when a "man has spent half a lifetime in neglect of his baptism, it can "sometimes, even thus late, take effect upon him, and produce, "after long delay, many of its legitimate and blessed results."

The writer, fearing that his food might prove too strong for his Protestant readers, in a note qualifies his statements, and then proclaims the monstrous doctrine of Rome and the Romanizers, that if ever a baptized person is brought out of the darkness of sin and made, what is termed by evangelical Churchmen, a truly converted man, that great and vital change must be attributed to his *baptism!* "I may take this opportunity of observing that, though we *cer-"tainly* affirm the presence of grace in baptism only in the case of "infants, who interpose no obstacle, yet even an adult, receiving, "through his impenitence and unbelief, nothing but a *dead form* "of baptism, must yet, if mercifully brought out of such a condi-"tion, look not to certain vicissitudes of feeling, but to his baptism "as the epoch of his second birth. This, then, is baptismal re-"generation, viewed in reference to the gift of the Spirit. That "gift is conveyed, a power is present, present in virtue of a Divine "covenant, with every baptized man, by whose aid he can over-"come all sin, and grow up unto perfect holiness."

Most readers of the Bible have been under the impression that the saints who lived during the Old Testament period—that the long array of faithful heroes, enumerated by St. Paul, in the eleventh chapter of Hebrews, were brought into God's family and born again; but the author of this tract, says, no, *they were not regenerate,* for "one great misconception on the subject of regeneration "has been the supposing it a grace known to the sons of men *be-"fore* the gospel dispensation. This is an altogether modern view of "the subject." The author believes that regeneration and the new birth are synonymous; and as our Lord expressly declares, *except* a man be born again he cannot see the kingdom of heaven, it is difficult to conceive how that noble band of Old Testament martyrs and heroes ever gained the kingdom of God. The fact is, the author of the tract knows not the gospel; he does not even see "men as trees walking;" he is a blind guide; and if the blind lead the blind, both must fall into the ditch.

The Protestant Episcopal Tract Society are responsible for this mass of unsound and Romish teaching. The whole thing is so entirely inconsistent with the spirit as well as the letter of our standards, that no arguments are needed to prove that this institution is a supporter of the views known as Puseyism. This is the tract society for the distribution of whose tracts High-Churchmen contribute their money; and for the influence of such teaching—for the fastening of such frightful errors upon the church they must be held accountable. Oh, when will men see the evil tendency of a system of theology which strikes at the very foundations of our holy and beautiful faith, and substitutes a mere mechanical theory, which must fill our church with cold and formal worshippers.

The newspaper press has been clear and unmistakable. The following extracts from the New York Churchman, which has for many years been the exponent of the extreme party, will show that in baptism, they believe the soul is regenerated, born again, converted.

"Were entrance into the covenant to be effected by man's own "act, or by a certain kind or degree of mental state,—if his own "virtue or his own *faith* were the means whereby he was to be admitted into the way of salvation, human weakness and ignorance "would be a perpetual source of delusion. But God has set in the "church those *by whom*, through a means and form [baptism] appointed by himself, he takes those who by nature are children of "wrath, and by giving them new birth into a state of salvation, "makes them the children of grace."

"We hold this doctrine of baptismal regeneration. The baptized infant is with us 'a member of Christ, a child of God, and "an inheritor of the kingdom of heaven,' and this he is made by "a *sacrament*, a mysterious and inscrutable means of conveying "God's grace, the regenerating influences of the Holy Spirit. "And this is no figure, no metaphor embodied in action, no type, no "bare symbol, no signifying that which may be or may not be; but "a *saving ordinance*, a reality tenfold more real than any phenomenon that is presented to us, either in time, or yet in space."

In another place it contains an article by Catholicus, upon the "doctrine of baptismal regeneration," regretting the denial of "the "saving effects of baptism"—asserting that though "repentance is "necessary to the receiving of baptism, yet it is BAPTISM which is "the means of conveying purifying grace to the soul;" that in the case of St. Paul, "though pardon and purity came from the Lord, "they were conveyed to him *only* through washing in the waters "of baptism."

It is distinctly declared in these extracts that *baptism* does the work in the soul,—even in the convert on the way to Damascus *it* is the instrument of the grace,—and hence the grace of pardon depends thereon.

Again, "In their earlier days, infants received Christ's sanctify-"ing influence, and this blessed sacrament was provided as the *chan-*

"*nel* of this grace. None may separate it from the grace He has con-"nected therewith. To *every baptized person,* Christ's message is "good news, for they have received the Master's gift of water and "the Spirit, that they may be cleansed; and now under the guidance "and help of the Holy Ghost they have power to become holy. "Another benefit of this sacrament *is remission of sin.* Those "baptized, thus gain a new relation unto God—pardoned and "cleansed—the blood of Christ applied to them. Our Lord himself "*connected the new birth with baptism.* I see not how any can "preserve the integrity of Scripture, and yet affirm that those who "have been *baptized* are not *thus* endowed with a *holy power* to "work their salvation out."

Again the Churchman—speaks "The catholic church has ever "held rebaptism a profanation, and therefore has ever taught that "in ALL CASES regeneration does *fully* and *completely* take place "in BAPTISM, and consequently that the power of the Holy Ghost "is ever present in God's ordinance to make that an *undoubted* "*fact* which the outward administration indicates and declares. "Regeneration is no more a matter of consciousness to the subject of "it than natural generation, and it is from the *delusive importance* "that men have attached to *frames and feelings and fleshly motions* "that *the heresy* of rejecting the truth of baptism has arisen."

We proceed to the True Catholic, another organ of the same opinions. In an article in the number for December, 1847, it is asserted that in those who come to baptism prepared, *it* effects "a real living union to the living body of Christ, which is "wrought by the agency of the Holy Ghost." Sin, whether original or actual, is remitted to him. Justification, or a title through the merits of Christ to be treated as just, is brought about, "conveyed to him." "He is not rendered inherently holy, just, "and pure." But "the Holy Ghost becomes an indweller of his "heart," "pervades him." "By the power thus imparted to him "he becomes capable of doing works acceptable to God in Christ "Jesus." "He acquires the power of working out his own salva-"tion." "This power is the germ of sanctification."

Our previous comments apply to these passages—their authors evidently hold the opinion charged—that regeneration is a part of the ordinance of baptism—is one and the same thing with it.

The design of this tract is not only to furnish evidence that Bishops of our Church, and some of the public exponents of its views, teach that outward baptism is coincident with spiritual regeneration, but also to show that clergymen, in their parishes, in their ordinary teaching, make this doctrine a prominent feature in their instruction.

The great body of the laity of the Church repudiate this sacramental view of conversion, and hence many of the clergy who hold it are somewhat cautious in its presentation. But there are others, who, Bishop of Exeter like, boldly proclaim their candid opinions, and who fearlessly unfurl the banner of Heresy.

We can give only a few extracts from some of the numerous sermons which have burdened the press within a few past years. First we call attention to a sermon preached at the funeral of the Rev. Palmer Dyer, of the Diocese of New York, by the Rev. John Alden Spooner, of Glens Falls, New York, in which we have a very candid and clear view of the principles of the Tractarians. Nor would they seem to be very offensive to High-Churchmen who reject that appellation, from the fact that no condemnation has come from the ecclesiastical authority of the diocese with which Mr. S. is connected, or the church papers which are supported by that class of churchmen.

But let Mr. Spooner be heard. Speaking of Mr. Dyer, he says—

"He was *baptized*. The record and proof of that his CONVER-"SION is in the Church-book at Granville, N. Y. At the sacred "fount there his sins were washed away, and he was regenerated."

The record of the baptism is the *proof of his conversion*. This certainly is very much like the inseparability of baptism and conversion, or regeneration. And this was as an *adult*, because Mr. Spooner states that, not being satisfied with any baptism "except "it were given by a Bishop, or by one ordained by a Bishop, he at "once ceased to rely on any other," and was rebaptized in the church, and *reconfirmed!*

In regard to Mr. Dyer's confirmation, Mr. Spooner states that "Bishop Brownell imparted to him the gift of the Holy "Ghost." The rite of confirmation being openly declared, as by the Romanist, one of the sacraments of the church.

"He was *confirmed*. There is left for us no doubt as to his "'receiving the Holy Ghost.' That gift was imparted to him in "the church, by 'the laying on of the hands' of Bishop Brownell; "and the record of it exists. Our ground of humble and scrip- "tural joy is thus enlarged. *Union with the mind of God* was "thus rendered more sure by the possession of the Holy Spirit to "enlighten and guide. The heart before *cleansed in baptism*, now "made the tenement of the Holy Ghost in the *lesser sacrament of* "*confirmation*, had double certainty of improvement."*

---

* As the reader may be a little curious to know the views of Mr. Spooner upon some other subjects which have occupied the minds of a certain class of men in our Protestant Church, it may be well to give a few extracts from this funeral sermon, in order to satisfy those, who are unwilling to believe that there *is* such a principle as Puseyism in the church, and that it is publicly professed, and is uncondemned by many who are in authority. Mr. Spooner is now a clergyman in good standing in the diocese of New York.

"*It is the absolution and the benediction of the Church for which God looks in* "*the individual to determine that he is in favour.* It is to the ministry that "God says, 'Whatsoever ye shall bind on earth shall be bound in heaven; and "whatsoever ye shall loose on earth shall be loosed in heaven.' St. Matthew "xviii. 18. Separated, then, from the church, we see no ordinary Bible hope of "heaven. Otherwhere than in the Church, and with that ministry which God "appointed, the individual is not 'loosed from sin.'

"Habitual religiousness demands *frequency in the stated forms and acts of* "*piety*. Among those forms, the restored elevation of the cross, and *habitual* "*and devout crossings of the person, should be distinguished.* In our poverty, "we cannot, it is true, witness the consecrated church at the end of every second "league; but if we would, we might at such intervals *behold the Cross, toward* "*which the traveller might turn, and near which the wayfarer might kneel.* "They might not be places for rural gatherings to listen to the word, as they "were of old, but they would stand as tokens by which at least all might be "continually reminded of the prevalence of Christianity, of the need and possi- "bility of mercy, and of the death of Christ. And *devout crossings of the* "*person, while in every emergency and in every act we might not by word* "*place ourselves in Christ, by this sacred symbol we should. Crossing ourselves* "*in the beginning of a duty and in its end, as when we kneel and when we rise* "*from our prayer; crossing ourselves at the appearance of danger, or in each* "*hourly act, we thereby invoke the power of Christ and place ourselves with him:* "and so, from every section could one go to his death from almost within the "shadow of the cross, and in any emergency close his eyes in the embrace of his "Lord. *To such an one no death could be a surprise.*

"Again, among those acts of piety that should be frequent, and that, next to "the holy communion, are of *chiefest* efficacy in making the soul ripe for even "an unwarned death, are, *habitual private confession, and the pastor's absolu-* "*tion and the pastor's blessing.* To the faithful person, living in the fulness of "confession,—*doing the required penance*, struggling with the exposed sin, la- "bouring after the desired virtue, being absolved and blest, *and bowing for the* "*holy Eucharist*,—there would be daily the surrounding atmosphere of the Di- "vine protection, and the calm if not ecstatic assurance daily of Divine accept- "ance. We speak of *features in the Christian plan of grace that have been* "*rudely thrown away or negligently lost from our plan.* It is our unworthiness "that has brought this calamity upon us. And while we may not define for "what sin it is that God does thus visit us; why it is that the *confessional is re-* "*moved, and penance no more required*, and why God suffers such blindness in "individuals that they rail at these and at absolution and benediction, and why "churches are taken out of our thoroughfares where men might most easily "frequent them, and pastors fixed in retired if not distant locations, so that ab-

From "REST FOR THE SOUL IN CHRIST," a sermon by the Rev. John V. Van Ingen, D.D., of Rochester, New York:—"Belief and baptism—in nature they differ strikingly, *not in* "*importance.*" "Of faith the Church has ever preached high "doctrine, but *just as high of baptism.*" Our baptism is made to us what our Divine Master meant it "should be; *an artery* "from the heart of Christ to us, the living channel now of life "to those actions which we shape by his commandments." Baptism is here styled an *artery*. According to Dr. Johnson, "An "artery is a canal from the heart to all parts of the body." Dr. Van Ingen in using this simile teaches that the ordinance of baptism is a channel of life from the heart of Christ to the soul of the baptized adult; for in this discourse he speaks of baptism in the abstract, applying it to those who would seek "*rest for the* "*soul.*" Again, "I am persuaded by the opposition I have "witnessed to high views of the baptismal rite and covenant and "its gifts, that opposition to such views springs from the deep "fountains of that passion which makes men scorn the thought "of being dependent, like blind and humble Saul, upon the touch "of a brother's hand for eyesight, and makes them hate those "words of inspiration, 'Brother Saul, the Lord, even Jesus who "appeared to thee, hath sent *me*, that thou mightest receive thy "sight and receive the Holy Ghost.'"

The lesson here designed to be taught is that which Dr. Pusey has already taught us, that Saul was not converted, not born again, at the time when the whole Protestant world believes he was converted, on his way to Damascus, and when Jesus appeared to him, but not until he was baptized; and also that in baptism, at the touch of a brother's hand, the blind and unconverted sinner receives spiritual sight, and is made a new creature in Christ Jesus.

"solution and a ready blessing could not be had if desired; while we may not "define the sin that has caused God to visit all this calamity upon us,—yet we "see a beginning dawn of the returning mercy of God in the awakening and extending earnest desire in many hearts to have these things otherwise, in their "uttered and unuttered prayers that God would forgive our sin, would remove "our blindness, would restore His gifts; and we have sure confidence, that, not "as now, to a few hearts, but before long to the many, it will be taught and by "them be felt, that the deepest wants of the soul can only be met through the "confessional: *that inflicted penance is the loving correction that maketh great;* "*and that the pastor's absolution and the pastor's frequent blessing are the purest* "*and richest gifts through Christ on this side heaven to fit to live, to fit to die,* "*and to insure the best destiny of eternity.* Frequency in the stated forms and "acts of piety is necessary to habitual religiousness."

Here is rest for the soul in baptism, but not in Christ! It is the pure sacramental system. It leads to Rome.

In a sermon by the Rev. Evan M. Johnson, of Brooklyn, he says, "The Head of the Church instituted the holy sacrament of "baptism, *in which* he implants (without reference to the fitness "of his earthly agent) through *his ministry* the *seed* of *divine life* "in the *soul* of man."

Again, "Individuals have been made, and are made, and will con-"tinue to be made members of this one body of Christ by *baptism*."

Again, Mr. Johnson says in another discourse, "The prayer-"book and all sound catholic divines that have ever lived, have "taught and do teach that by the Holy Spirit *given in the sacra-"ment of baptism*, because it is Christ's sacrament, administered "by his agent, (however unworthy,) the *divine life* is implanted in "the *soul* of man. Those who embrace the new doctrine, since "called Evangelical, teach and hold that the divine life is not im-"planted in holy baptism, but that individuals are converted to "Christianity by the direct agency of the Holy Spirit, and are "thus made members of an invisible church."

Mr. Johnson is a prominent man in the High-Church ranks, and is one of their most active and energetic members. He speaks not particularly of infant baptism, but baptism in general. He has acuteness sufficient to perceive that if baptism has in *itself* the power to regenerate the infant, it must possess the same in every case where it is applied. The enlightened Christian may very easily decide which view of baptism is most in accordance with Scripture,—that set forth by Mr. J., or that entertained by those whom he justly terms "Evangelical," in contradistinction to the "Catholic" or "High-Church" or "Sacramental" teacher.

We have thus laid before our readers the proof upon which we rely to sustain our allegation, that the opinions upon the subject of baptismal regeneration which Mr. Faber controverts, are those of the parties who now deny them. The extracts we have given, are from writers, it will be observed, which are to be found upon the counters of any theological bookstore. Had a well-furnished controversial library been carefully sought, evidence fuller and more striking had certainly been found. Evidence more conclusive we do not need. What has been adduced, however, does show directly and indirectly that the writers who are followed and approved by a number of our clergy and laity, *do hold* that in the *article* of baptism regeneration is effected, that this is the *invariable* effect of baptism, and that this regeneration, so far from being a mere change of condition, involves all that evangelical writers are accustomed to express in the term conversion, no less than a *moral change*, rescuing the recipient from a bondage of sin, and making him one with Jesus Christ. That it is shown *directly* may be seen in various expressions which must have attracted the notice of the reader, and which are so strong that stronger words could hardly be spoken of any thing relating to the methods of grace. If we were to say, for instance, that faith in Jesus Christ and regeneration are inseparable, the assertion would also be liable to those qualifications under favour of which the opponents of Mr. Faber endeavour to escape the force of his reasoning. For in that acknowledged statement a *genuine* faith would necessarily be understood, a faith in Him as the one Mediator and God—and when baptism and regeneration are said to be inseparable, it is said with the like qualifications. And yet *it is apparent from their own admissions* that some of the advocates of this doctrine do not stop here, but hold that even the hypocritical Simon Magus, coming to baptism for base hire, is necessarily regenerated, gifted with a new nature, cleansed and made one with Christ, though all these effects were immediately obliterated, and the sinner left as before in the pollution of his former iniquity. By direct words to that effect it is then shown that the writers we have quoted do hold that baptism and regeneration are identical.

But *indirectly* these quotations prove the same thing. Only upon the supposition that the *article* of baptism is the instrument of the soul's regeneration can the language of these writers be reconciled to the ordinary rules of speech. In the Bible itself, in the burning words of its most eloquent preacher, Paul of Tarsus, when his lips utter the gratitude of his soul for the gift of salvation by Christ, you will scarcely find stronger expressions than these writers apply to baptism. Its preponderating and paramount importance vivifies every page. It is the subject of continual exhortation and argument. It is the mission of the Church of Christ to an unbelieving world. From the apostolic commission—"He "that believes and is baptized shall be saved," should you strike out the first member of the sentence, these men will scarcely miss it. Their current and sincere reading of that passage is, "Go ye "into all the world and make disciples of every creature: he that is "*baptized* shall be saved."

No one can open their books and newspapers, from Mant and Pusey to the Churchman and the Remembrancer—from the dreams of Froude to the extravagancies of Mr. Spooner—without perceiving that baptism is something of transcendent import, utterly beyond a sign or seal, and no less than the actual and effectual instrument of the change from the darkness of a carnal nature to fitness for the inheritance of the saints in light. But besides this, we would earnestly impress upon our thoughtful readers, that the inseparability of baptism and regeneration is a *necessary consequence* of the doctrines, in whatever form we meet them, which are known as the scheme of baptismal regeneration. Doubtless many of those who have read Mr. Faber, have been sincere in thinking his position a "caricature" of their sentiments. But it is merely because they have not carried out their opinions to their legitimate conclusions. There can be but two schemes on this subject. One is, that *baptism* regenerates the soul: the other is, that baptism is the seal or sign of a regeneration which is otherwise done. In the latter case it is the Spirit of God which has effected, or is presumed to have effected, a change which the ordinance sets forth, or else the covenant relation of the recipient is altered so that the Spirit of God can hereafter effect such a change. But it is the *Spirit of God* which directly does the whole work which baptism sets forth. A peculiar grace may attend it. It may be indispensable to the proper religious growth of a Christian, but the *regenerating* work is a work independent of baptism. Baptism is a commanded and therefore necessary ordinance; but the conversion of the soul is only sealed or set forth, not effected therein. But in the other view it is the sacrament which does this work; the Spirit of God is tied to this instrument; conditions therefore cannot be attached to its operation. To assert that repentance and faith are necessary when regeneration is tied to the ordinance, is a contradiction in terms. For repentance and faith constitute a change of heart. Repentance is not alone sorrow for sin, but such a turning from sin as, according to the direct words of Scripture, can only be effected by the Spirit of God. Faith is such a casting of the soul upon Jesus Christ as unites the sinner to the Saviour. To say then that these are necessary before baptism, is to say that the *moral change* from the condition of sin to acceptance with God, is necessary before baptism; and he who believes this cannot believe in spiritual regeneration in baptism. So on the other hand, he who does believe in this view of baptismal regeneration, must believe in it unconditionally. He must believe that it is produced by the ordinance. He cannot suppose any prevenient grace or any conditions of faith and repentance to be necessary, for then the change is effected without baptism. He has no shadow of a pretence for saying that sometimes it does, and sometimes it does not regenerate. If this be the Gospel, God has made baptism the instrument of salvation—God is a covenant God—upon his covenant we rely—therefore baptism and this effect are identical. If we believe in baptismal regeneration, we must believe that baptism and regeneration are inseparable.

But if baptism and regeneration are inseparable, then Mr. Faber's charge is true. Now it will be observed that the opponents of Mr. Faber have not denied the strength of his arguments; they have admitted them, for they have only denied his premises. These have now been established. They had their choice either to deny his position, or invalidate his inferences; so far from doing this last, they have agreed that the opinion he controverts is *contrary to daily experience*, is *against the Word of God*, is *against the formularies of the Church*, and *is against any fair consensus of its divines*, —for such are the inferences he establishes. Nay, they have, in so many words, consented themselves to condemn them, if any man held them. Does not this pamphlet say to them trumpet-tongued, Thou art the man? Are they not convicted by their direct words, by the force of their indirect expressions, and by the undeniable truth that the doctrine of regeneration by baptism involves necessarily the inseparability of regeneration *and* baptism. It is impossible, therefore, to pass in silence a denial which is unsupported by the facts, and comes either from a blind desire to defend a position, or a real ignorance of the legitimate character of their views. It is the purpose of this tract to persuade those, who avow themselves believers in and supporters of the doctrine of baptismal regeneration, and yet reject Mr. Faber's argument as inapplicable to them, to believe that his argument does apply to them—to persuade them that the holders of that doctrine in general have really the view he opposes, and that any views of baptismal regeneration, in its ordinary acceptation, involve the position controverted by him; and therefore, that the opinions *they* hold are, as he has proven, 1st, contradicted by daily experience; 2d, are adverse to Holy Scripture; 3d, cannot fairly be deduced from the formularies of the Church, nor from any fair consensus of its divines. That they are views which lie at the root of the most disastrous error; that they must result, if followed out, in the exaggeration of an ordinance to an equality with the irresistible spirit of grace, and prepare the mind for the reception of that impure faith, the well-spring of whose error consists mainly in maintaining the EFFICACY of the ordinances and the ministry over the Word and Spirit of God. Do not say you hate Rome, and so quiet conscience; you are never safe unless you hate error, and love the pure gospel of Christ. This is another gospel. The true gospel of God teaches that man is a sinner; that his nature is adverse to holiness; that by faith in the Son of God only, and entirely, can he be accounted holy, and be reconciled to Heaven. That to him who has this faith there is no more condemnation. That the Church with its ordinances is established to teach this truth to sinners, to preserve and build them up therein. Baptism is a witness of our dependence on this faith, in which its promises and privileges are visibly signed and sealed to us, and our faith quickened, strengthened, and confirmed. If the Scriptures say baptism saves us, it is as St. Paul says he "saved some," that is, the Gospel of the Grace of God, which it sets forth and seals, saves us. He who teaches that *baptism* saves us, denies Christ, who died for us. He limits the work of grace. He puts something between Christ and the sinner. He makes vain the gospel Paul preached. He substitutes another. AND THOUGH WE, OR AN ANGEL FROM HEAVEN, PREACH ANY OTHER GOSPEL THAN THAT PAUL PREACHED UNTO YOU, LET HIM BE ACCURSED.

THE END.

BAPTISMAL VOWS

AND

WORLDLY AMUSEMENTS.

BY THE

RIGHT REV. WILLIAM MEADE, D.D.,

BISHOP OF THE PROT. EPIS. CHURCH IN THE DIOCESE OF VIRGINIA.

NEW-YORK:

PROTESTANT EPISCOPAL SOCIETY FOR THE PROMOTION OF EVANGELICAL KNOWLEDGE.

NO. 11 BIBLE HOUSE, ASTOR PLACE.

1855.

JOHN A. GRAY,
PRINTER AND STEREOTYPER,
95 and 97 Cliff street, N. Y.

BAPTISMAL VOWS

AND

WORLDLY AMUSEMENTS.

AT the time of our baptism, whether in infancy or riper years, we make, either by our sureties or in person, a solemn renunciation of certain things believed to be offensive to God. The same renunciation is required in confirmation, when the baptismal covenant is renewed. Of course, all evil things whatsoever must be comprehended in that renunciation, or it could not be satisfactory to an holy God. These things are set forth under three heads. 1st. The devil and all his works. 2d. The pomps and vanities of this wicked world. 3d. All the sinful lusts of the flesh. It is not our purpose to enumerate all those evil and sinful things which come under the above-mentioned heads; but, as the title of this tract calls for, to make inquiry whether certain things for which some plead and which are usually called by the less offensive name of fashionable amusements, may not come under one or more of these heads. The Scriptures are so full of warnings against the Devil and his works, the world and its vanities, the flesh and its lusts, that the Church in drawing up a renunciation of sin for those who profess, in humble penitence, to seek admission to the fold of Christ, is bound to include them all.

The history of this form of renunciation is interesting. We trace it clearly to God's ancient people, unto whom we should always look for instruction, with filial reverence. Baptism itself was adopted by our Lord from the Jewish Church. Gentile converts were introduced into that by baptism as well as by circumcision. An entire renunciation of all the vanities of pagan worship, and all the sinful lusts of the people, was required of adults, for themselves and their children, whom they were allowed to bring with them. The Jewish writers inform us, that a most searching inquiry was made of adults as to the purity of their motives in wishing to join the Jewish Church. If there was reason to fear that secular or mercenary considerations led to this desire, they were rejected. When symbolically washed in the waters of baptism from all Gentile uncleannesses, they were said to be born again or regenerate, old things having passed away from them and all things having become new. There was a positive stipulation between the candidate and the Church as to this renunciation. If the candidate was a true-hearted convert, he became an *Israelite indeed*, a true son of the God of Abraham. It was to this stipulation, as well as to the adoption of a similar one by the Christian Church, in relation to her converts that St. Peter alludes, when in connection with baptism, he speaks of the "answer of a good conscience towards God," as that which saves. Now, it may be that the renunciation on the part of the Gentile converts when they were "baptized into Moses," or became Jews, may help us to discover what was the renunciation of those who were baptized into Christ or became Christians. Of course, the Jews would be particular in requiring the Gentile converts to forsake and renounce those things which were regarded as most hateful in their religion and morals. The following facts taken from the Abbe Fleury's history of the Ancient Israelites, and from Josephus, their great historian, may throw some light on the subject:

The Abbe Fleury says: "They had no profane shows among them; and as to games of chance, they were entirely ignorant of them, for we do not find the name of such things as the latter in Scripture. As to hunting, though we read of nets and snares in Scripture, yet he says there is no account of dogs being raised and kept for the chase as in modern days, such hunting belonging to the vast forests and untilled lands of cold countries. The testimony of Josephus is also very satisfactory. In his history and defense of the Jewish nation, he justifies their avoidance of intercourse with foreigners, by the example of the Athenians and Lacedemonians in their earlier and purer days, when they feared the contamination of intimacy with older and more corrupt nations, and forbade much association with them. Speaking of the manners of the heathen, he says: 'Our law does not permit us to make festivals at the birth of our children, and thereby afford occasion of drinking to excess; but it ordains that the very beginning of our education should be immediately directed to sobriety.' Again: 'Our laws take care of righteousness, they banish idleness and expensive living, instruct men to be content with what they have, and be laborious in their callings; courageous in defending laws; inexorable in punishing malefactors.' His account of the first introduction of heathenish amusements among them is quite affecting. No public exhibitions of the kind were ever known among them, until after the death of Alexander the Great, when some apostate Jews obtained leave of Antiochus to build a gymnasium at Jerusalem, as they 'wished to follow the Grecian way of living.' After that, the wicked Herod, abandoning the laws and customs of his fathers, built a theatre in the city, and a large amphitheatre in the plain, to exhibit such shows as Josephus says, 'had never been delivered down to them as fit to be used.' He spared no pains and expense to make them as entertaining as possible, by getting performers from all parts of the world. 'To native Jews,' says Josephus, 'this was no better than a dissolution of those customs for which they had so great a veneration.' Most violent was the opposition made to the representations of the theatre, and Herod had need of all his skill to prevent some great outbreak of the people. As it was, his life was assailed by some, who died declaring their readiness thus to suffer in defense of their ancient customs."

Who, after reading this account, can doubt but that the Jews in requiring that renunciation of the works of darkness, which was demanded of every Gentile convert, included these wicked and profane diversions? Who can question but that the Apostles alluded to such things, in many of their condemnations of heathen abominations? And can it be that the Christian Church in proposing terms of admission to Jewish and Gentile converts, should fall below those which had been established under a dispensation which inspiration has called "a beggarly element" compared with Christianity? The New Testament is too full of warnings against worldly conformity, pleasure-loving, revellings, banquetings, and abominable idolatries, to allow such a supposition. The discipline of the early Church also in relation to such things is strong in favor of the belief that she only followed in the path marked out by the Jewish and Apostolic Church. In proof of which I quote the following canons and testimonies:

"In the Laodicean Canons, passed in 367, it is decreed that Christians ought not to use wanton dancing at their weddings, but to have a modest dinner and supper. That they of the priesthood and clergy (those called the clergy being inferior officers in the Church, as singers, readers, etc.) ought not to gaze on fine shows at weddings or other feasts, but before the musicians enter, to rise up and retreat. 'That they of the priesthood and clergy, or even the laity, ought not to club together for great eating and drinking-bouts.' These latter were probably among those things which St. Paul denominated 'revellings, banquetings,' etc. In the African code of 418 it is ordered: 'Let not the sons of clergymen (that is, of the inferior ministers of the sanctuary) manage public shows, nor even be spectators of them; and it has always been enjoined on all Christians, that they go not where blasphemy is used.' 'That clergymen do not go to victualling-houses to eat or drink, but only upon necessity on their travels.' These places were doubtless much abused, as many in these days are. 'That reconciliation (that is, admission to the communion) be not denied to actors or stage-players, or apostates on their conversion.' All such persons were by canon excluded on account of their profession. 'That if any one desired to forsake any ludicrous exercise, and become a Christian, no one be allowed to tempt or force him to such exercise.' It seems that to become a Christian, involved the necessity of forsaking such things. All parents and older Christians should think of this in relation to their children and the younger ones of the Church."

THE TRULLAN CANONS OF 683.

These forbid making lascivious pictures; acting of farces, baiting beasts with dogs; dancing on the stage; the lewd festivities on the Kalends—attending feasts in honor of the god Pan; the public mystic dancings, both of men and women; tragical and comical masks, that either sex wear the habit of the other; also the bacchanalian feasts; on pain of deposition to the clergy and excommunication to the laity. Those called apostolical canons, and which are of doubtful date, being by some ascribed to the second century, say: "Let the bishop, priest, or deacon, who spends his time in dice or drinking, either desist, or be deposed; the sub-deacon, reader, singer, or layman, be excommunicated."

TESTIMONIES OF BINGHAM AND CAVE.

The following passages from Bingham's Antiquities of the Christian Church, and Cave's Primitive Christianity, will add force to these canons and to the remarks preceding and accompanying them. Mr. Bingham, in various places of his sixth volume, refers to the ancient canons as forbidding the public shows, games, theatres, dancings, etc., and says that they were condemned for two reasons: 1st. Because they were against the spirit of the second and seventh commandments, which forbid all encouragement of idolatry, and all impurity; both of which attended these exhibitions. 2dly. Because they were the very works of the devil, and the pomps and vanities of the world, which they renounced at their baptism as ministering to the sinful lusts of the flesh. "All who had any concern in the exercise or management of these unlawful sports, and all frequenters of them, were obliged either to quit these practices, or be liable to excommunication, so long as they continued to follow them, not only because a great deal of impurity and cruelty was committed in them, but also because they contributed to the maintenance of idolatry, which was an appendage to them. All these were comprised in the pomp and service of the devil, which every Christian had renounced at his baptism." (Vol. VI. 191.) Even the holding such offices under the civil government, where the heathen had rule, as required them to have any thing to do with such things, was forbidden; or if the offices were accepted, those holding them were debarred communion during the term of office. The plea of curiosity, he says, was not allowed as sufficient excuse for witnessing a heathen sacrifice; a servant, however, attending his master on duty was excused. Bingham also shows that the writing or reading of lascivious books and plays was forbidden, and mentions an instance of a bishop who wrote one, and was deprived of his office because he would not recant it. He shows, in like manner, that immodest apparel and decoration were forbidden to Christians. In vol. iii. we have a particular account of the baptismal renunciation, from various authors. One of the forms, according to St. Ambrose, was: "I renounce the devil and his works, the world and its luxury and pleasures." Another, according to St. Jerome, was: "I renounce thee, Satan, and thy pomp, and thy vices, and thy world." Sometimes, he says, "the games and shows, which were part of the devil's pomp, were expressly mentioned in this form of renunciation," as it is in Salvian. "I renounce the devil, his pomps, and his shows, and his works;" and this was after idolatry was removed from the public shows. The same form substantially has continued to this day in the Christian Church, and is meant to condemn substantially the same vain, lewd, and improper things. If not, then is it an unmeaning service. Moreover, the ancients traced it to the time of St. Peter, who speaks of "the answer of a good conscience towards God" as being the saving thing in baptism. At the time, however, that idolatry ceased, though lewdness still remained in their public entertainments, the Church had become degenerate, discipline was relaxed, though the canons were the same; and in many instances, the only opposition made to worldly conformity was the faithful denunciation of these things by those bishops, priests, and laymen, who themselves continued faithful. Some such there ever have been, making an uninterrupted stream of testimony on the part of the Church against these things.

In proof that very many of the early Christians were, from principle and in practice, opposed to such things, though discipline was needful to restrain many, especially when all catechumens and all the baptized, who then also became communicants, though infants, were to be governed, I adduce a few passages from Cave's History of the Early Christians. After speaking of the simplicity of their manners, dress, and entertainments, he says: "Nor were they more studious of pleasures and recreations abroad, than they were of fineness and bravery at home. They went not to public feasts, nor frequented the public shows, that were made for the disport and entertainment of the people, and this was so notorious, that the heathen charged it upon them as part of their crime." Observe how he, in Minutius Felix, draws it up: "The Romans (says he) govern and enjoy the world, while you in the mean time are careful and mopish, abstaining even from lawful pleasures; you visit not the shows, nor are present at the *pomps*, nor frequent the public feasts; you abhor the holy games, the sacrificial meats and drinks, crown not your heads with garlands, nor perfume your bodies with sweet odors—a ghastly, fearful, and miserable people." To which it is replied: "That they could not be present at such places without affronting their modesty, and offering a distaste and horror to their minds;" that at their baptism they had solemnly engaged "to renounce the devil and all his works, pomps, and pleasures; that is, says St. Cyril, the sights and sports of the theatre, and such like vanities."

If it be said that such places and amusements have greatly changed, and are not now liable to the same objections, we reply that there is enough left to bring them under the full condemnation of baptismal vows. Human nature is the same in every age, and is born into the same world of sin and temptation. In its unsanctified state, it delights in the indulgence of the same lusts, in the same gratifications. Even in its sanctified state, there is a remainder of sin ever ready to return to such things. The devil is the same unchanged being that he was at the first; still bent upon the injury of our race, as when he tempted our first parents to gratify appetite, curiosity, and ambition, saying: "Ye shall not surely die, but shall be as gods." His children are the same now as ever, sons of Belial, and daughters of pleasure, tempting even the sons of God. He uses fullness of bread and abundance of idleness as means of corruption still, and destroys as many souls as ever in the snares of pleasure. The children of God have the same conflict as ever, and the kingdom of heaven still suffereth violence, and can not be taken but by force. The Canaanites are yet in the land. The heathen in heart are all around us, and we must come out from among them, as we hope to be the sons and daughters of God. The same heaven is to be won; the same hell to be escaped. If, from these general remarks, we descend to particulars, we shall find a closer resemblance than some might imagine between the pleasurable vices of the former and latter days, as well as all other sins. Games of chance, for instance, are the same absorbing, time-wasting, and soul-destroying things now that they were in the first days of the Church, and among the heathen. If gladiatorial combats were discontinued, other combats took their place, in different parts of Christendom, and have not been entirely abandoned to this day. If the shows of wild beasts and their deadly combats with each other, and with men, passed away, combats between domestic animals have been carried on to the destruction of thousands, and have been attended in many parts of Christendom by thousands of baptized Christians, sometimes even on the Sabbath. As to the theatre, are not sentiments continually there uttered, and in the most imposing manner, just as contrary to our religion and offensive to God, and pernicious to morals, as any idolatrous ones in those of old? Is there not indelicacy and lewdness in the dress and action of performers now as of old, and are not actors and actresses excluded now as of old, not only from the communion, but from respectable society? Are not the theatres the very places where the most abandoned of the female sex come to use all their arts for the seduction of the other, and where thousands of the other sex rush into the snare? Is it not shocking to think that our sisters and daughters are sitting beneath the same roof with these wretched beings, delighted with the same exhibition, applauding the same false sentiments, and even amused at the same indecent and licentious jests, or gestures, from persons perhaps of the same character? And as to dancing, can there have been any thing in ancient times more immodest than the half-dressed female performers on the stage, who attract so many to behold the shameful exposure of their persons, while engaged in an unnatural use of their limbs? Would any persons in such a garb be admitted into respectable houses? Would not the very boys follow and hiss at such along the streets, if any attempted to walk them in such an undress? But is this all? Do not some who go to admire such actresses, return to imitate them, so far as will be tolerated? Is it not a matter of complaint, regret, and shame, not merely with pious Christians, but with many of the purer minded of this world, that dances are introduced, utterly inconsistent with that shamefacedness and modesty which the Apostle recommends; in which there is an indelicate familiarity between the sexes which would not be allowed on other occasions? Again, is it asked whether there be any thing in modern times which may be compared with the pictures of ancient days? We ask if there has not been a growing disposition to exhibit in a condition altogether different from that in which God himself placed our first parents, when with his own hands he made them garments for a covering, the pictures and statues of human beings, to be objects of admiration to the youth of both sexes?*

* In another instance, also, may we trace a resemblance between modern and ancient times. The Apostle Paul, in his 1st Epistle to Timothy, enjoins it on "women professing godliness," "to adorn themselves with modest apparel, with shamefacedness and sobriety, not with broidered hair," etc. Some of the early canons also forbid certain decorations of the person, "whereby to ensnare the beholders." It has ever been supposed that the attire of female performers at the theatres and other places was here alluded to, and that Christians were forbidden to imitate their unbecoming fashions. And is it not a fact undisputed, that the theatres of Paris and London have, at some times, had no little to do with setting the fashions for the ladies of Europe and America, and that some of their fashions have been wanting in shamefacedness, sobriety, and modesty, as enjoined by the Apostle?

It must be acknowledged that the public mind and taste are becoming more and more familiarized with such things. Indecent gestures, and smutty inuendoes and libertine sentiments in the theatre, receive nothing but a mild rebuke from the gentlemen, as being contrary to good taste, and are resented by the ladies, only by the uplifted fan or handkerchief. All kinds of exhibitions, indeed, which are transported from place to place, must now have something to gratify the corrupt taste of the people, in order to insure their support.* It should have great weight in determining the judgment and regulating the conduct of Christians as to all such things, to know that in all ages there have been numbers not enrolling themselves with communicants, and some even doubting the truth of our holy religion, who, on principles of mere morality, have condemned them. What a testimony does the Emperor Julian furnish! Wishing to adopt the most effectual means for supplanting Christianity and establishing Paganism, he presented the ministers and members of the Christian Church as models to his priests and people, positively forbidding the former to have any thing to do with the public amusements of that day, and saying that it was by the holy lives of

* A young member of the Church not long since stated, that he was induced, for the first time, to attend a circus, being led thither by the example of other professors, and among the first things he heard, was blasphemy from the clown, who came forth calling himself "The great I am."

Christians and their abstaining from such things, that their religion had made such progress, and that Paganism could only regain what it had lost in the same way. This of itself proves that, though many professing Christians had been false to their profession, many had been faithful to it; enough to force this commendation from an enemy.

That the early Reformers condemned those sins, of every class, which the Fathers did, and that they brought them to the same tests, namely, the moral law, understood in its spirit, as well as in its letter, and to the baptismal renunciation, is clear from their writings. Thomas Becon, chaplain to Archbishop Cranmer, says: "That the seventh commandment forbids, among other things, reading of amorous books, idle jesting, vain pastimes, idleness, banquetings, and evil company, as being provocations to lust." He enjoins it on young women "to avoid idleness, and to be engaged in diligent employment; not to run about unto vain spectacles, games, pastimes, plays, interludes, etc.;" "not to keep company with vain, light, and wanton persons, whose delight is in singing, dancing, etc." Speaking of Christmas festivals, he says: "These be no Christmas banquets, but Christless and devilish banquets. They be not feasts for Christian men, but for Gentiles and Ethnicks." He also condemns sumptuous funerals as exhibiting the pomps and vanities of the world; quoting one of the Fathers, who said: "Our Lord arose naked from the grave, and his followers ought not to desire superfluous and unprofitable cost, proud and vain charges. Simply, not sumptuously, honestly, not honorably, may I be buried." It is pleasing to see how this sentiment was felt and acted out by Queen Adelaide, of England. During her life she had been a most exemplary Christian, abounding in alms-deeds and good works; and at her death, she requested that her funeral should be conducted in the most simple manner, not with that expense and parade which she considered among the pomps and vanities that she had renounced at her baptism; which request was faithfully complied with by the present Queen.

I will only add that the Reformers were united in their strong condemnation of extravagance and indelicacy of dress, gluttony, and voluptuousness of living, regarding them as belonging to pomps and vanities, or the sinful lusts of the flesh. In our book of Homilies, all of these sins are specially treated of and faithfully condemned.

IMPORTANT TESTIMONIES IN RELATION TO THE THEATRE.

On the subject of the theatre, we need little else than to select a few passages from the celebrated work of Bishop Collier. Dr. Johnson says of him: "Being a fierce and implacable non-juror, he knew that an attack on the theatre would never make him suspected for a Puritan; he therefore published a short view of the immorality of the English stage, I believe with no other motive than religious zeal and honest indignation. His onset was violent. Those passages, which, while they stood single, had passed with little notice, when they were accumulated and exposed together, excited horror. The wise and the pious caught the alarm, and the nation wondered why it had suffered irreligion and licentiousness to be openly taught at the public charge." (*Life of Congreve.*)

A part of Bishop Collier's work consists of quotations from philosophers, orators, historians, from the laws and constitutions of states, etc., and from the Fathers and Councils of the Christian Church. From this we make the following selections:

"Plato says: 'That plays raise the passions, and pervert the use of them, and by consequence are dangerous to morality. For this reason he banishes these diversions his commonwealth.'"

"Aristotle says: 'That the law ought to forbid young people the seeing of comedies,' 'that where the representation is foul, the thoughts of the company must suffer.'"

"Cicero says: 'That licentious plays and poems are the bane of sobriety and wise thinking.'"

"Livy says: 'That plays among the Romans were first brought in to pacify the gods, and remove a mortality, but that the remedy was worse than the disease.'"

"Valerius Maximus, speaking of certain bloody riots at the theatre, says: 'The state first blushed, then bled for the entertainment.'"

"Seneca: 'That scarce any one would apply themselves to the study of nature and morality, unless when the play-house was shut, or the weather foul.' 'That there is nothing more destructive to good manners, than to go idling to see sights; for there vice makes an insensible approach, and steals upon us in the guise of pleasure.'"

"The Athenians, though fond of the stage, 'thought a comedy so disreputable a performance, that they made a law that no judge of the Areopagus should make one.'

"The Lacedemonians, a more sober people, never tolerated the theatre under any form.

"The Romans degraded play-actors, and deprived them of the rights of citizenship.

"In the code of Theodosius, 'players were called "personæ inhonestæ," or blemished persons, and had a mark of infamy set on them.'

"In the English constitution, at an early period, 'players and all such characters were adjudged rogues, vagabonds, and sturdy beggars, and subjected to penalties.'

"In the reign of Elizabeth, on application to the throne from a number of worthy citizens of London, the play-houses were put down, and the players thrust out of the city."

"On the continent of Europe, various laws by different states and authorities, and at different times since the Reformation, have been passed against theatrical exhibitions and performers the latter being regarded as outlawed, both by churches and civil governments."

It is not to be wondered at, if with all these testimonies of pagans and civil rulers against the stage, that the Christian Church, which was set up by the pure and holy God, to be the "salt of the earth and light of the world," should also condemn it. It would be most strange if it did not.

Council after Council has condemned all actors or actresses, and forbidden the encouragement of them, or intermarriage with them, or their admission to the communion, while thus engaged. The third Council of Carthage, of which Augustine was a member, "ordains, that the sons of bishops, or other clergy, should not be permitted to furnish out shows, or plays, or be present at them—such sort of pagan entertainments being forbidden to all the Laity. It being always unlawful to Christians to come amongst blasphemers."

The second Council of Chalcedon sets forth: "That clergymen ought to abstain from all over-engaging entertainments in music or show; and as for the smutty or licentious insolence of players and buffoons, let them not only decline the hearing of it themselves, but likewise conclude the laity obliged to the same conduct."

The testimony of the Fathers is uniform and strong on this subject.

Tertullian, in his book on the diversions of the heathen, of which the play-house was one, says: "That the tenor of their faith, the reason of principle, and the order of discipline, had barred them the entertainments of the town." He therefore exhorts them to "refresh their memories, to run up to their baptism, and recollect their first engagements; for without care, pleasure is a strange bewitching thing."

"Nothing," he says, "will serve to settle some, but a plain text of Scripture. They hover in uncertainty, because it is not said as expressly, 'Thou shalt not go to the play-house,' as 'tis, 'Thou shalt not kill.' But this looks more like fencing than argument. For we have the meaning of the prohibition, if not the sound, in the first Psalm: 'Blessed is the man that walketh not in the counsel of the ungodly, nor standeth in the way of sinners, nor sitteth in the seat of the scornful.' What though the performance may be in some measure pretty and entertaining? What though innocence, yea, and virtue, shine through some part of it? It is not the custom to prepare poison unpalatable, nor make up ratsbane with rhubarb and senna. No. To have the mischief speed, they must oblige the sense, and make the dose pleasant. Thus the Devil throws in a cordial drop to make the draught go down, and steals some few ingredients from the Dispensatory of Heaven."

Clemens Alexandrinus says: "What part of impudence, either in words or practice, are omitted on the stage? Don't the buffoons take almost all manner of liberties, and plunge through thick and thin to make a jest? If," he says, "it be said that these diversions are only taken to unbend the mind, and refresh nature a little. To this I answer, that the spaces between business should not be filled up with such rubbish. A wise man has a guard upon his recreations, and always prefers the profitable to the pleasant."

St. Chrysostom says to those who can not see the unlawfulness of the stage: "Let us not only avoid downright sinning, but the tendencies to it. Some indifferent things are fatal in their consequences, and strike us at the rebound. Now, who would choose his standing within an inch of a fall, or swim upon the verge of a whirlpool? He that walks upon a precipice, shakes, though he does not tumble; and commonly his fright brings him to the bottom. The case is much the same in reference to conscience and morality. He that won't keep his distance from the gulf, is oftentimes sucked in by the eddy, and the least oversight is enough to undo him." But he does not admit that there ought to be any doubt as to the unlawfulness of theatres. He asks how they would tolerate such things in their families, their children, servants, and visitors, which they permit to amuse them at the theatre. He will not listen to the excuse, that themselves are not injured in their characters by the scurrilities of the theatre; but even if that could be, he dwells upon the injury done to others by their example. He particularly dwells on the sinfulness of going to those places where evil women, improperly dressed, exhibit themselves so as to tempt to the violation of the seventh commandment, as explained by our Lord, and concludes by saying: "Observe me, I speak to you all, let none who partake of this holy table disqualify himself by such mortal diversions."

Thus much for the ancients, whether among the better portion of the Heathen or the Primitive

Christians. It is impossible, while reading the account which they give of the ancient theatres, of the arguments in their behalf, of the pleas put in for attending them by some professing Christians, and not feel as if we were reading about modern theatres and the excuses for them by some in our day. The truth is, that the difference between them is, on the whole, but slight. They always have been, and will be, adapted to corrupt human nature, and designed to gratify its depraved affections. They are the works of the Devil, the pomps and vanities of this wicked world, and the very things which tempt all the sinful lusts of the flesh to action, all which are renounced in baptism and confirmation. Bishop Collier, who examined the history of the stage, and the plays acted on it, in every age, declares that its main features have been always the same, and that so far from the modern theatre being reformed so as to be worthy the patronage of Christians, it is in some respects worse than the ancient. If the theatre should ever be so purified as to be a school of virtue and religion to Christians, it would become so much like a temple of religion, and its performers so like ministers of the Gospel, that there would be no need of both.

LATER TESTIMONIES.

A few testimonies from more modern authorities will suffice to prove what I have said as to the resemblance in their worst features between ancient and modern theatres.

The great and good Sir Matthew Hale thus speaks of them: "Gaming and plays as they are pernicious and corrupt youth, so, if they had no other fault, they are justly to be declined in respect to their excessive expense of time and habituating men to idleness and vain thoughts and disturbing passion when they are past as well as when they are used." Mr. Wilberforce says: "There has been much argument concerning the lawfulness of theatrical amusements. Let it be sufficient to remark, that the controversy would be short, indeed, if the question were to be tried by the criterion of *love to the Supreme Being.* If there were any thing of that sensibility for the honor of God and of that zeal in his service, which we show in behalf of our earthly friends or of our political connections, we should not seek our pleasures in that place which the debauchee, inflamed with wine, or bent on the gratification of other licentious appetites, finds most congenial to his state and temper of mind;—in that place, from the neighborhood of which decorum and modesty and regularity retire, while riot and lewdness are invited to the spot, and invariably select it for their chosen residence; where the sacred name of God is often profaned; where sentiments are often heard with delight, and motions and gestures often applauded, which would not be tolerated in private company." To this we add the opinion of Sir John Hawkins, who, as one said, has never been considered over rigid or illiberal: "Although it be said of plays that they teach morality, and of the stage that it is the mirror of life; these assertions are mere declamations and have no foundation either in truth or experience. On the contrary, the play-house and the region about it are the very hot-beds of vice."

Even the infidel Rousseau says: "Where is the imprudent mother who would dare to carry her daughter to this dangerous school, and how many respectable women would think they dishonored themselves in going there?"

We conclude our European authorities by referring to one of the best treatises against the stage that ever was written. It came from the pen of Mrs. Hannah More, who has often been quoted in favor of the stage, because in early life she wrote two plays which were acted with applause on the London theatre. It is not, however, mentioned, as it ought to be, in connection with this fact, that about the very time that her plays were acted she awoke to the evil of the stage, and absented herself from her own applauded performances. Perhaps she was at that very time meditating that admirable argument by which she hoped to counteract any evil from her own previous example.

AMERICAN AUTHORITIES.

As to American authorities, I quote first, and as of itself sufficient, a resolution of Congress when it appealed to Heaven for aid in the mighty conflict in which our country was engaged.

On the 12th of October, 1778, the following preamble and resolution were adopted: "Whereas, true religion and good morals are the only solid foundation of public liberty and happiness, Resolved, That it be, and is hereby recommended to the several States, to take the most effectual measures for the encouragement thereof, and for suppressing theatrical entertainments, horse-racing, gaming, and such other diversions as are productive of idleness, dissipation, and a general depravity of manners." Eighteen members only voted against it. Among those in its favor we are happy to see such names as those of Samuel Adams, and Gerry, of Massachusetts; Sherman and Ellsworth, of Connecticut; Robert Morris and Robert Dean, of Pennsylvania; Richard Henry Lee and Marsden Smith, of Virginia; Laurens and Mathews, of South-Carolina.

The earliest protest against the theatre, in any thing like an argument of which I have heard, was one set forth by the clergy of all denominations in Philadelphia, and ascribed either to Bishop White or Dr. Green.

Whether Bishop White or Dr. Green was the author of that Protest, we find in the Lectures on the Church Catechism, by the former, a passage yet more to our purpose than any in the Protest. In that he says: "That after the stage was purged of idolatry by Christian emperors, still lewdness continued, and therefore the baptismal vow was continued; and even if that had been banished from the stage, there would always have been something of the kind in the world to require such a vow and promise."

In connection with this I can not but adduce the opinion of one whose memory must be dear to every American Episcopalian, especially to those in the diocese of Maryland: I mean Dr. Thomas Bray, who was sent to this country as Commissary for the Church of Maryland, and substitute for a bishop when bishops were denied us. Dr. Hawks has given us a painfully interesting account of his labors for the Church in Maryland, in his history of that diocese. Dr. Bray attracted the attention of the Bishop of London, who appointed him to this office, by some catechetical lectures which he published in England. In one of these he says: "That which approaches nearest in these our days, to those sorts of heathenish pomps, and which in pompousness and magnificence of scene are not much inferior to them, are the profane and lewd plays acted, in our public play-houses, where, for aught I know, more souls are murdered than were bodies in the former; more profaneness and lewd assignations made than at the pagan theatres; and how infinitely unfit it is that those kinds of diversions should be permitted in a Christian state, or that persons professing Christianity should be permitted to go near them. It can be demonstrated, he says, that the stage can never cease to be a school of vice; for were nothing exhibited thereon that is congenial to the corrupt inclinations of the depraved heart of man, it would attract no spectator, and could not be supported. If an attendance on the amusements of the theatre be not explicit and positive breach of the baptismal covenant, it will be difficult to prove that it can be broken at all." Such are the words of one of whom Mr. Biddulph says: "He was neither a Puritan nor a Methodist, but a staunch member of the Church of England."

I have only to add, that the various Christian bodies in our land have, in different ways and at various times, most solemnly condemned the stage as contrary to our holy religion, and required their members to abstain from the same. I will only quote the words of our House of Bishops, when at the suggestion of the clergy and laity of the other House, it expressed its opinion of the same. After warning, in general terms, against "an indulgence in those worldly pleasures which may tend to withdraw the affections from spiritual things," they add: "And especially on the subject of gaming, of amusements involving cruelty to the brute creation, and *of theatrical entertainments*, to which some peculiar circumstances have called their attention, they do not hesitate to express their unanimous opinion, that these amusements, as well from their licentious tendency as from the strong temptations to vice which they afford, ought not to be frequented."

Similar resolutions have been adopted by several of the Diocesan Conventions.

THE QUESTION OF DANCING CONSIDERED.

There is one amusement, whose inconsistency, with the spirit of our holy religion is not so obvious to some; and yet it has been as clearly objected to, by the great body of pious Christians, as some other things of a grosser character. A few remarks as to its origin, history, and usual effects are subjoined. It is the more proper to do it, because Scripture is often appealed to for its authority and sanction.

Considered as a mere movement of the limbs, unstudied and untaught, it is the natural and innocent expression of the light and joyous feelings of children in their pastimes, and in which the voice will be apt to take some part. Older persons, also, of a peculiar temperament, when under some high pleasurable excitement, whether from wine, strong drink, or other stimulus, are apt thus to leap and sing. Deranged persons, too, if of a happy instead of melancholy turn, are sometimes disposed to this use of the limbs and voice. Wherefore we find Cicero, in condemning the exercise as unbecoming a Roman citizen, says: "Scarcely any sober person dances, unless he is deranged." We read of dancing also at an early period in the history of all nations, in connection with some religious celebration: as when the Israelites had passed through the Red Sea, and sang a song of praise to Jehovah, accompanied with music and dancing; and again at the foot of Sinai, when they danced around the golden calf. David also leaped and danced before the ark. This act of David was for a long time commemorated among the Jews by an annual dance in the temple, with music and clapping of hands. Even in the time of our Lord, at the Feast of Tabernacles, the elders and doctors danced in the court of the temple to the sound of its music. We read also of some Christians in the East celebrating the resurrection of Christ at Easter, in the same way. In our country at this day, there are some Christians who worship God with singing, dancing, and clapping of hands. Whatever sanction, therefore, Scripture lends to dancing, is in favor of those religious exercises, which were very different from the studied exhibitions of after-times. As paganism in all its forms was only a corruption of the true patriarchal religion, so many modes of its worship were borrowed from God's ancient people, and most probably this. Athenæus tells us: "That at the first, when they believed that the gods were their invisible guests, their dancing after sacrificial feasts was modest, and their eating and drinking temperate." Afterwards, both himself and Plato say that they degenerated into occasions of impurity and excess. Nothing can be more clear from all history, than that dancing, both before and after its corruption, formed a large part of heathen worship, and that as unworthy views of their deities prevailed, so their worship became more corrupt. Nor was it to be expected that this use of the body should always be employed only in the service of their gods. From praising the deity or deities, men began to praise their heroes and heroines in the song and dance, and to gratify all their own corrupt tastes, lusts, and passions in the same. From the sacrificial feasts, music and dancing found their way to other entertainments, though something of a religious character may have gone with them—for the heathen had their household gods, whom they sought to propitiate. Cicero, Atticus, and others inform us, that the more sober-minded among them, instead of music and dancing at their feasts, performed by a band of persons hired for the purpose, would have some one to read choice passages from their best books, to those who were at supper.*

* To such music and dancing our Lord most probably refers in the parable of the prodigal son. Approbation, however, of such can not fairly be inferred. It is only a comparison instituted between the joy of an earthly father, at the reformation and return of a son, exhibited by a feast of the good things of this world, and that of angels at the conversion of a sinner to God. If we press the analogy further than this, we shall feel called upon to celebrate the conversion of a sinner to God at this day by feasting and mirth, which all would condemn. Our Lord and all the inspired writers were in the habit of representing heavenly by earthly things, even by some confessedly sinful. Thus, in the very next chapter, our attention to the future welfare of the soul is urged by ths parable of the unjust steward, whose wise forethought is commended to our imitation, but surely not his unjust manner of showing it. St. Paul, in several places, refers to the races and bloody combats of the ancient amphitheatres, when he exhorts Christians to "be temperate in all things," "to press towards the prize," "to strive as in an agony," "to resist even unto blood:" following the example of those who, after much previous training, put forth all their strength in the combat, were often covered with blood,

In pursuing the history of dancing, we find that it was entirely diverted from religious worship, and

and sometimes died in the strife, amidst the shouts of the spectators. He even compares all that host of holy men mentioned in his Epistle to the Hebrews, "of whom the world was not worthy, and who died in the faith," to those thousands, and sometimes hundreds of thousands, of idle, dissolute, and blood-thirsty persons, who hung like clouds in the air on the seats around and above the combatants, and bids Christians be animated by the invisible presence of these faithful departed ones, in running their race, and fighting their fight, as these others were by those who encouraged them to the contest. And yet, horrid as were these amusements, the Apostle in using them as comparisons does not stop to condemn them. If, indeed, we had heard of our Lord or any of the Apostles frequenting such places for amusement, then their silence might fairly be considered as approbation, and we might follow their example as to similar things of the present day. Our Lord did once honor with his presence a marriage in Galilee, as his ministers have done ever since, when called on to legalize and bless the nuptials; and we have reason to believe that music and dancing, more or less unbecoming, were oftentimes, then as now, introduced, though the mode may have differed much. But as in far the greater number of marriages at this day they are not admitted, being objected to by the more pious and sober-minded, so it doubtless was then, since we find even some of the pagans banishing them from their feasts and substituting more sober enjoyments. Even some ministers of religion, it must be acknowledged, have, in every age, preferred the more festive and merry weddings, while the graver and more devoted ones have discouraged them, and soon left the places where they were introduced, as the primitive canons enjoined it on all Christians to do. Whether our Lord preferred the more sober or the others—whether, if now on earth, he would unite in practice with those few of his ministers who encourage such things by their presence, or with those many who disapprove, let the reader judge. There is a circumstance mentioned in connection with the marriage in Galilee which merits a passing notice, as it has perplexed and distressed cultivated as an art by certain persons, in connection with music, for purposes of gain. It was seen with more or less that was objectionable, at private or public entertainments. Others, with a view to pleasure and admiration, imitated the exquisite skill of these performers. Thus we find the daughter of Herodias so delighting Herod, whose family had introduced all Roman and Grecian amusements into Judea, as to lead to the tragic death of John the Baptist. At the time of the introduction of Christianity into the world, dancing by practised performers made a part of all the public shows and theatrical performances of Greece and Rome, as well as of many private entertainments. Together with its

some pious persons, to whom it seems to represent our Lord as encouraging not only merry-making, but drunkenness. The wine being consumed, more was wanted, and our Lord, by a miracle, furnished some of the best kind. The master of the feast institutes a comparison between our Lord and others, as to the supply of wine, his being the best, theirs of a meaner sort. There is not the slightest intimation of any thing like intemperance at that feast. That our Lord should, by a miracle, have increased it, and thereby given a perpetual sanction to intemperance, while Scripture declares that drunkards should never enter heaven, is utterly incredible. The fact which is stated of its being the best wine is worthy of notice. It is well established, that the purest and best wine in ancient times was the least intoxicating. He who did all things well, doubtless furnished the guests with that least liable to be abused to intemperance, while it was still most healthful and pleasant. We only add, that if figures, parables, and allusions justify all those things from whence they are drawn, and to which they refer, then may almost any evil custom or act be sanctioned, not only by Scripture, but by every sermon that is preached, or book that is written.

accompaniments, it was denounced as being a part of that "lust of the flesh, lust of the eye, and pride of life," which the Scriptures declare to be not of God, but of the world; and the Church reckoned it to be one of those pomps and vanities which were renounced at baptism.* We do not find any recognition of it as practised in any form so as to be encouraged among Christians; but as the Romans thought it unbecoming a citizen to dance, so the Fathers speak of it as unbecoming Christians, taught and practised as it was at that day. Wherefore we find St. Ambrose saying of such things: "*Let mothers teach their children prayers, not dances.*" As to the places where it was practised, he says: "*Where timbrels sound, the pipe makes a noise, the harp clatters, the cymbals shake together, what fear of the Lord can there*

* The perversions of things moral and sacred to immoral and profane uses are worthy of notice. Dancing, from being a religious exercise, accompanied with sacred music and hymns of praise, was corrupted into unhallowed and licentious gratification. Lotteries, appointed of God as appeals, with prayer to him for the division of property, the choosing of persons for certain duties, and settling many difficult questions, became corrupted into games of chance, and appeals to the heathen goddess, *Fortune.* Even the sacred supper, appointed of Christ, was soon abused by some into an intemperate meal, and at a later period has been perverted into the idolatrous worship of the mass. The Egyptian custom of having a skeleton at their feasts, as a "*memento mori*" to the guests, to warn them against excess, was abused by the Grecians and Romans into an excuse for it. "Let us eat and drink, for to-morrow we die," was their use of it, as we learn from many other authorities beside St. Paul.

be?" St. Chrysostom says of the act itself: "*God hath not given us legs to dance, but to walk modestly.*" "*Where wanton dancing is, there the devil is present.*" St. Basil says: "*Instead of stirring up thy feet, and jumping furiously, thou oughtest to bend thy knees in prayer.*"

These expressions show that the same pleas were put in for the amusement at that day which are now used, and that the same answers were made. The exciting and engrossing entertainment, however, still continued, and as the days of thick darkness and deep depravity came on, was more and more the delight and happiness of those who knew not the nature of true religion. It surely ought to be a source of jealousy and apprehension with the Christian as to this amusement, that, not content with appropriating to itself a portion of the time allotted to worldly pursuits, it has made such large inroads upon that blessed day which God has commanded us to keep holy; and this, too, without the least pretense of restoring the exercise to its original use. If that, indeed, were attempted, the amusement would soon be abandoned by those most devoted to it. If religion were seen "mingling in the dance," as has been said, the ball-room would soon be deserted. For many centuries it has, with some kindred diversions, possessed itself of a portion of the Sabbath—that is, wherever the Romish Church prevails—which thus not only robs us of one half of a sacrament, but gives up one half of the Lord's day to the world.

Such being the history of this exercise, the question is, as to its continuance, whether as a religious act, or as an amusement? Since it was never enjoined as a part either of Jewish or Christian worship, we are under no obligation to restore it, and can have no sufficient inducement to do it, seeing that it could only suit, even in its best form, a very early and simple state of society. As an amusement, seeing that it is a perversion of an ancient religious exercise, and has ever been discouraged by the sober-minded and pious of all nations, on account of its evil tendencies and accompaniments, we ought conscientiously to inquire, whether its great liability to abuse, and its many acknowledged abuses, should not make us frown upon it in all its forms? I will briefly allude to some of the objections to it.

1st. When taught to the young at an early age, it is attended with an expense of time and money which might be far better employed; it promotes the love of dress and pleasure, to which the young are already too prone; it tempts to vanity and the love of display; it induces a strong desire to enter on the amusements of the world at an early period, in order to exhibit the accomplishments thus acquired, and to enjoy the pleasures for which a taste has been formed; it promotes forwardness instead of modesty; it leads the young ones exactly in the opposite direction to that pointed out by the word of God, and pledged in the baptismal vows. Thus educated, they are, in this respect at least, trained not in the way they ought to go, but in the way they should forsake, according to almost universal consent, if by divine grace they are ever turned to God in true penitence and faith.

2dly. In relation to those more advanced in years, it is liable to all the above objections in a still higher degree, beside some others. It is acknowledged to be, by the help of exciting music and the mingling together of both sexes, and quick action of the limbs, the most exhilarating, fascinating, and absorbing of all exercises; quite different from any of those to which it has been compared, and by which it is sought to be justified, so that it is almost always indulged to excess; extended to a late hour of the night; followed by exhaustion of mind and body, and sometimes sickness. Instead of being sober-minded, as young men are exhorted to be by the Apostle, those engaged in this exercise are more or less beside themselves through high excitement, uttering idle words in great abundance, and being light-minded and mannered. Great is the temptation not only to expensive dressing, but to improper dressing and exposure of the person, to the display of vanity, the seeking after admiration for qualities having no real worth in them. Those who think they excel in a more private way are tempted to exhibit themselves in some more public one. Those who see it performed with great skill in private, are tempted to see it performed more admirably in the theatre, and this will reconcile them to the more immodest performances in private, which at first were offensive to the feelings.

Is this a proper entertainment or practice for the Christian? It has always been considered so disreputable to excel in this as a public performer, that such an one has been excluded, sometimes from civil, and always from religious privileges, and from respectable society. Can the practice of it then, even in a more private way, be suitable and becoming to a serious Christian? Very few persons can be found who do not answer, No. How many there are who say that the ministers of the Gospel need not, should not, preach against it, but only seek to insinuate religion into the heart; for if that be changed, this, and all such things, are forsaken as insipid and uncongenial. Young converts feel this to be so, and are distressed at the suggestion that they may one day be drawn back to the love of these things; but when their love grows cold, when they cease to watch and pray against temptation, but go into it, then old tastes and desires return, and if they yield, then are they brought into still closer intimacy with the lovers of pleasure, and if they do not relinquish their profession, continue it only to be a burden to themselves, a matter of grief to some and of raillery to others. If such persons could only know what is thought, and often said of them, by many of the votaries of pleasure who wonder at their inconsistency, it surely would not be without its effect upon their conduct in this matter. The men of this world are wise in their generation, and good judges of consistency. In such matters let their testimony be heard. Only one remark more, and I am done. Let any persons doubting or hesitating on this subject, just compare their feelings and views, when first converted to the Lord, if truly so—their preparation for renewing the baptismal vows, for kneeling the first time at the Holy Table and their exercises while there, with their preparation for the ball-room and their exercises of mind and body while there, and thus test the compatibility of the two; and if any should still say, as some have said, that they have been as pious in a ball-room or theatre as at the table of the Lord, let them seriously inquire whether the piety they have exercised in either place is such as will be accepted in the great day, or make them meet for the purer joys of that great temple above, where the sons of God shall shout for joy, and every member of their glorified bodies be made to take some part in the heavenly worship?

THE LIFE AND LABORS

OF

REV. CHARLES SIMEON.

THE FAITHFUL SERVANT.

THE

LIFE AND LABORS

OF THE

REV. CHARLES SIMEON.

SELECTED FROM THE LARGER WORK OF

REV. WILLIAM CARUS.

BY

RT. REV. WILLIAM MEADE, D.D.

PHILADELPHIA:
EDWARD GASKILL.
1853.

PHILADELPHIA:
T. K. AND P. G. COLLINS, PRINTERS.

PREFACE

TO THE

SELECTIONS.

THE work from which these selections are taken, was prepared by the Rev. William Carus, who succeeded to Mr. Simeon as minister of Trinity Church, and in all respects most faithfully and successfully supplied his place in Cambridge, until removed to another sphere of duty. The compiler of these selections had once the pleasure of being present at one of these evening parties, referred to in the following pages, in the large College room in which they were held by Mr. Simeon, at which time Mr. Carus, in like manner, conversed and prayed with the young gownsmen who came thither for their edification. Sacred is that place. May it ever be applied to such holy uses. The memoir as published by Mr. Carus, occupies an octavo volume of eight hundred and forty-eight pages, and is a rich treasury of important information touching the times in which Mr. Simeon lived, and of holy sentiments drawn from his private memoranda and correspondence. It has been republished in this country, it is believed, at the suggestion of the Hon. William Appleton, of Boston, who subscribed for five hundred copies, which were gratuitously circulated by him, chiefly among the Clergy of the Episcopal Church. Most devoutly is it to be wished that the volume was possessed, and had been read, by every minister of every denomination in our land, and by all the reading laity thereof. But, in this age of many and cheap books, it is not to be expected, that a volume of such cost would be purchased, or one of such size be read by many. Neither is it probable, that even those who possess and have read it, no matter how much delighted and edified at the time, would, to the neglect of those new books which are continually claiming their attention, open anew so large a volume for a second perusal. How much of holy pleasure and profit to souls may thus be lost? To prevent this, so far as is practicable, is the object of these selections, now offered to the public. What a service was rendered to society by Dr. Caspar Morris, of Philadelphia, when he reduced the four English volumes in which the sons of Mr. Wilberforce recorded their father's life and correspondence to one American volume, which thousands read, who would never have seen the others. Nor is there so much lost by a well-executed abridgment, or judicious selection, as some might imagine. There is the rich cream to milk, which contains nearly all the butter. There are the substantial essences to many other things which chemistry extracts, and which are applied to so many valuable purposes. Readers of books well know, that in some of the best of them, there is a comparatively small part, that is worth all the rest, and which they therefore carefully mark for a second perusal, or for future reference.

Such was the method pursued by the author of these Selections on his first reading of Simeon's Memoirs; and while thus engaged, he was ever saying to himself, O that all men could read these things. He has never ceased thus to feel, and indeed has made repeated proposals to those, who were believed to have more time and talent for the task—to make a selection, which would enable and induce thousands to enjoy, what is now locked up from them in a large octavo. Having failed in all these efforts, he has attempted the work himself; and now offers to all, but especially to the ministers and members of the Episcopal Church, the result of his labors. Perhaps he ought not to allow himself to use the term labor, for it was a most delightful exercise, and a work far more easy of accomplishment than he had imagined. He has never met with so large and so rich a volume, which as readily admitted of such reduction, without doing great injustice to the author, or the subject thereof. What has been retained, gives a faithful, though of course not a full-length portrait of Mr. Simeon. If he is not much mistaken, many ministers of our church will not only delight to read it themselves, even though they possess and have rejoiced over the larger volume; but will earnestly recommend it to their people; and sometimes offer it to those who, from birth or education, are tempted to ask concerning our church, "Can any good thing come out of Nazareth?"

Those also of our own communion, whether of the Clergy or Laity, who may entertain prejudices against that portion of the Clergy of our Mother Church, which, during the last century, received the denomination of Evangelical—may in these pages read a true history of their character and opinions. Those of the Clergy who are also thus denominated, in our own Church and country, will, I am sure, desire to be judged of, as to their general views of the great doctrines of the gospel, by those who first had and still hold that title in England; while they earnestly seek that spirit of holy zeal in all devotional exercises in private, and good works at home, and missionary labors abroad, which so remarkably characterized them.

CONTENTS.

CHAPTER I.

CHAPTER II.

CHAPTER III.

CHAPTER IV.

CHAPTER V.

CHAPTER VI.

SELECTIONS

FROM THE

MEMOIR OF THE REV. CHARLES SIMEON.

CHAPTER I.

CHARLES SIMEON, the subject of this Memoir, was the fourth and youngest son of Richard Simeon, Esq., of Reading, by his marriage with Elizabeth Hutton, the descendant of a family remarkable for having numbered among its members two archbishops of York. His immediate ancestors, in the two preceding generations, had been the incumbents of the living of Bucklebury in Berkshire; a circumstance which may possibly have had some influence in directing his thoughts to that profession of which he afterwards became so distinguished and influential a member. The family trace their descent directly from the ancient house of the Simeons of Pyrton in Oxfordshire, in which county, and that of Stafford, they formerly held very large possessions. Their only male representatives are now to be found in Mr. Simeon's branch of the family, the other branches having terminated in females; one of whom intermarried with the celebrated John Hampden, and others are merged in the families of the Welds of Lulworth Castle, and the Lords Vaux of Harrowden.

The eldest son of Richard Simeon, who was named after his father, died early in life. John, the second son, was bred to the bar; he became Senior Master of the Court of Chancery, and was one of the Commissioners, conjointly with Sir Herbert Taylor and Count Munster, for the management of the private property of George the Third. For many years he represented the Borough of Reading in Parliament, and in 1815 was created a baronet, an honor previously held by the family from a period almost coeval with the institution of the order. The third brother, Edward, was an eminent merchant in London, and for many years one of the Directors of the Bank of England. He realized a large fortune, of which, however, he had but little enjoyment, being cut off prematurely by a peculiar and distressing malady, during which he derived the most important benefit from the devoted attention and faithful instruction of his youngest brother.

Charles Simeon was born at Reading, September 24, 1759, and was baptized at the parish church October 24, following. Very little can be ascertained with accuracy respecting his early history. Whilst yet very young, he was sent to the Royal College of Eton, where he was in due course admitted on the foundation; and when nineteen years of age he succeeded to a Scholarship of King's College in the University of Cambridge. The energy and vigor which so remarkably distinguished him through life were much noticed in his youth. Horsemanship was his favorite exercise; and few persons, it is well known, were better judges of the merits of a horse, or more dexterous and bold in the management of one. In feats of strength and activity he was surpassed by none; of some of these he was pleasantly reminded in the decline of life by his early schoolfellow and constant friend, Dr. Goodall, the late Provost of Eton, who, in a letter, September 29, 1833, writes to him, "I much doubt if you could *now* snuff a candle with your feet, or ump over half a dozen chairs in succession. *Sed quid ego hæc revoco?*—at 73, *moniti meliora sequamur.*"

With regard to his moral character and habits, there is every reason to believe, from observations that occasionally escaped from him, that he was by no means profligate or vicious in the usual sense of the terms. It would rather appear that, though exposed to scenes and temptations, which he often spoke of with horror, he was on the whole in early life regular in his habits, and correct in his general conduct. His failings were principally such as arose from a constitutional vehemence and warmth of temper, the more easily provoked from certain feelings of vanity and self-importance, which, during the whole of his life, were a subject of conflict and trial to him. These feelings would display themselves at school in too great attention to dress, and in little peculiarities of manner, which quickly attracted the notice and provoked the ridicule of his companions.

It seemed necessary to premise thus much respecting Mr. Simeon's early habits and behavior, as it might easily be supposed, from the strong language he has used when describing "the vanity and wickedness" of his youth, that he had been guilty of some gross violations of morality. Those, however, who are accustomed to searching self-examination, and habitually compare their lives and tempers with the requirements of God's holy law, will have no difficulty in understanding Mr. Simeon's unreserved expressions of sorrow and humiliation when reviewing the past. It should be remembered, too, that the statements of the following autobiography are those of an advanced Christian, recording with matured views his judgment of the unprofitableness of his youth. We now enter upon Mr. Simeon's own narrative:—

MEMOIR WRITTEN IN 1813.

"I begin then with *my early life*. But what an awful scene does that present to my view! Never have I reviewed it for thirty-four years past, nor ever can I, to my dying hour, without the deepest shame and sorrow. My vanity, my folly, my wickedness God alone knoweth, or can bear to know. To enter into a detail of particulars would answer no good end. If I be found at last a prodigal restored to his father's house, God will in no ordinary measure be glorified in me; the abundance of my sinfulness will display in most affecting colors the superabundance of his grace.

"There is, however, one remarkable circumstance which I will mention. About two years before I left Eton, on one of the fast days during the American war, I was particularly struck with the idea of the whole nation uniting in fasting and prayer on account of the sins which had brought down the divine judgments upon us, and I thought that, if there was one who had more displeased God than others, it was I. To humble myself therefore before God appeared to me a duty of immediate and indispensable necessity. Accordingly I spent the day in fasting and prayer. But I had not learned the happy art of 'washing my face and anointing my head, that I might not appear unto men to fast.' My companions therefore noticed the change in my deportment, and immediately cried out Οὐαὶ, οὐαὶ ὑμῖν, ὑποκριταὶ (Woe, woe unto you, hypocrites), by which means they soon dissipated my good desires, and reduced me to my former state of thoughtlessness and sin. I do not remember that these good desires ever returned during my stay at school, but I think that they were from God, and that God would at that time have communicated richer blessings to me if I had not resisted the operations of his grace, and done despite to his blessed Spirit."

[The late Rev. J. H. Michell, Rector of Kelshall, who was Mr. Simeon's schoolfellow at Eton, from the year 1768 to their removal together to King's College, gives the following account of this circumstance in a letter to the editor in 1837:—

"On the fast day in 1776 we attended the chapel twice, and heard a sermon from Dr. Barnard, the Provost. Though few of us had any clear notion of a fast, except that we were to abstain from meat and amusement till the afternoon after the second service, yet we could not forbear from observing and ridiculing our schoolfellow, who shut himself within his study, and, instead of joining us in the public hall, contented himself with one hard egg. His dress and manners from this time became more plain and unfashionable. This was very observable to myself, who slept within a few feet of his bed. As it was the custom for the upper boys to meet, after the outward doors were closed, in their lower chamber, many a direct and indirect jest was uttered against him. . . . . . We learnt, also, that he kept a small box with several divisions, into which, on having been tempted to say or do what he afterwards considered as immoral or unlawful, it was his custom to put money for the poor. His habits from that period became peculiarly strict." He adds: "We used to have a song about him, ridiculing his strictness and devotion; and the chorus of that song, referring to his box, I am ashamed to say I once joined in, and it haunts me to this day."]

"On my coming to college, January 29, 1779, the gracious designs of God towards me were soon manifest. It was but the third day after my arrival that I understood I should be expected in the space of about three weeks to attend the Lord's Supper. What! said I, *must* I attend? On being informed that I *must*, the thought rushed into my mind that Satan himself was as fit to attend as I, and that, if I must attend, I must *prepare* for my attendance there. Without a moment's loss of time I bought the old *Whole Duty of Man* (the only religious book that I had ever heard of) and began to read it with great diligence, at the same time calling my ways to remembrance, and crying to God for mercy; and so earnest was I in these exercises, that within the three weeks I made myself quite ill with reading, fasting, and prayer. From that day to this, blessed, forever blessed, be my God, I have never ceased to regard the salvation of my soul as the one thing needful.

"I am far from considering it a good thing that young men in the university should be compelled to go to the table of the

Lord; for it has an evident tendency to lower in their estimation that sacred ordinance, and to harden them in their iniquities; but God was pleased to make use of that compulsion for the good of my soul, and to bring me to repentance by means, which for the most part, I fear, drive men into a total disregard of all religion.

"I soon became a member of the Society for Promoting Christian Knowledge, because I thought that the books of that society would be the most useful of any that I could procure, and that I might do good to others by the circulation of them. The first book which I got to instruct me in reference to the Lord's Supper (for I knew that on Easter Sunday I must receive it again) was Kettlewell on the Sacrament; but I remember that it required more of me than I could bear, and therefore I procured Bishop Wilson on the Lord's Supper, which seemed to be more moderate in its requirements. I continued with unabated earnestness to search out, and mourn over the numberless iniquities of my former life; and so greatly was my mind oppressed with the weight of them, that I frequently looked upon the dogs with envy; wishing, if it were possible, that I could be blessed with their mortality, and they be cursed with my immortality in my stead. I set myself immediately to undo all my former sins, as far as I could, and did it in some instances which required great self-denial, though I do not think it quite expedient to record them; but the having done it has been a comfort to me even to this very hour, inasmuch as it gives me reason to hope that my repentance was genuine. One little instance of quite inferior consideration was this: On leaving Eton, I took a receipt in full of every person with whom I had dealt; but one man, who let out boats, had charged me, as I verily believed, at least double the amount of my just debt; and therefore I paid him only half; and gave him his option, to receive that or none. This, on reflection, appeared to me an act of oppression; for though the man was certainly not in high repute for honesty, I could not *prove* that he had imposed upon me; and it was better that I should suffer loss, than run any risk of doing an unjust thing. I therefore determined to pay him the other half of his bill, the very first moment I should see him. This also was a relief to my mind, because it was doing as I would be done unto.*

* It is a curious fact, however, that this very man, a year or two after I had executed my purpose, met me in Eton, and claimed from me the original bill; but as, for three or four years, I carried in my

"My distress of mind continued for about three months, and well might it have continued for years, since my sins were more in number than the hairs of my head, or than the sands upon the sea-shore; but God in infinite condescension began at last to smile upon me, and to give me a hope of acceptance with him. The circumstances attendant on this were very peculiar. My efforts to remedy my former misdeeds had been steadily pursued, and in a manner that leaves me no doubt to whose gracious assistance they were owing; and, in comparison of approving myself to God in this matter, I made no account of shame, or loss, or anything in the world; and, if I could have practised it to a far greater extent, with the hope of ultimate benefit to myself and others, I think I should have done it. In proportion as I proceeded in this work, I felt somewhat of hope springing up in my mind; but it was an indistinct kind of hope, founded on God's mercy to real penitents. But, in Passion-week, as I was reading Bishop Wilson on the Lord's Supper, I met with an expression to this effect: 'That the Jews knew what they did when they transferred their sin to the head of their offering.' The thought rushed into my mind, What! may I transfer all my guilt to another? Has God provided an offering for me, that I may lay my sins on his head? then, God willing, I will not bear them on my own soul one moment longer. Accordingly I sought to lay my sins upon the sacred head of Jesus; and on the Wednesday began to have a hope of mercy; on the Thursday that hope increased; on the Friday and Saturday, it became more strong; and on the Sunday morning (Easter-day, April 4) I awoke early with those words upon my heart and lips, 'Jesus Christ is risen to-day! Hallelujah! Hallelujah!' From that hour peace flowed in rich abundance into my soul; and, at the Lord's table in our chapel, I had the sweetest access to God through my blessed Saviour. I remember on that occasion, there being more bread consecrated than was sufficient for the communicants, the clergyman gave some of us a piece more of it after the service; and, on my putting it into my mouth, I covered my face with my hand and prayed. The clergyman seeing it smiled at me; but I thought, if he had felt such a load taken off from his soul as I did, and had been

pocket the small card on which all the receipts were written, I showed him his receipt, and brought to his remembrance all the circumstances that had passed. From that day I have been very careful in keeping my receipts; and have, on one occasion in particular, saved a great deal of money by it.

as sensible of his obligations to the Lord Jesus Christ as I was, he would not deem my prayers and praises at all superfluous.

"The service in our chapel has almost at all times been very irreverently performed :* but such was the state of my soul for many months from that time that the prayers were as marrow and fatness to me. Of course, there was a great difference in my frames at different times; but, for the most part, they were very devout, and often, throughout a great part of the service, I prayed unto the Lord 'with strong crying and tears.' This is a proof to me that the deadness and formality experienced in the worship of the Church arise far more from the low state of our graces, than from any defect in our Liturgy; if only we had our hearts deeply penitent and contrite, I know from my experience at this hour, that no prayers in the world could be better suited to our wants, or more delightful to our souls.

"From the time that I found peace with God myself, I wished to impart to others the benefits I had received. I therefore adopted a measure which must have appeared most singular to others; and which, perhaps, a more matured judgment might have disapproved; but I acted in the simplicity of my heart, and I am persuaded that God accepted it at my hands. I told my servant that, as she and the other servants were prevented almost entirely from going to church, I would do my best to instruct them on a Sunday evening, if they chose to come to me for that purpose. Several of them thankfully availed themselves of the offer, and came to me; and I read some good book to them, and used some of the prayers of the Liturgy for prayer; and, though I do not know that any of them ever received substantial benefit to their souls, I think that the opportunities were not lost upon myself; for I thereby cultivated a spirit of benevolence, and fulfilled in some measure that divine precept, 'Freely ye have received, freely give.'

"In the long vacation I went home; and carried with me the same blessed desires. I had then a brother, eight years older than myself, living with my father, and managing, as it were, his house. I wished to instruct the servants, and to unite with them in family prayer; but I had no hope that a proposal to that effect would be acceded to either by my father or my brother: I therefore proposed it to the servants, and established it myself, leaving to my brother to join with us or not, as

---

* Contrasted with this painful state of things, we cannot but notice here, with thankfulness, the reverence and devotion which now prevail in this and our other College Chapels.—Ed.

he saw good. To my great joy, after it was established, my brother cordially united with me, and we statedly worshipped God, morning and evening, in the family. I take for granted that my father knew of it; but I do not remember that one word ever passed between him and me upon the subject.

"As yet, and indeed for three years after, I knew not any religious person, and consequently continued to have my society among the world. When the races came, I went to them, as I had been used to do, and attended at the race-balls as usual, though without the pleasure which I had formerly experienced. I felt them to be empty vanities; but I did not see them to be sinful; I did not then understand those words, '*Be not conformed to this world.*' At the latter ball, Major B., of Windsor, asked me to go over with him the next day to Windsor, to join in a match at cricket, and to spend a few days with him: this I did; and it led to an event which I desire ever to remember with the deepest shame, and the most lively gratitude to God. On the Sunday he proposed to go and visit a friend about fifteen miles off; and to that proposal I acceded. Here I sinned against God and my own conscience; for, though I knew not the evil of races and balls, I knew full well that I ought to keep holy the Sabbath day. He carried me about ten miles in his phaeton; and then we proceeded the remainder of our way on horseback. The day was hot; it was about the 26th day of August, 1779, and when we arrived at the gentleman's house, I drank a great deal of cool tankard. After dinner, not aware of the strength of the cool tankard, I drank wine just as I should have done if I had drunk nothing else; and when I came to return on horseback I was in a state of utter intoxication. The motion of the horse increased the effect of the liquor, and deprived me entirely of my senses. Major B. rode before, and I followed; but my horse, just before I came to a very large heath, turned in to an inn; and the people seeing my state took me off my horse. Major B., not seeing me behind, rode back to inquire for me: and when he found what condition I was in, he put me into a postchaise, and carried me to the inn whence we had taken our horses. Here we were forced to stop all night. The next morning we returned in his phaeton to Windsor. I do not recollect whether my feelings were very acute that day; I rather think not. The next morning we went to a public breakfast and dance at Egham, which at that time was always on the Tuesday after the Reading races. There I passed an hour or two, and after returning with him to Windsor proceeded on horseback to Reading.

I went through Salthill, and seeing Mrs. Marsh standing at her inn-door, I entered into a little conversation with her. She asked me whether I had heard of the accident that had happened to a *gentleman of Reading* on the Sunday evening before; and then told me that a gentleman of Reading had fallen from his horse in a state of intoxication, and had been killed on the spot. What were my feelings now! I had eighteen miles to ride, and all alone; how was I filled with wonder at the mercy of God towards me! Why was it not myself, instead of the other gentleman? Why was he taken, and I left? and what must have been my state to all eternity if I had then been taken away! In violating the Sabbath, I had sinned deliberately; and for so doing God had left me to all the other sins that followed! How shall I adore his name to all eternity that He did not cut me off in these sins, and make me a monument of his heaviest displeasure!

"There have been two seasons in my life when God might have cut me off in most righteous judgment; namely, in August, 1778, when my horse fell with me in Piccadilly, and broke my spur, but without my falling off; (at which time I was at the very summit of all my wickedness, without one serious concern about my soul; and when the stumbling of my horse called forth only a bitter curse at him, instead of a thanksgiving to God;) and, on this occasion, when, after having received so much mercy from God as I had since done, I sinned so grievously against him. On either of these occasions he might well have made me a monument of his heaviest indignation. Never have I since gone through Egham without the most lively emotions of gratitude, blended with the deepest humiliation of soul before God. I always look for the Assembly Room, that I may begin there my acknowledgments to my heavenly Father; and it is remarkable that on the very day of August in the last year (1812), I went through Egham with my dear invalid brother, in our way to the Isle of Wight. What a mercy did I feel it that, after the lapse of thirty-three years, the mercy was as fresh in my remembrance as at the first, and that all my feelings, if not quite so acute as at first, were quite as sincere. Blessed, forever blessed, be my God, who has not to this hour cast off my soul!

"During this vacation, and all the following vacations till I entered into Orders, I used to attend the parish-church at Reading every afternoon, and frequently in a morning; and I used to find many sweet seasons of refreshment and comfort in the use of the stated prayers.

"After this I went on, through the goodness of God, comfortably for nearly a year; but having read a great deal of Hervey's works, I was much perplexed in my mind respecting the nature of saving faith. I have some idea that I expressed a wish to my father to have some person who could give me information on the subject; and that it was he who advised me to apply to Dr. Loveday of Caversham for instruction. To him I did apply, and he lent me Archbishop Sharp's third volume, containing his casuistical sermons; these I read with great profit; they showed me that Hervey's view of saving faith was erroneous; and from that day to this I have never had a doubt upon the subject. I think it clear, even to demonstration, that *assurance* is not necessary to saving faith; a simple reliance on Christ for salvation is that faith which the word of God requires; assurance is a privilege, but not a duty. The true source of all the mistakes that are made in the religious world about assurance is, that men do not distinguish as they ought, between an assurance of *faith* and an assurance of *hope*. There are three kinds of full assurance spoken of in the Scriptures (as I have shown in one of my printed Skeletons); a full assurance of understanding (Col. ii. 2), of faith (Heb. x. 22), and of hope (Heb. vi. 11). The first relates to a clear view of revealed truth in all its parts; the second, to the power and willingness of Christ to save to the uttermost all that come unto God by him; and the third (which is generally understood by the word *assurance*), to our own personal interest in Christ. This last may doubtless be enjoyed; but a person may possess saving faith without it, and even a full assurance of faith without it; he may be fully assured of Christ's power and willingness to save him, and yet not be assured that Christ has actually imparted salvation to him. The truth is, that these two kinds of assurance, namely, of faith and of hope, have respect to very different things; assurance of faith having respect only to the truth of God in his word, whilst assurance of hope is founded on the correspondence of our character with that word: the one believes that God will fulfil his promises to persons of a particular description; and the other, that we ourselves are of that very character to whom they are and shall be fulfilled. This latter, therefore, I say again, is not a duty, but a privilege (an inestimable privilege no doubt); and it is certain that our Lord himself very highly commended the faith of the Canaanitish woman and others, who possessed the former assurance without one atom of the latter.

"This shows, I think, that we ought to read all human compositions with caution. The best of writers have their favorite notions, which they are apt to carry too far; and this I consider to be the case with Hervey, both with respect to the doctrine of assurance, and that also of imputed righteousness. I do myself believe the doctrine of imputed righteousness; but I do not approve of refining upon it, and insisting upon it, in the way that Hervey does: I love the simplicity of the Scriptures; and I wish to receive and inculcate every truth precisely in the way, and to the extent, that it is set forth in the inspired volume. Were this the habit of all divines, there would soon be an end of most of the controversies that have agitated and divided the Church of Christ.

"During my Scholarship at King's College, I made many attempts to benefit my friends, and sometimes thought I had succeeded in conveying to them some spiritual good: but I now see that I expected too much from my own exertions, and from their resolutions. If good be done to any, the work must be God's alone; 'the help that is done upon earth, he doeth it himself.'

"I am not aware of anything very particular occurring previous to my becoming a Fellow of King's; but there were certainly some great benefits which I received from my religious turn of mind.

"Though by nature and habit of an extravagant disposition, I practised the most rigid economy; and in this I was very much assisted by allotting my small income so as to provide for every the minutest expense, and at the same time consecrating a stated part of my income to the Lord, together with all that I could save out of the part reserved for my own use: This made economy truly delightful; and enabled me to finish my three years of scholarship without owing a shilling, whilst others, my contemporaries, incurred debts of several hundred pounds. To this hour do I reap the benefit of these habits; for though my income is now very large, I never indulge in any extravagance. I have, it is true, my establishment on rather a high scale in comparison of others; but I never throw away my money in foolish indulgences, nor spend more of my income upon myself than I believe God himself approves. I appear to spend a great deal; but by constant and careful economy, I in reality spend scarcely half of what I should in general be thought to spend; and of the indulgences I have, I am persuaded I could sacrifice far the greater part without a moment's regret, if there were occasion for my so doing."

It appears from his books of accounts, which from the first were kept with remarkable neatness and accuracy, that his whole income in 1780 (the second year of his residence in College) was only £125; and after gradually increasing for fourteen years, it became in 1793 about £300 per annum. On examining the mode of its disbursement during this period, it seems to have been his plan regularly to dispose of *one-third* of his income in charity.

CHAPTER II.

"I NOW come to the time of my Ordination. On May 26th, 1782 (Trinity Sunday), I was ordained by the Bishop of Ely; and began my ministry in St. Edward's Church (in good old Latimer's pulpit), serving that parish for Mr. Atkinson during the long vacation. The way in which I became acquainted with him was this. I had endeavored to find out some minister who preached those truths which I loved and delighted in; and I attended at St. Mary's for a long time to but little purpose. At last I heard Mr. A. at St. Edward's; and he came nearer to the truth than any one else that I could hear. I therefore, from the time that I became a Fellow of King's, attended regularly at his church. Being the only gownsman that attended there, I rather wondered that he did not take any notice of me; I thought that, if I were a minister, and saw a young gownsman attending as regularly and devoutly as I did, I should invite him to come and see me; and I determined, if he should do so, I would avail myself of the opportunity to get acquainted with him. I longed exceedingly to know some spiritual person who had the same views and feelings with myself; and I had serious thoughts of putting into the papers, as soon as I should be ordained, an advertisement to the following effect: 'That a young Clergyman who felt himself an undone sinner, and looked to the Lord Jesus Christ alone for salvation, and desired to live only to make known that Saviour unto others, was persuaded that there must be some persons in the world whose views and feelings on this subject accorded with his own, though he had now lived three years without finding so much as one; and that if there were any *minister* of that description he would gladly become his curate, and serve him gratis.' At last he did invite me to come and drink tea with him; and invited a Mr. D., an artist, to come and meet me. The conversation did not take a useful turn, for Mr. D. was not what I should call a religious man; and we parted without any profitable communication of our sentiments. In a few days I invited Mr. Atkinson to sup with me, and asked Mr. D. to meet him: it happened that Mr. D. could not come; so that Mr. A. and I were *tête-à-tête*. I soon dropped some expressions which conveyed the idea of my feeling myself a poor, guilty, helpless sinner; and Mr. A. was quite surprised, for he had set it down as a matter of course that I must be a stanch pharisee; he had, even for the whole space of time that I had been at college, noticed my solemn and reverent behavior at St. Mary's, so different from that which is generally observed in that place, and concluded, as three of his pious friends had also done, that I was actuated by a proud pharisaical spirit: when therefore he found that I was of a very different complexion, he manifested a union of heart with me, and introduced me the very next day to an excellent man, my dear friend, Mr. John Venn, who, alas! is just now deceased (July, 1813). Here I found a man after my own heart, a man for whom I have retained the most unfeigned love to his last moments, and of whom I ever shall retain the most affectionate remembrance. He, Mr. J. Venn, soon took me over to Yelling, and introduced me to a man of no ordinary character, his own dear and honored father. O what an acquisition was this! In this aged minister I found a father, an instructor, and a most bright example: and I shall have reason to adore my God to all eternity for the benefit of his acquaintance. This blessed man had often heard his son speak of this singular gownsman of King's College, and had advised him to get acquainted with him: but God, no doubt for wise and gracious reasons, had kept far from me all spiritual acquaintance; by which means he made it to appear the more clearly that the work in me was 'not of man, or by man, but of God alone.'

"Being now acquainted with Mr. Atkinson, I undertook the care of his church during the long vacation; and I have reason to hope that some good was done there. In the space of a month or six weeks the church became quite crowded; the Lord's table was attended by three times the usual number of communicants, and a considerable stir was made among the dry bones. I visited all the parish from house to house, without making any difference between Churchmen and dissenters:

"In October, my poor brother Richard died: and as there was then no one living with my aged father, it was thought desirable that I should leave College, and go to live with him. To this I acceded; but feeling the indispensable necessity of serving God according to my conscience, and of seeing my own acquaintance without restraint, I secured a promise that I should have a part of the house to myself, where I might see my friends without interfering with my father. Everything was settled: my books, &c., were just going to be packed up; and in a fortnight I was to leave College for good. But behold! in that juncture an event took place that decided the plans of my whole life. I had often, when passing Trinity Church, which stands in the heart of Cambridge, and is one of the largest churches in the town, said within myself, 'How should I rejoice if God were to give me that church, that I might preach his Gospel there, and be a herald for him in the midst of the University!' But as to the actual possession of it, I had no more prospect of attaining it, than of being exalted to the See of Canterbury. It so happened, however, that the incumbent of it (Mr. Therond) died just at this time, and that the only bishop, with whom my father had the smallest acquaintance, had recently been translated to the See of Ely. I therefore sent off instantly to my father, to desire him to make application to the bishop for the living on my behalf. This my father immediately did; and I waited in College to see the event of his application. The parishioners of Trinity were earnest to procure the living for Mr. Hammond, who had served the parish as curate for some time; and they immediately chose him lecturer, concluding that the living without the lectureship would not be worth any one's acceptance; it being, even with the surplice-fees, not worth more than forty guineas per annum. They all signed a petition to the bishop in behalf of Mr. H., informing him, at the same time, that they had appointed him to the lectureship. The parish being so extremely violent for Mr. H., I went to the vestry, where they were assembled, and told them that I was a minister of peace; that I had no wish for the living but for the sake of doing them good; and that I would, *if upon further reflection it did not appear improper*, write to the bishop to say that I declined any further competition. Accordingly I went home, and wrote to the bishop precisely to the effect that I had stated in the vestry; but it so happened that my letter was too late for the post. This being the case, I had the whole night for reflection; and upon reconsidering the matter, I found I had acted very foolishly; for, whether the bishop designed to give it me or not, it was unwise: if he did not intend to give it me, my declining it was superfluous; and, if he did, it was throwing away an opportunity that might never occur again. I therefore determined to keep back the letter, which indeed my own declaration at the vestry had authorized me to do. But still, having in appearance pledged my word, what was to be done? This I determined with myself: I will wait the event; if the bishop gives Mr. H. the living, it is well; and, if he give it me, I will appoint Mr. H. my substitute, with the whole profits of the living, and continue him in the situation as long as he chooses to hold it; and then, if I am alive when he wishes to leave it, I can go and take possession of it as my own, without any risk of having another bishop in that see, or of meeting with a repulse on renewing my application for it. Thus I shall keep my word most fully with the parish, and yet avoid all the evils which a hasty declining of the living might have occasioned.

"Here, then, behold to what a situation I was reduced! the living now could not possibly be mine, at least for years to come. Whether the bishop should give it him or me, I was equally precluded from possessing it. But God, in submission to whose will I had made the sacrifice, most marvellously interposed to deliver me from this difficulty. No sooner had I made the declaration in the vestry, than the parishioners, without any authority from me, wrote to the bishop that I had declined: and this brought me a letter from the bishop, saying, that if I chose to have the living it was at my service; but that, if I declined it, Mr. H. should not have it on any account.*

"Here the knot was untied: my word was kept to all intents and purposes; everything was done by me that truth and honor could dictate: to decline the living now would in no respect answer the wishes of the parish, and to execute my intentions

---

* The bishop's words were: "The parishioners have petitioned for Mr. Hammond, and, unless gratified, insinuate their intentions of bestowing their lectureship on a different person than my curate. I do not like that mode of application, and if you do not accept it, shall certainly not license Mr. H. to it. I shall await your answer." Nov. 9, 1782.

The next day Mr. Simeon preached for the first time in Trinity Church.

in reference to Mr. H. was impossible. Thus did God interpose to deliver me from a difficulty which seemed absolutely insurmountable; and the parish themselves, through their indiscreet and indecent earnestness to accomplish their own wishes, were the very instruments whom God made use of to fix me among them as their stated pastor. How little did they think what that letter of theirs would effect! It was that which irritated the bishop, and caused him to send me such a letter as relieved me at once from all embarrassment, and fixed me in a church which I have now held for above thirty years, and which I hope to retain to my dying hour. Truly 'the judgments of God are unsearchable, and his ways past finding out.'

"The disappointment which the parish felt proved very unfavorable to my ministry. The people almost universally put locks on their pews, and would neither come to church themselves, nor suffer others to do so: and multitudes from time to time were forced to go out of the church, for want of the necessary accommodation. I put in there a number of forms, and erected in vacant places, at my own expense, some open seats; but the churchwardens pulled them down, and cast them out of the church. To visit the parishioners in their own houses was impracticable; for they were so imbittered against me that there was scarcely one that would admit me into his house. In this state of things I saw no remedy but faith and patience. The passage of Scripture which subdued and controlled my mind was, 'The servant of the Lord must not strive.' It was painful indeed to see the church, with the exception of the aisles, almost forsaken; but I thought that if God would only give a double blessing to the congregation that did attend, there would on the whole be as much good done as if the congregation were doubled, and the blessing limited to half the amount. This has comforted me many, many times, when, without such a reflection, I should have sunk under my burthens.

"The opposition thus formed continued for many years. The lectureship being filled by Mr. Hammond, I had only one opportunity of preaching in the whole week. I therefore determined to establish an evening lecture;* but scarcely had I established it, before the churchwardens shut the church doors

* July 16, 1783. Mr. Simeon writes to Rev. J. Venn: "Coulthurst established an extempore lecture at six in the evening, for the first time on the last Sabbath; and I intend, with God's grace, now he has led the way, to begin the same at the same hour in Trinity Church next Sunday. I much need your prayers, my dear friend, being very insufficient for so arduous a task."

against me. On one occasion the congregation was assembled, and it was found that the churchwarden had gone away with the key in his pocket. I therefore got a smith to open the doors for that time, but did not think it expedient to persist under such circumstances.

"Yet what was to be done? If those whose minds were impressed by my preaching had not some opportunity of further instruction, they would infallibly go to the dissenting meetings, and thus be gradually drawn away from the church. The only alternative I had was to make them meet in a private room; I therefore hired a small room in my parish, and met them there, and expounded to them the Scripture, and prayed with them. In time the room was too small to hold us all, and I could not get one larger in my parish; I therefore got one in an adjoining parish, which had the advantage of being very spacious and very retired. Here I met my people for a considerable time. I was sensible that it would be regarded by many as irregular; but what was to be done? I could not instruct them in my church; and I must of necessity have them all drawn away by the Dissenters, if I did not meet them myself; I therefore committed the matter to God in earnest prayer, and entreated of Him, that if it were His will that I should continue the room, He would graciously screen me from persecution on account of it; or that if persecution should arise on account of it, He would not impute it to me as sin, if I gave up the room. He knew the real desire of my heart; He knew that I only wished to fulfil his will: I told him a thousand times over that I did not deprecate persecution; for I considered *that* as the necessary lot of all who would 'live godly in Christ Jesus;' and more especially, of all who would preach Christ with fidelity; but I deprecated it as arising from that room.

"My friends, as I expected, were all alarmed; and at last they prevailed on my dear and honored friend, Mr. Henry Venn, to speak to me on the subject. His word would operate more forcibly with me than the words of a thousand others, because I knew him to be governed by no carnal policy, but to be given up wholly unto God. On his dissuading me from it, I told him all my transactions with God respecting it; I told him that none of my friends were more fearful of injuring the cause of God than I was; that the motion of a finger was sufficient to turn me in this matter, if only I could ascertain the mind of God; and that, in order to learn the will of God respecting it, I had with many prayers committed it to Him in that way; entreating Him to prevent its being an occasion of offence, if he willed that I should continue it; and that He would pardon me for giving it up, in case it should excite a clamor and persecution against me. Mr. V. then said, 'Go on, and God be with you:' and verily God was with me there on many occasions, to the abundant edification of my people in faith and love. The persecutions in my parish continued and increased; but during the space of many years no persecution whatever arose from that room, though confessedly it was the side on which my enemies might have attacked me with most effect.

"My parish, after two or three years, made a formal complaint against me to the bishop; they complained that I preached so as to alarm and terrify them, and that the people came and crowded the church, and stole their books. The bishop wrote to me, and I answered him at great length, vindicating my preaching, and denying the charges which were brought against me. I still possess a copy of my answer; but it was certainly not drawn up in a judicious way. I remember it contained my answers in distinct heads, 1, 2, 3, somewhat like a syllabus, and not in a continued strain of argument; and the bishop was rather displeased with it; but I was not then skilled in writing to bishops; were I to answer the same accusations now (1813), I should frame my reply in a different way; as indeed my late answer to similar accusations, no longer than the year before last, sufficiently shows.

"In my preaching I endeavored to approve myself to God with fidelity and zeal; but I do not now think that I did it in a judicious way. I thought that to declare the truth with boldness was the one object which I ought to keep in view; and this is a very general mistake among young ministers. I did not sufficiently attend to the example of our Lord and his apostles, in speaking as men were able to hear it, and in administering milk to babes, and meat to strong men. My mind being but ill-informed, my topics were necessarily few; and the great subjects of death, judgment, heaven, and hell, were prominent in every discourse, particularly as motives to enforce the points on which I had occasion to insist. Were I *now* to enter on a new sphere, especially if it were in a town and not in a village, I would, in the Morning Services especially, unfold the parables, and endeavor rather to take the citadel by sap and mine, than by assault and battery. I would endeavor to '*win* souls,' and 'speak to them the truth in *love;*' not considering so much what I was able to say, as what they were able to receive. But this requires more extensive knowledge, and a more chastised mind than falls in general to the lot of young ministers, especially of such as have never had one letter of instruction given them on the subject.

"After about five years, Mr. Hammond vacated the lectureship; and a son of a parishioner became a competitor for it. By this time I had gained some footing in the parish; and I believe at this hour that if matters had been carried fairly, I had the majority of votes; but there was a bitter and persecuting spirit among all the heads of the parish; and, whether justly or unjustly, they carried it against me. The greater part of the pews also still continued shut; but though I was persuaded that the parishioners had no right to lock them up, there being only one faculty pew in the church, I was restrained from attempting to open them by that divine declaration, 'the servant of the Lord must not strive.' Many hundreds of times has that one word tied my hands, when a concern for immortal souls, and a sense of the injury done to my ministry, would have prompted me to take off the locks. I hoped that God would at last effect a change; and I found, after about ten years, that I was not disappointed.

"Little did I think, in all the years that the parishioners prevailed to shut the church against me, how great a mercy it was both to me and the church of God; for if I had been able to labor to the full extent of my wishes, I should infallibly have ruined my health in a short time: but being actually bound, as it were hand and foot, I was constrained to keep within my strength, and was thus enabled to go on for twenty-four years, without ever being laid by one single Sabbath. How mysterious are the designs of God, and how marvellously does he make the wrath of man to praise him!"

During the period of his residence at King's (as Mr. H. informed the editor in 1837), Mr. Simeon invariably rose every morning, though it was the winter season, at four o'clock, and, after lighting his fire, he devoted the first four hours of the day to private prayer, and the devotional study of the Scriptures. He would then ring his bell, and calling in his friend with his servant, engage with them in what he termed his family prayer. Here was the secret of his great grace and spiritual strength. Deriving instruction from such a source, and seeking it with such diligence, he was comforted in all his trials, and prepared for every duty. The copy of the Scriptures, which became the favorite companion of his devotional hours from this period, was a quarto volume of Brown's *Self-interpreting Bible*, which, to the end of his life, he was continually enriching with valuable notes of his own. So much did he prize this commentary, that in 1787, Jan. 19, he wrote to the author at Haddington, "Your Self-interpreting Bible seems to stand in lieu of all other comments, and I am daily receiving so much edification and instruction from it that I would wish it in the hands of all serious ministers. I have conceived a thought of purchasing a few to give to those godly ministers who would find it very inconvenient to purchase it for themselves. But having no very great affluence myself, it is needful that I should proceed upon the most saving plan. I take the liberty therefore of asking whether you (whose heart seems to be much set upon forwarding the cause of Christ) could procure me forty at the booksellers' price for *that purpose alone*, and to inform me whether there will be a new edition soon."

As a conspicuous memorandum in his pocket-book for this year, Mr. Simeon has written in large characters, twice over, on separate pages :—

Talk not about myself.
Speak evil of no man.

This trial from within he continues to deplore when writing to Mr. Thornton the following year :—

"A thousand thanks to you, dear sir, for many valuable observations in your last letter, especially that which I hope to remember, that ministers, when truly useful, and more perfectly instructed in the ways of God, are 'off their speed,' and not so full of their success. Alas, alas! how apt are young ministers (I speak feelingly) to be talking of that great letter I. It would be easier to erase that letter from all the books in the kingdom than to hide it for one hour from the eyes of a vain person. Another observation, in a former letter of yours, has not escaped my remembrance, the three lessons which a minister has to learn—1. Humility; 2. Humility; 3. Humility. How long are we learning the true nature of Christianity!"

We now come to a most eventful period in Mr. Simeon's history. His thoughts and efforts were no longer to be limited to the scene of his immediate duties at Cambridge. The report of his labors and zeal had at this early period been carried to India; and he was henceforth to be prominently engaged in carrying out a design for the evangelization of that immense territory. At the commencement of 1788, he received an Address from Calcutta, relative to a mission, which the Rev. David

Brown, in conjunction with Mr. Chambers, Mr. Grant, and Mr. Udny, was anxious to establish in that country. "From the inclosed papers (they write) you will learn the project of a mission to the East Indies. We understand such matters lie very near your heart, and that you have a warm zeal to promote their interest. Upon this ground we take the liberty to invite you to become agent on behalf of the intended mission at home. We humbly hope you will accept our proposal, and immediately commence a correspondence with us, stating to us, from time to time, the progress of our application," &c.

On the front of this document Mr. S. has written: "It merely shows how early God enabled me to act for India; to provide for which, has now for forty-two years been a principal and an incessant object of my care and labor."

This project of a mission to India led to Mr. Simeon's consideration of the subject upon a still more extensive scale; and, as will presently appear, gave rise to those important discussions on "the education of missionaries," and on "the propriety and mode of attempting a mission to the heathen from the Established Church," which issued in the formation of the Church Missionary Society.

The zeal and devotion, which he displayed on behalf of the spiritual destitution of the heathen, were equally ready to be exerted for the relief of temporal distress at home. About the close of the year 1788, during the great scarcity of bread, a subscription was raised in the University, and by the inhabitants of the town, to which Mr. Simeon very largely contributed, to enable the poor in Cambridge to obtain bread at half price. It occurred to Mr. S., who was well acquainted with the state of the villages in the neighborhood, that they must be equally distressed with the town: "What is to become of *them?*" he asked. "That is more than we can undertake to answer for," was the reply. "Then," said Mr. Simeon, "that shall be *my* business." Accordingly, he set on foot a plan, by which they too might be included in the benefit; and taking himself a large share of the expense and most of the trouble, he set about it with all his wonted energy—inspired others with the same desire to extend more widely the circle of relief—and every Monday rode himself to the villages within his reach, to see that the bakers performed their duty in selling to the poor at half price.

During the year 1788, he entered for the first time upon a college office, being elected Junior Dean of Arts, and the following year he was appointed to the important office of Dean of Divinity. He was now in a position to exercise great moral influence in his college, especially over its junior members, and, as may be supposed, he was not slow to avail himself of this opportunity for doing good and reforming evils.

CHAPTER III.

"After some years I prevailed, and established an evening lecture, with the consent of the churchwardens (July 18, 1790). I had long before consulted Sir W. Scott about the right of the churchwardens to shut the church, and of the parishioners to lock up the pews, and his opinion was that the right of prohibiting me from using the church in canonical hours was vested in the bishop alone, and that none but faculty pews could legally be shut up in the manner that mine were. I did not, however, choose to exercise my right in reference to either the one or the other, but desired rather to wait till God himself should accomplish my wishes in his own time and way. To this I was led by various considerations. My own natural disposition would have instigated me to maintain my rights by force, and I knew I could never do wrong in resisting my corrupt nature. Like a bowl with a strong bias, I could not go far out of the way on the side opposite to that bias, or, if I did, I should have always something to bring me back; but if I leaned to the side where that force was in operation, I might be precipitated I knew not whither, and should have nothing to counteract the impulse, or to bring me back. There was no doubt therefore in my mind which was the safer and better path for me to pursue.

"In the year 1796, a Scotch minister, whom I think it one of the greatest blessings of my life ever to have known, Dr. W. Buchanan, of Edinburgh, was introduced to me; and I went with him to Edinburgh and through [the Highlands, and again in 1798 to] Inverness and Tain; and from thence through Ross shire to the Hebrides, and back through Glasgow, &c. In almost all the places that we went to I preached; and I established a lecture in Edinburgh, which has been continued ever since. Except when I preached in Episcopal chapels,

I officiated precisely as they do in the Kirk of Scotland; and I did so upon this principle: Presbyterianism is as much the established religion in North Britain as Episcopacy is in the South; there being no difference between them, except in church government. As an Episcopalian, therefore, I preached in Episcopal chapels; and as a member of the Established Church, I preached in the Presbyterian churches; and I felt myself the more warranted to do this, because, if the king, who is the head of the establishment in both countries, were in Scotland, he would of necessity attend at a Presbyterian church there, as he does at an Episcopalian church here; and I look upon it as an incontrovertible position that where the king *must* attend a clergyman *may* preach. I was informed indeed that Archbishop Usher had preached in the Kirk of Scotland, and I know that some very high churchmen had done so; but without laying any stress on precedents, I repeat that, where the king and his court must attend, a clergyman may preach. And I believe many will bless God to all eternity that ever I did preach there. But I cannot help recording here, to the honor of the Church of England, that, on all the three times that I have visited Scotland, and have attended almost entirely the Presbyterian churches, I have on my return to the use of our liturgy been perfectly astonished at the vast superiority of our mode of worship, and felt it an inestimable privilege that we possess a form of sound words, so adapted in every respect to the wants and desires of all who would worship God in spirit and in truth."

In speaking of the comparative excellencies of extempore prayer and written forms, Mr. Simeon would frequently observe: "If *all* men could pray, at *all* times, as *some* men can *sometimes*, then indeed we might prefer extempore to precomposed prayers."

"In 1794 I was chosen Lecturer of Trinity Church without opposition; and as I thought it unprofitable for one minister to labor three times a day in the same Church, I invited my dear and honored friend Mr. Thomason to become my assistant, and procured the curacy of Stapleford, in which he might minister in the morning, and I in the afternoon. Thus we both were fully employed; and it was a great joy to me to have such a colleague to labor with me. On his becoming my assistant (Oct. 1796), I judged it inexpedient to continue meeting my people altogether in one body, because there was not now the same necessity as formerly, and because he no less than myself would be involved in any obloquy that might attend it. To have some opportunities of meeting my people I considered as indispensable; for how could I know my sheep, if I did not see them in private? and how was it possible for me to visit so many at their own houses, and to find out all their different states and trials? If there were regular seasons for us to meet together, I could from time to time invite them to state to me, either before others, or in private, whatever they might wish to say: and I could learn by conversation something respecting the state of their souls before God. I could learn, too, whether any were in danger of being drawn away by the Dissenters, or were imbibing any erroneous tenets, or were acting in any respect unworthy of their holy profession. I am aware that even such societies as these are by many accounted irregular, and that very few of the governors of our Church would sanction them. Indeed it is a curious fact, that the establishing of such societies is generally supposed to indicate an indifference towards the Church when it actually proceeds from a love to the Church, and a zeal for its interests. Were the Bishops acquainted with the ministers who are called Evangelical, they would soon see the importance, yea, and the absolute necessity, of such meetings, not merely for the edification of the people, *but chiefly for the preservation of the Established Church.* The Dissenters in general, and the Methodists in particular, have such meetings; and they are found to be of the highest utility for the cultivation of mutual love, and for the keeping of their respective members in one compact body. Where nothing of that kind is established, the members of any church are only as a rope of sand, and may easily be scattered with every wind of doctrine, or drawn aside by any proselyting sectary. What influence can a minister maintain over his people, if he does not foster them as a brood under his wings? As to the idea of such meetings being contrary to our obligations as ministers of the Establishment, let any one read the Bishop's Charge to the Priests in the Ordination Service, and say, whether a clergyman can fulfil his duties without them? I am well persuaded he cannot; and experience proves that wherever there is an efficient ministry in the Church without somewhat of a similar superintendence, the clergyman beats the bush, and the Dissenters catch the game: whereas, where such a superintendence is maintained, the people are united as an army with banners. This has been the case in Cambridge to an extraordinary degree; for in the thirty years that I have ministered at Trinity Church, the Dissenters have not (as far as I recollect) drawn away three whom I was not glad to get rid of. It has only been the refuse, who have first lost all simplicity of mind, if not wholly departed from God, that they have been able to steal from me. The number of my people, I mean of those who appeared to be spiritually enlightened, were about 120 (those who came to my Church from the adjacent villages being of course omitted, on account of their distance from me); and these I divided into six societies, of about twenty each; so that by meeting two societies and one in every alternate week, I could see them all in the month. In these societies I separated men and women, and associated together those who were most suited to each other. One society in particular I made of those who were more judicious and experienced, and who were denominated stewards, from their having to dispose of the alms which we regularly collected in all the societies for the relief of the poor. A select number had been separated to this office even whilst we were meeting altogether; and therefore it seemed highly expedient that they should constitute a separate society now.—Besides, I had now a further view in forming them into one society; for as now I could only meet the different individuals once a month, instead of once a week, it was desirable that I should have some in whose judgment I could confide, to inform me of all that was passing among the people; for instance, whether any were turning back from God, or inclining to the Dissenters, or in any view whatever needing my peculiar care: by them, too, I could learn, far better than by any other means, the state of those who were desirous of uniting themselves with us. Moreover, I could make use of them in the first instance to rectify any little disorders, and reserve myself to interpose in matters which they were unable to accomplish. I considered myself as a coachman upon the box, and them as the reins, by which I had immediate access to every individual in my church: and from the most mature reflection, I cannot but consider this as of the greatest importance to the welfare of any people. That it is open to abuse is certain; and what is there that may not be abused? Even the Apostolic Churches were more or less distracted by the conceit of some, or the violence of others; and whilst human nature is what it is, we cannot hope to find any society of men on earth free from some kind of evils; but whilst I was able to attend to all the societies myself, there was as little evil arising from this arrangement, as can be expected in any society on earth. It pleased God, however, to afflict me at last with almost a total loss of my voice, so that for the space of two years I could do very little in public, and nothing at all in private; and during that time several of the people became conceited and headstrong. Long before I changed the plan from one society to six, there had been a weekly meeting for prayer (as there was in many other places through the kingdom) on account of the war; and when the change was made, that prayer-meeting was continued, being carried on by the people without me; for, on account of my numerous societies and engagements, I could not be present at them. This was an evil, but it was one which I could not remedy. Could I have superintended and conducted them myself, I have no reason to think that any evil would have arisen from them; but, where people are left to themselves, the most conceited and the most forward will take advantage of it to show their evil dispositions; and if they can gain an ascendency (which they too frequently will), they will prove a plague and a grief to the minister that is placed over them. So I found it; and when I returned among my people, I strove in vain to reduce them to a better state. Not that any great evil immediately appeared; but I saw that some of the chief stewards had lost a measure of their simplicity and tractableness; and the general rage which had recently arisen through the nation for itinerant preaching, had visibly infected some amongst them. This I endeavored to stop; being well convinced, that, whether it was evil in itself or not, it was not possible for me, as a minister of the Established Church, to countenance such proceedings amongst my people, since I should assuredly be represented by my enemies as a patron and encourager of those irregularities. To a certain extent I prevailed; for I summoned the stewards to make known to them my views of the subject, and actually expelled from my societies one, who had taken out a license as a preacher. But within these two years (*i. e.* about 1811), matters have been brought to a crisis; and the lamentable state of my people has fully appeared."

At a later period Mr. Simeon says: "I cannot ascribe the whole of this disorderly spirit to the circumstance of their having been invested by me with a portion of authority; for, the same spirit manifested itself, in a far greater degree, among Mr. Robinson's people at Leicester, where no such society had been formed. There, a hundred went off from his Church at once; and many who remained behind, were as thorns in his side for several years. The true state of this case is, that the corruption of human nature will, sooner or later, show itself in every church. There were those who said to Moses, 'You take too much upon you,' whilst the charge was, in truth, applicable only to themselves. There ever was, and ever will be, some Diotrephes, 'who loves to have the pre-eminence,' and who will find some occasion or other to manifest and diffuse his own evil dispositions. If even St. Paul found this to be the case, yea, and the loving John too—who am I, that I should minister for thirty-three years, and not find it? This is only a fresh proof that human nature is the same in every country, and in every age. I pray God to give them a better spirit, and to endue me, as he did Solomon, with wisdom, that I may go in and out before them with a wise and perfect heart."

The subject of Missions to the Heathen continued to be one of absorbing interest to Mr. Simeon; and he spared no pains to excite the zeal, and secure the aid of his most influential friends in furthering the sacred cause. His earnestness and love were felt to be worthy of imitation, even by Mr. Wilberforce himself, as appears from his journal:—

"Thursday, July 20. To dine at Henry Thornton's, where Simeon and Grant, to talk over mission scheme.

"July 22. Simeon with us; his heart glowing with love of Christ. How full he is of love, and of desire to promote the spiritual benefit of others. Oh! that I might copy him, as he Christ. My path is indeed difficult, and full of enemies. But God in Christ can and will strengthen and uphold us, if we trust in him."

The many excellent and warm friends, whom Mr. Simeon had attached to himself during his late tour through Scotland, began now to press him with earnest solicitations to repeat his visit to the North. Amongst the rest, not the least frequent and persuasive, were the requests of his beloved friend at Edinburgh, Dr. Buchanan. In a letter, the next spring, he reminds him of the deep interest that had been excited on all sides by his preaching, and holds out a prospect of increased good from his return.

. . . "You have very great encouragement, indeed, to come among us, you remember the crowds that followed you wherever you preached; and many, many are the inquiries that have been made about your return, by persons of all ranks. I have reason to think that you were the instrument of doing much good when you were here; and, should it please God to bring you among us again, I hope it will be with joy, and for a blessing to many."

Early in the month of May, Mr. Simeon prepared to comply with the pressing requests of his Northern friends.

"His visits to Edinburgh," observes a friend, in a letter to Mr. Preston, "were always felt as a refreshment and useful stimulus, by the good people there. The doctrine he preached and expounded to them, was the same; but the manner and the illustrations, and the zeal and fervor of his ministrations, both in public and in private, were very different; and were calculated to produce, and did produce, a great effect. I remember well his preaching a most striking sermon on ministerial duties and faithfulness; in which he introduced, with a view to illustration, the keeper of the lighthouse on Inch-keith, the island situate in the middle of the Firth of Forth, between Mid-Lothian and Fife. He supposed the keeper to have let the light go out, and that in consequence the coast was strewed with wrecks, and with dead and mangled bodies; and that the wailings of widows and orphans were everywhere heard. He supposed the delinquent brought out for examination before a full court and an assembled people; and, at last, the answer to be given by him, that he was 'asleep!'—'asleep!' The way in which he made this 'asleep!' burst on the ears of his audience, who were hanging in perfect stillness on his lips, contrasting the cause with the effects, I remember to this day. I remember on another occasion in Edinburgh, after having finished an impressive discourse, his standing up in full size and with impassioned gesture, and stopping a merry jig which was commencing from the organ."

The unusual earnestness and fervor of Mr. Simeon's manner in all his addresses, whether in public or private, liable as it was to be misapprehended by strangers, was now thoroughly understood and appreciated by his friends. His evident sincerity, his unwearied and disinterested exertions, and entire consistency of character, had won for him the devoted attachment of those who had the opportunity of most intimately observing him. Prejudices began to yield to sentiments of respect, and even of admiration, in the minds of many, who had at one time regarded him with doubt, if not with dislike. Thus his early friend and schoolfellow, Mr. Michell, writes respecting the change in his own views, and, more particularly, in those of Dean Milner: "During the year 1795 to 1800, I was in college (King's). My very frequent intercourse with him (Mr. Simeon) daily increased my admiration of his character, and my desire to render him any assistance, by every public and private effort within my power. During my proctorship with Mr. Vickers, of Trinity Hall, we zealously united in defending him from those insults, which he occasionally experienced in his church, on the Sunday evenings and his weekly lectures. Dr. Milner's sentiments respecting him were a memorable instance of the Dean's Christian candor and judgment. In the presence of Dr. Jowett and myself, he more than once declared that he had rigorously for some years scrutinized the character and conduct of Mr. Simeon, and, for a time, entertained some doubts of his sincerity; but was now perfectly convinced of his truly Christian spirit and usefulness, and of his unreserved devotedness to the glory of God."

The great subject of Missions to the Heathen, which had so long engaged Mr. Simeon's earnest attention, and for which he had labored to enlist the zeal of his friends, was at length to receive the consideration due to its importance. Measures began to be proposed for forming a Missionary Society "in direct connection with and under the sanction of the Church of England." Certain resolutions of a practical character were suggested by Mr. Venn, to be considered in detail at the Eclectic; and as the subject had originally been discussed at Mr. Simeon's desire, "the Society felt the propriety of inviting him to assist at their next meeting." Accordingly, Mr. Venn undertook to write to him, and requested his attendance on the occasion.

This meeting was held March 18th. "Fourteen members were present. Mr. Venn opened the discussion, by insisting upon the duty of doing something for the conversion of the Heathen. Mr. Charles Grant urged the founding of a Missionary Seminary. The Rev. Josiah Pratt advocated the adoption of the Resolution, as 'breathing a quiet, humble, dependent spirit.' The Rev. Charles Simeon, with characteristic distinctness of purpose and promptitude of zeal, proposed three questions: '*What can we do?— When shall we do it?—How shall we do it?——What can we do?* We cannot join the [London] Missionary Society; yet I bless God that they have stood forth. We must now stand forth. We require something more than resolutions—something ostensible—something held up to the public. Many draw back because we do not stand forward.—*When shall we do it?* Directly: not a moment to be lost. We have been dreaming these four years, while all England, all Europe, has been awake.—*How shall we do it?* It is hopeless to wait for Missionaries. Send out Catechists. Plan two years ago. Mr. Wilberforce.'—The result of this meeting was a general consent that a Society should be forthwith formed, by inviting a few of those upon whose concurrence in their own views they could rely; and that a Prospectus of their proceedings should be afterwards prepared, and that then their plans should be laid before the Heads of the church. The next meeting of the Eclectic was devoted to the same subject, and the Rules of the proposed Society were considered and settled. On the 12th of April, a meeting was held at the Castle-and-Falcon Inn, Aldersgate Street, '*For the purpose of Instituting a Society amongst the Members of the Established Church for sending Missionaries among the Heathen.*' The Rev. J. Venn was in the chair, and detailed the objects of the Meeting." Sixteen clergymen and nine laymen were all that composed that small assembly; but the blessing of God was manifestly with them in their "work of faith and labor of love." "The Society for Missions to Africa and the East," then formally established, grew and advanced like the grain of mustard-seed; and in less than half a century it has carried the knowledge of "the unsearchable riches of Christ" to Western Africa and New Zealand—to India, North and South—to Ceylon and Bombay—to the West Indies—to the shores of the Mediterranean—to the wild Indian in North West America;—and, at length, has extended its holy efforts to the vast field opened to us among the countless multitudes of China. May the Spirit of the Lord Jesus Christ rest abundantly upon all who are connected with this and kindred institutions; and may the language of their prayers ever be, 'God be merciful unto us, and bless us; and cause his face to shine upon us, that thy way may be known upon earth, thy saving health among all nations!'

Among many incidents of lighter moment, which from time to time arose to encourage Mr. Simeon amidst much opposition and trial, perhaps the following is not unworthy of being recorded. He had recently endured considerable loss on account of his self-denying benevolence, when very unexpectedly he received, from an unknown hand, this somewhat remarkable token of confidence and respect:—

CAMBRIDGE, *October* 8, 1800.

"As one of the executors of the late Mr. ———, it is my duty to inform you, that he has by his will left you a legacy of eight hundred pounds, in the words mentioned on the other side; and the further sum of one hundred pounds for your trouble in the disposition thereof."

Upon the front of this letter, Mr. Simeon has written: "I had about a year before suffered great loss in my fortune (no matter how) for doing good with my money. Here a man, *whom I never saw*, left me £800 to do good with, and no responsibility in accounting for it. *No one needs to tell me whence this came.*"

In the course of the following year, Mr. Simeon completed the design, which he had before announced, of adding another series of Skeletons to the former volumes. These, amounting in number to five hundred, were published in two large volumes, and arranged systematically under the following heads: Types, Prophecies, Parables, Miracles, Warnings, Exhortations, Promises, Examples. The first volume being reprinted uniformly with these two, the whole work was now designated "Helps to Composition," and was introduced to the public by a very important doctrinal preface, in which Mr. S. states his object to be "freely and without reserve" to express his sentiments upon the great controversy of those times, being "exceedingly desirous to counteract that spirit of animosity which had so greatly prevailed against those who adhere to the principles of the Established Church." The statements contained in that preface Mr. Simeon deemed so important (at least in this point of view), that in his "Answer to Dr. Marsh's Inquiry, respecting the neglecting to give the Prayer-Book with the Bible" (published in 1812), he introduces nearly the whole of these remarks, that his readers might "know how far these sentiments are repugnant to the Articles or Liturgy of the Church of England." And he observes further, "that this part of the preface was originally written *on purpose to prevent even a possibility of misrepresentation* on the part of those who are so forward to designate their brethren by injurious and obnoxious appellations." On the margin of his own copy Mr. Simeon has written: "The reader is requested to bear in mind that the extract could not possibly have been shortened without mutilating the subject, which is of extreme importance both in itself and in reference to Dr. M.'s pamphlet. The author hopes that this will plead his excuse for the length of the extract." As Mr. Simeon continued to attach "extreme importance" to this preface, to the end of his life, and always referred to it as the best exposition of his views on the Calvinistic controversy, it is here given entire.

EXTRACT FROM THE PREFACE OF THE "HELPS TO COMPOSITION."

"In the discussion of so many subjects, it cannot fail but that every doctrine of our holy religion must be more or less canvassed. On every point the author has spoken freely, and without reserve. As for names and parties in religion, he equally disclaims them all; he takes his religion from the Bible, and endeavors, as much as possible, to speak as that speaks.* Hence, as in the Scriptures themselves, so also in this work, there will be found sentiments not really opposite, but apparently of an opposite tendency, according to the subject that is under discussion. In writing, for instance, on John v. 40, '*Ye will not come to me, that ye might have life,*' he does not hesitate to lay the whole blame of men's condemnation on the obstinacy of their own depraved will; nor does he think it at all necessary to weaken the subject by nice distinctions, in order to support a system. On the contrary, when he preaches on John vi. 44, '*No man can come to me, except the Father who hath sent me draw him,*' he does not scruple to state, in the fullest manner he is able, 'That we have no power to do good works, pleasant and acceptable to God, without the grace of God, by Christ, preventing us, that we may have a good will, and working with us when we have that good will;'† nor does he judge it expedient on any account to soften, and palliate, and fritter away this important truth. While too many set these passages at variance, and espouse the one in opposition to the other, he dwells with equal pleasure on them both, and thinks it, on the whole, better to state these apparently opposite truths in the plain and unsophisticated manner of the Scriptures, than to enter into scholastic subtleties that have been invented for the upholding of human systems. He is aware that they who are warm advocates for this or that system of religion will be ready to condemn him as inconsistent, but if he speak in exact conformity with the Scriptures, he shall rest the vindication of

---

* "If in anything he grounded his sentiments upon *human* authority, it would not be on the dogmas of Calvin or Arminius, but on the Articles and Homilies of *the Church of England.* He has the happiness to say that he does *ex animo*, from his inmost soul, believe the doctrines to which he has subscribed; but the reason of his believing them is not that they are made the Creed of the Established Church, but that he finds them manifestly contained in the Sacred Oracles."

† The Tenth Article.

his conduct simply on the authority and example of the inspired writers. He has no desire to be wise above what is written, nor any conceit that he can teach the Apostles to speak with more propriety and correctness than they have spoken.

"It may be asked, perhaps, how do you *reconcile* these doctrines which you believe to be of equal authority and equal importance? But what right has any man to impose this task on the preachers of God's word? God has not required it of them; nor is the truth or falsehood of any doctrine to be determined absolutely by this criterion. It is presumed that every one will acknowledge the holiness of God and the existence of sin, but will any one undertake to reconcile them? or does any one consider the inability of man to reconcile them as a sufficient ground for denying either the one or the other of these truths? If, then, neither of these points are doubted, notwithstanding they cannot be reconciled by us, why should other points, equally obvious in some respects, yet equally difficult to be reconciled in others, be incompatible, merely because we, with our limited capacity, cannot perfectly discern their harmony and agreement?

"But, perhaps, these points, which have been such a fruitful source of contention in the Church, are not so opposite to each other as some imagine; and it is possible that the truly scriptural statement will be found, not in an exclusive adoption of either, nor yet in a confused mixture of both, but in the proper and seasonable application of them both; or, to use the language of St. Paul, 'in rightly dividing the word of truth.'

"Here the author desires to speak with trembling. He is aware that he is treading upon slippery ground, and that he has but little prospect of satisfying any who have decidedly ranged themselves under the standard either of Calvin or Arminius. But he wishes to be understood; he is not solicitous to bring any man to pronounce his Shibboleth, much less has he any design to maintain a controversy in support of it; he merely offers an apology for the sentiments contained in his publication, and, with much deference, submits to the public his views of Scripture truth; and, whether they be perfectly approved or not, *this* he hopes to gain from all parties, a favorable acceptance of what they do approve, and a candid forbearance in the points they disapprove.

"This being premised, he will proceed to state the manner in which these apparently opposite tenets may, in his judgment, be profitably insisted on.

"It is supposed by many, that the doctrines of grace are

incompatible with the doctrine of man's free-will; and that therefore the one or the other must be false. But why so? Can any man doubt one moment whether he be a free agent or not? he may as well doubt his own existence. On the other hand, will any man who has the smallest spark of humility affirm, that he has 'made himself to differ; and that he has something which he has not received' from a superior power? Will any one refuse to say with the Apostle, 'By the grace of God I am what I am?'

"Again; as men differ with respect to the first beginnings of a work of grace, so do they also with respect to the manner in which it must be carried on; some affirming, that God has engaged to 'perfect that which concerneth us;' and others, that even St. Paul had reason to fear 'lest he himself should become a cast-away.' But why should these things be deemed incompatible? Does not every man feel within himself a liableness, yea, a proneness, to fall? Does not every man feel, that there is corruption enough within him to drive him to the commission of the greatest enormities, and eternally to destroy his soul? He can have but little knowledge of his own heart, who will deny this. On the other hand, who, that is holding on in the ways of righteousness, does not daily ascribe his steadfastness to the influence of that grace which he receives from God; and look daily to God for more grace, in order that he may be 'kept by *his* power through faith unto salvation?' No man can in any measure resemble the scripture saints, unless he be of this disposition. Why, then, *must* these things be put in opposition to each other, so that every advocate for one of these points must of necessity controvert and explode the other? Only let any *pious* person, whether Calvinist or Arminian, examine the language of his prayers after he has been devoutly pouring out his soul before God, and he will find his own words almost in perfect consonance with the foregoing statement. The Calvinist will be confessing the extreme depravity of his nature, together with his liability and proneness to fall; and the Arminian will be glorifying God for all that is good within him, and will commit his soul to God, in order that 'HE who has laid the foundation of his own spiritual temple, may also finish it.'

"Doubtless either of these points may be injudiciously stated, or improperly applied. If the doctrines of Election and Predestination be so stated as to destroy man's free agency, and make him merely passive in the work of salvation, they are not stated as they are in the Articles and Homilies of our Church, or as they are in the Holy Scriptures. On the other hand, if the doctrines of free-will and liableness to final apostasy be so stated as to rob God of his honor, and to deny that he is both 'the *Author* and the *Finisher* of our faith,' they are equally abhorrent from the sentiments of our Established Church, and from the plainest declarations of Holy Writ.

"The Author humbly apprehends, that there is a perfect agreement between these different points; and that they are equally salutary or equally pernicious, according as they are properly or improperly applied. If, for instance, on hearing a person excuse his own supineness by saying: 'I can do nothing, unless God give me his grace;' we should reply: 'This is true; it is God who alone can give you either to will or to do'—what would be the consequence? we should confirm him in his sloth, and encourage him to cast all the blame of his condemnation upon God himself. But if we should bring before him the apparently opposite truths, and bid him arise and call upon God; we should take the way to convince him that the fault was utterly his own, and that his destruction would be the consequence, not of God's decrees, but of his own inveterate love of sin.

"Let us suppose, on the other hand, that a person, having 'tasted the good word of life,' begin to boast that he has made himself to differ, and that his superiority to others is the mere result of his own free-will: if, in answer to him, we should immediately descant on our freedom to good or evil, and on the powers with which God has endued us for the preservation of our souls, we should foster the pride of his heart, and encourage him, contrary to an express command, to glory before God:* whereas, if we should remind him, that 'by the grace of God we are what we are,' and that all must say, 'Not unto us, O Lord, not unto us, but unto thy name be the praise,' we should lower his overweening conceit of his own goodness, and lead him to acknowledge his obligations to God.

"Let us illustrate the same in reference to the two other doctrines we mentioned, namely, The perseverance of the saints, and our liableness, in ourselves, to 'make shipwreck of the faith.' Suppose a person say, 'I need not be careful about my conduct;' for 'God has begun the good work within me, and has engaged to perform it till the day of Christ:' if we were to begin extolling the covenant of grace, and setting forth the truth of God in his promises, we should countenance his error

* 1 Cor. i. 29. Rom. iii. 27.

at the very time that he was turning the grace of God into licentiousness. But if we should warn him against the danger of being given over to a reprobate mind, and of perishing under an accumulated load of guilt, we should counteract his sinful disposition, and stimulate him to flee from the wrath to come.

"On the other hand, if a humble person should be drooping and desponding under a sense of his own corruptions, and we should spread before him all our difficulties and dangers, we should altogether 'break the bruised reed, and quench the smoking flax:' but if we should point out to him the fulness and stability of God's covenant; if we should enlarge upon the interest which Christ takes in his people, and his engagements that 'none shall ever pluck them out of his hand;'* it is obvious, that we should administer a cordial to his fainting spirit, or (as God requires of us) we should 'strengthen the weak hands, and confirm the feeble knees, and comfort the fearful heart.'

"These sentiments may perhaps receive some confirmation from the conduct of the apostle Paul. In administering the word, he consulted the state of his auditors, and apportioned to them either 'milk or strong meat,' according to their ability to digest and improve it.† In reference to this we may say, that the doctrines of human liberty, and human frailty, together with the other first principles of Christianity, are as milk, which those who are yet 'babes in Christ,' must have set before them: but that the doctrines of grace, or 'the deep things of God,' are rather as strong meat, which none can digest, unless they have grown to some stature in the family of Christ, and had their spiritual senses long exercised in discerning good and evil:‡ and that, as strong meat, which would nourish an adult, would destroy the life of an infant; and milk, that would nourish an infant, would be inadequate to the support of a man oppressed with hard labor; so it is with respect to the points which we have been considering. Or, if we may be permitted a little to vary this illustration, the one sort of truths are as food proper to be administered to all; whereas the other are rather as cordials for the support and comfort of those who need them.

"In a word, there seems to be a perfect correspondence between God's works of providence and grace: in the former, 'he worketh all things according to the counsel of his own will,' yet leaves men perfectly free agents in all that they do; so, in

* John x. 27, 28. † 1 Cor. iii. 1, 2. ‡ Heb. v. 12, 14.

the latter, he accomplishes his own eternal purpose both in calling, and in keeping, his elect; but yet he never puts upon them any constraint, which is not perfectly compatible with the freest operations of their own will.

"The Author well knows that these doctrines *may be*, and alas! *too often are*, so stated as to be really contradictory. But that they *may be* so stated as to be profitable to the souls of men, he hopes is clear from the illustrations that have been just given.*

"He trusts he shall be pardoned if he go yet further, and say that, in his judgment, there not only is no positive contradiction in this statement, but that there is *a propriety* in it, yea, moreover, *a necessity* for it, because there is *a subserviency in these truths, the one to the other.* God elects us; but he carries his purpose into effect by the free agency of man, which is altogether influenced by rational considerations. So also he carries on and completes his work in our souls, by causing us to feel our proneness to apostatize, and by making us cry to him daily for the more effectual influences of his grace. Thus, while he consults his own glory, he promotes our greatest good, in that he teaches us to combine humility with earnestness, and vigilance with composure.

"The Author would not have troubled the Reader with this apology, were it not that he is exceedingly desirous to counteract that spirit of animosity, which has of late so greatly prevailed against those who adhere to the principles of the Established Church. Not that he has himself any cause to complain; on the contrary, he has reason to acknowledge that his former volume met with a far more favorable reception from the public than he ever dared to expect. But he would wish his work to be brought to this test—Does it uniformly tend

"TO HUMBLE THE SINNER?
"TO EXALT THE SAVIOUR?
"TO PROMOTE HOLINESS?"

* "Many have carried their attachment to system so far, that they could not endure to preach upon any passage of Scripture that seemed to oppose their favorite sentiments; or, if they did, their whole endeavor has been to make the text speak a different language from that which it appeared to do. In opposition to all such modes of procedure, it is the Author's wish in this preface to recommend a conformity to the Scriptures themselves without any solicitude about systems of man's invention. Nor would anything under heaven be more grateful to him, than to see names and parties buried in eternal oblivion, and primitive simplicity restored to the Church."

"If in one single instance it lose sight of any of these points, let it be condemned without mercy. But, if it invariably pursue these ends, then let not any, whatever system they embrace, quarrel with an expression that does not quite accord with their views. Let them consider the general scope and tendency of the book: and, if it be, as he trusts it is, not to strengthen a party in the Church, but to promote the good of the whole; then let smaller differences of sentiment be overlooked, and all unite in vindicating the great doctrines of SALVATION BY GRACE THROUGH FAITH IN CHRIST."

We must now return to the narrative. The loss Mr. Simeon had sustained by the early removal of his honored coadjutor, Mr. Sowerby, was ere long to be supplied by the services of one, whose praise is in all the churches. During the period of Mr. Sowerby's labors at Trinity Church, a student of St. John's College had become a regular attendant there, who the next year (1801) was about to attain the same honors as Senior Wrangler, and afterwards to discharge the sacred duties of the ministry in the same Church.

Henry Martyn had for some time been deeply impressed by the preaching of Mr. Simeon; and amidst the labors and anxieties almost inseparable from the preparation for a high degree, he had found the unspeakable importance of unremitted attention to his spiritual progress. "The chief cause, under God, of his stability at this season," writes Mr. Sargent, "in those religious principles, which by divine grace he had adopted, was evidently that constant attendance, which he now commenced, on the ministry of Mr. Simeon; under whose truly pastoral instructions, he himself declares, that he gradually acquired more knowledge in divine things." It was during the summer vacation of this year that their acquaintance became more intimate. "Having long listened with no small degree of pleasure and profit to Mr. Simeon as a preacher, he now began to enjoy the happiness of an admission to the most friendly and unreserved intercourse with him; and was in the habit of soliciting and receiving on all important occasions his counsel and encouragement." In the course of the following year, his thoughts appear to have been for the first time directed to the idea of entering upon the arduous and holy work of a Christian Missionary. "The immediate cause of his determination to undertake this office, was hearing Mr. Simeon remark on the benefit which had resulted from the services of a Missionary in India; his attention was thus arrested, and his thoughts occupied with the vast importance of the subject." For another year he was continually engaged in the contemplation of this great work; and by diligent 'attendance to reading, to exhortation, to doctrine,' prepared himself for the solemn rite of Ordination. This he received at Ely, Oct. 22, 1803, and immediately commenced his pastoral duties as Curate of Trinity Church, undertaking also the charge of the small village of Lolworth, in the neighborhood. What must have been Mr. Simeon's consolations in the ministry at this period, enjoying as he now did the rare privilege of the devoted affection and invaluable co-operation of two such friends as Thomason and Martyn! This happy triumvirate, however, was not long to continue. Mr. Martyn was soon to leave his native shores forever, and to have the deeply-cherished desires of his soul at length gratified by an appointment to Missionary labor in India. On Wednesday, April 3, 1805, he went to Mr. Grant's, and found that the question about his obtaining a Chaplaincy had that day been settled. The following morning he returned to Cambridge, to take leave of the University and his beloved flock. His Journal gives us the touching narrative of his few remaining days there.

In the summer previous to his leaving Cambridge, Mr. Martyn had been introduced to a young man of rare genius and piety, whom Mr. Simeon had been anxious to commend to his regard, and to place at his college. The warmest sympathy in behalf of this extraordinary young student had already been felt by all who knew the touching history of his early life; whilst the highest expectation had been formed of his future career, in consequence of his matchless talents and industry. Every academical distinction, whether classical or mathematical, was considered to be easily within his reach. But the highest attractions of Henry Kirke White, in the view of Mr. Martyn, were the loveliness of his character and the fervor of his piety. Here, indeed, he found "a kindred spirit with himself;" and consequently, Mr. Martyn "took the liveliest interest in his behalf, and used his utmost endeavors to facilitate his entrance upon that course at college, which afterwards proved so brilliant and so transient." Through Mr. Simeon's counsel and kind promise of assistance, Kirke White was at length enabled, amidst all his difficulties, to indulge the long-cherished hope of entering the University. "I can *now* inform you," he writes, July 9, 1804, to his generous friend and biographer, Mr. Southey, "that I have reason to believe my way through college is clear before me. From what source I know not; but through the hands of Mr. Simeon, I am provided with £30 per annum; and while things go on so prosperously as they do now, I can command £20, or £30 more from my friends, and this, in all probability until I take my degree." According to Mr. Simeon's advice he had consented to defer his coming to college for a year, and was placed under the tuition of Rev. Mr. Grainger, of Wintringham, that he might be the better prepared to enter on that career of honor, which appeared to open so brightly before him. In consequence of this delay, he lost the advantage he had fondly looked forward to, of the society and friendship of Mr. Martyn, who was gone from the University before he came into residence. But he found in Mr. Simeon all the tenderness and solicitude, which a kind and wise father could bestow upon a beloved son. And besides the regard and sympathy he met with from him in private, he had the benefit of his public ministry, which he appears to have highly valued. "Mr. Simeon's preaching," he says, "strikes me much." And well did he profit by those faithful instructions. What he had learned to esteem as a privilege of the first importance to himself—the opportunity of hearing sound and earnest sermons—he cordially commended to those nearest and dearest to him. "It is well for you," he observes to his sister, "that you can still enjoy the privilege of sitting under the sound of the Gospel; and the wants of others, in these respects, will, perhaps, teach you how to value the blessing. All our comforts, and almost all our hopes here, lie at the mercy of every succeeding hour. Death is always at hand to bereave us of some dear connection, or to snatch us away from those who may need our counsel and protection." Alas! how soon did he realize the truth of his own remarks. "The seeds of death were in him, and the place, to which he had so long looked on with hope, served unhappily as a hot-house to ripen them." His unrivalled talent had placed him, after his first college examination, at the very head of his year; and, through the kindness of his tutor, Mr. Catton, he was provided with additional help to prosecute his fatal studies during the ensuing summer. With rare delicacy, he now determined to relinquish the aid he had been permitted to draw from Mr. Simeon. "I have of course signified to Mr. Simeon," he writes, "that I shall have no need whatever of the stipend which I have hitherto received through his hands. He was extremely kind on the occasion, and, indeed, his conduct towards me has ever been *fatherly*. It was Mr. —— who allowed me £20 per annum, and Mr. Simeon added £10. He told me that my conduct gave him the most heartfelt joy; that I was so generally respected, without having made any compliances, as he understood, or having, in any instance, concealed my principles. Indeed, this is a praise which I may claim, though I never conceived that it was at all an object of praise. I have always taken some pains to let those around me know my religious sentiments, as a saving of trouble, and as a mark of that independence of opinion, which I think every one ought to assert; and, as I have produced my opinions with frankness and modesty, and supported them (if attacked) with coolness and candor, I have never found them any impediment to my acquaintance with any person whose acquaintance I coveted." Not many weeks after he had penned this truly Christian letter to his brother, he fell before the resistless progress of that wasting malady, which his intense study had so fearfully quickened; and on Sunday, Oct. 19, 1806, he entered into rest, exchanging his earthly honors for an incorruptible and unfading crown.

The departure of Henry Martyn to a foreign land rekindled a desire in Mr. Thomason, which he had strongly felt before, to engage in missionary labors among the heathen. In the spring of 1805, Mr. Simeon had gone to London, to communicate with Mr. Grant upon the subject; but at that time there was no opening to the East Indies, "where it had been thought most advisable for him either to accompany or to follow Henry Martyn." Still, he by no means relinquished the idea of yet enjoying the privilege of following his beloved friend. The desire was strengthened by his having lately written a Review, which had led him to consider the zeal and devotion of Wesley and Whitfield in their Saviour's service. In reference to this he wrote to his mother, March 6, 1805: "The reading the life and labors of these excellent ministers fills me with admiration of their zeal, and with shame that I am such a blank in creation. My sphere is contracted, and I long for a more extensive field of labor. God has given me an education and a spirit, I trust, which might render me far more useful in the Church than I now am. Where my present thoughts will lead me, I know not; but I look round upon this lovely spot with all the indifference of a man who would, with the greatest cheerfulness, part with all, if a situation of greater usefulness, however laborious, should offer itself. Here I am; Lord, what wilt thou have me to do?" Deeply trying must have been this season of suspense to the sensitive heart of his affectionate mother. In reply to a letter of hers on the subject, Mr. Simeon expresses himself with his usual tenderness and Christian feeling.

"Your letter fills me with deep concern, and I am extremely

anxious to remove, as far as possible, the load from your mind. To convey on paper all that I have to say, would be tedious. I have judged it better, therefore, to set off instantly, for the purpose of making known to you everything that has arisen, and precisely as it has arisen; and, at the same time, to mention some circumstances, which, in all probability, will operate to prevent the execution of the plan your son proposed when he saw you last. From the beginning, I have endeavored to yield to no bias, but to suggest everything as it occurred to my mind. I have, in this respect, manifested disinterestedness, at all events; for, next to yourself, there certainly is no person living, who would feel his loss so much as I. Indeed, I can scarcely yield to you in this particular; for, though your sensibilities are beyond all comparison more exquisite than mine, and your bereavement would be more pungent, your habits of life would remain the same: whereas, mine would be wholly changed. I should lose not only a dear friend, but the friend with whom I live in daily habits of communion; the friend that is as my own soul. I know no loss that would come so near to my feelings, or leave such a blank in my life. Should I be called to bear the loss, I hope that grace will be given me suitably to improve it. I trust that you also, if such an event should take place, will be enabled to adopt the resolution of a widowed lady, who lost her only three children, one after the other, in quick succession: 'I see that God is determined to have my whole heart, and so he shall.'"

At the beginning of 1807, Mr. Simeon's strength had become so impaired by over-exertion, and his voice was so feeble, that he was compelled to reduce, for a season, his ministerial duties, and to devolve on Mr. Thomason an important part of the service, in which he had so greatly delighted.

CHAPTER IV.

An important trait of Mr. Simeon's character, noticed by Mr. Preston, "was the delight with which he observed the spiritual progress and growing usefulness of other ministers, even when there might seem to be a temptation to the feeling of jealousy, as if another were rising to supersede himself. On such occasions he would say, with evident joy and sincerity,

'He must increase; I must decrease.' This truly Christian feeling was manifested in a striking manner on his return to Cambridge from the Isle of Wight. During his residence there, and for some time before, his friend and curate, Mr. Thomason, who had previously performed only a subordinate part in the ministrations at Trinity Church, had been called out to the vigorous exercise of all his powers in the work of the ministry. Through the grace of God he had been enabled to rise to the occasion. No one, who remembers his sermons at Cambridge during that year, when Mr. Simeon was for the most part disabled from duty, will be backward to acknowledge, that his improvement, in the course of a few months, was extraordinary. There was, at that time, a richness and fulness in Mr. T.'s discourses, such as was not always found in Mr. Simeon's. This devoted servant of Christ, who loved his Lord with all his heart, and was thankful, for his sake, either 'to be abased or to abound,' was much struck and delighted, on his return, with what he saw and heard from his beloved colleague. After hearing him preach, he turned to a friend and said, 'Now I see *why* I have been laid aside; I bless God for it.'

"The generous and affectionate feeling which he habitually cherished, and, on suitable occasions, manifested towards those who have successively stood to him in the relation of curates, is gratefully remembered by every one of them. Considering that the term 'curate'—honorable as it is, and elsewhere attached to the office of the principal—is commonly regarded in this country as implying inferiority of rank, he was disposed to discard it. 'Not my *curate*,' he would say, 'my *brother*.' 'Now, *my brother*, which part of the duty shall I take?' The privilege formerly enjoyed by these gentlemen, of supping with him in private, after the conclusion of the evening service on the Lord's day, has been spoken of by more than one of them as peculiarly delightful and refreshing. So congenial were the duties of that holy day with the temper and taste of his renewed soul, that he generally appeared at the close of the day to be invigorated rather than exhausted by them. 'I am an eight-day clock,' said he; 'now I am wound up for another week.' His prayers on these occasions (for he always closed with prayer) were, it may be presumed, some of the least reserved of his supplications addressed to the throne of Grace. A dignitary of the Church, who was once present, remarked to the curate, in returning, how much he had been affected with the deep humiliation indicated by Mr. Simeon's prayers, particularly with the confession (taken from Bishop Beveridge, but which appeared to be new to him) that our very tears need to be washed in the atoning blood of Christ."

During the season of his retirement from public duties, Mr. Simeon was indefatigable in his attention to his beloved brother Edward. Little hope, indeed, remained of his recovery from the painful disorder under which he labored; but Mr. S. had the unspeakable consolation of observing a manifest improvement in his spiritual estate; though his outward man seemed to be decaying, his inward man was evidently "renewed day by day." Mr. Simeon's tenderness and earnestness on this and other matters of private and minor interest may be traced in the letters, written at this period, to Mr. Lloyd, and his much loved friends at Reading.

In the year 1808, Mr. Simeon was called to undergo a sacrifice, which, perhaps, he felt more acutely than any he had hitherto endured. He was, at length, to part with his beloved and faithful friend, Mr. Thomason: "The friend, with whom I live in daily habits of communion, the friend that is as my own soul." Mr. Thomason's "long-meditated design of consecrating his powers through life to the service of his God and Saviour in a distant land," was now to have its accomplishment. "Certainly, God is doing a great work in India," he writes; "the laborers are few, and the field amazingly extensive; they want men who will work, and whose habits are such as to render them useful workmen in a business, where application and study are much wanted. In this respect, my habits and inclinations are favorable. . . . *I consider that what others expose themselves to for lucre and worldly honors, ministers ought to endure for nobler ends.*"

In a few days after he had written these truly Christian remarks, he received his appointment from the Court of Directors; and on the 7th of June, 1808, he reached St. John's, in the Isle of Wight, ready to sail with the first fair wind.

As on the departure of his "beloved" Martyn, so now, when about to separate from his "dear brother" Thomason, Mr. Simeon remained with him to the very last; and not only went on board the vessel, but actually proceeded with him on his voyage as long as it was practicable to return. Mr. Thomason, in a few parting lines to his deeply-sorrowing mother, endeavored to comfort her by a reference to this last act of Mr. Simeon's love.

"TRAVERS, UNDER WEIGH, *June* 10, 1808.

"This morning we were summoned on board. The wind has become fair, and we are proceeding out to sea. Our dear and honored friend, Mr. Simeon, accompanied us to the vessel, and is now with us. We all retired to our cabin, and united in prayer, desiring to consecrate this spot to God, and to commit ourselves, and all the ship's company, to his gracious care. Blessed be God, we know what it is to draw nigh to Him, and we feel but one concern, that we may glorify Him in this world, and enjoy Him in the next. O, it is an unspeakable mercy to part with a good hope that we shall one day meet where sorrow and parting shall be no more."

Mr. Simeon's feelings on the occasion were intensely exercised. "Adored be the name of God!" he writes to Mr. Thomason, "for so uniting our hearts in love. For a long time I could not even look up; but, at last, I cast an eye of grief and affection towards your ship, and repeated it at intervals till you were about fifteen miles off; then, finding you were almost out of sight, I went down into the cabin. I arrived at home at twelve o'clock at night, thankful that I had been permitted to enjoy in our separation a pledge that we should meet again at the right hand of God. Our love will be there the same—it is the expression of it only that will be different."

Allusions have occasionally been made in the foregoing Memoir to certain meetings of Mr. Simeon's clerical friends, which were of a peculiarly instructive character, and regarded by all who attended them with feelings of no ordinary gratification. As a description of them has already been given by one, who of all others is the most competent to write on the subject, the account here subjoined is taken without alteration from Mr. Preston's "Memoranda."

"Of the many recollections of Mr. Simeon, on which it is now delightful to his friends to dwell, one, not the least interesting or profitable, is that of the annual meetings of clerical parties, which assembled, by his invitation, at the house, first of Mr. Thomason, at Little Shelford, near Cambridge; and afterwards of his successor, who subsequently removed to Aspeden Hall in Hertfordshire, where the meetings were continued. These were distinguished from most other clerical meetings, which are now not uncommon, by being composed, not of persons collected from the immediate neighborhood, but of those with whom, from circumstances or from choice, Mr. Simeon had been in habits of more than ordinary intimacy, and also by the married clergymen being invited to bring their wives with them; Mr. Simeon, with kind consideration, wishing that that sex, which often contributes largely, like 'the beloved Persis,' to the success of ministerial labors, should enjoy the benefit of the general conversation which took place after dinner, and also be enabled to compare together their several schemes of parochial usefulness, as the helps-meet of their respective partners. The whole of the party, consisting sometimes of from twenty to thirty persons, were accommodated on the spot; and continued together two entire days, besides the days of arrival and departure. The clergy spent the mornings, after breakfast, in conference, principally on the Scriptures; Mr. Simeon, generally assisted by some one, presiding. A favorite book of Mr. Simeon, on these occasions, was *Warden's System of Revealed Religion*, which contains a digest of Revelation under separate heads, composed in the express words of Scripture. The passages were usually read; first, as collected together, and then separately, in the Old and New Testaments; copies of the original being provided, and continually consulted. These conferences, divested as much as possible of stiffness, which was the more easily effected from the harmony and mutual confidence of the brotherly circle, were exceedingly delightful, and doubtless profitable. God, being thus honored, in being inquired after in His own word by those whose province it was to dispense it to others, the search after His will being begun and ended with prayer, did assuredly manifest Himself to them as He does not to the world. They have often said in words, and oftener in their hearts, 'It is good for us to be here.' This imperfect record will perhaps meet the eye of some who were present; and they will with one consent confirm it.

"While the clergy were thus employed, the ladies were in another room, where they read together, and endeavored to edify one another. At the hours of repast and in the evenings, all met together. After tea, there was usually some leading topic of conversation, likely to be interesting and profitable to both sexes; letters also, or any religious intelligence, or schemes of usefulness likely to be generally acceptable, were then brought forward.

"This narrative, divested of all mystery, will perhaps abate the fears of some persons, who have apprehended they scarcely know what lurking mischief from such 'unauthorized assemblies.' If any who felt jealousy, or suspected evil, could have seen and heard without being seen, they would haply have fallen upon their knees and confessed that God was in that place. They would at least have witnessed there, what is recorded on high authority to have taken place in olden time; when 'They that feared the Lord spake often one to another; and the Lord hearkened, and heard it; and a book of remembrance was written before him for them that feared the Lord, and that thought upon his name. And they shall be mine, saith the Lord of hosts, in that day when I make up my jewels; and I will spare them, as a man spareth his own son that serveth him.'* Certainly not one of those who have been present at those privileged seasons now repents, except of not having profited more from such opportunities. Never, probably, will some of them know more than they then experienced of the delight of the communion of saints, till they shall again meet with Martyn, and Jowett, and Lowe, and Thomason, and Sargent, and Simeon, and Farish, and (we name one only of those still on earth, because he is out of the immediate reach of this record) Daniel Wilson, and others whom we could name, men honored of God, and much esteemed in the Church, at the Supper of the Lamb, in heaven."

CHAPTER V.

It will have been frequently observed in the foregoing Memoir, how strong and constant was Mr. Simeon's regard for the Liturgy and Services of our Church. From an early period in his college life, when he says that the prayers were as 'marrow and fatness' to him, during the space of thirty years after, until the season of his late indisposition, when he remarks, "surely the Liturgy is of more service than is generally imagined," his attachment to our ritual had been unwavering. This long cherished and cordial regard for the formularies of our Church induced him, when appointed at length *select* preacher at St. Mary's, to deliver a course of Sermons on "The Excellency of the Liturgy." These were preached before the University during the month of November (1811), from the text: Deut. v. 28, 29: "They have well said all that they have spoken: O that there were such an heart in them!" On

---

* Mal. iii. 16, 17.

publishing these four Sermons the following spring, Mr. Simeon prefixed to them a Letter addressed to Dr. Marsh, the Lady Margaret's Professor of Divinity, as an "Answer" to his "Inquiry respecting the neglecting to give the Prayer-Book with the Bible." In the course of his argument, Dr. Marsh had endeavored to draw a parallel between the Assembly of Divines, who set aside the Liturgy, and the friends of the British and Foreign Bible Society, whom he accused of "neglecting to give it away." To heighten the representation, he says: "There was another feature in the Assembly of Divines, which we may distinctly perceive in the modern Society; it consisted chiefly of Calvinists; and the Calvinistic Clergy of the Church of England are generally members of the modern Society. Now a man who adopts the doctrines of Calvin cannot be zealously attached to our English Liturgy; a Calvinist may in many respects have a great regard for it; but he cannot have much pain in parting with it; as it abounds with passages so decisive of conditional salvation, that no ingenuity can torture them into the language of absolute decrees. Indeed, we know that the English Liturgy was so offensive to the Calvinists of Scotland, that the very attempt to introduce it in that country produced an insurrection, which ended in the Solemn League and Covenant, to which the English Calvinists acceded."

"In this passage," replies Mr. Simeon, "you avail yourself of a popular cry against a great body of the Clergy as espousing Calvinism, and as carrying their tenets to a very dangerous extent. But, Sir, it is greatly to be regretted that those who impute such sentiments to the Clergy here alluded to, will not tell us from whence they take their statements. If they would quote the obnoxious passages, they would put it into the power of those who might be supposed to be implicated in the charge, to say, whether they maintained such opinions or not. As for a great number of opinions which they are supposed to hold, I dare to assure the public, that Socinianism, or even Atheism itself, is not farther from their real sentiments, than such expressions as are often put into their mouths.

"Among the Clergy designated as Calvinists, I have no doubt but that I am ranked (with what justice that name, in its obnoxious sense, can be given me, the reader will see in the Sermons here brought before him): and I believe, indeed I am sure, that my sentiments in general do coincide with those which the great body of the Clergy here referred to maintain. And, that the readers of your pamphlet may know how far these sentiments are repugnant to the Articles or Liturgy of the Church of England, I shall here present them with an extract from the Preface to my work, entitled, 'Helps to Composition.'"

[Here follows the extract which has been given entire in pages 44–50.] Mr. Simeon then proceeds: "Now, Sir, I do not say that every individual of those whom you designate as Calvinistic Clergy, would express himself in precisely the same terms as I have done, or that there are not shades of difference between them; for you cannot find any ten men in the world, or indeed any two, whose minds are so constructed as to have no discordance of sentiment upon anything; for as, in the countenances of men, there are points of difference in persons between whom there exists the most perfect family likeness, so in the minds of men no two are perfectly alike. But I defy contradiction when I affirm, that the great mass of Clergy, who are now invidiously called Calvinistic, do preach in a way perfectly consonant with what is expressed in that preface; and I challenge the whole world to say that it is not perfectly in harmony with the articles, the Homilies, and the Liturgy of the Church of England."

Mr. Simeon's memoir now concludes:—

"I must here state at large a persecution which arose against me in my parish, which, by some circumstances connected with it, led to the crisis which I have referred to [page 38]. Bishop D—— had now succeeded to the See of Ely, and in his first charge he had spoken in no very favorable terms of those who maintain what I believe to be the Gospel of Christ. Aware, from the moment he was appointed, what were his dispositions towards persons of my sentiments, and towards myself in particular, I had used the most prudent means in my power to conciliate him. But the state of his mind being pretty clearly understood, as well from his charge as from general report, my enemies in the parish thought it a favorable time for them to stir, and to see if they could not raise a persecution against me.

"The precise hour in which my parishioners met together, to carry into effect their malicious designs, is worthy of particular observation. I had been lamenting in my mind that so little good was done in my parish, and contriving how I might benefit them after my death. I thought that a sermon which I had very recently printed, on the subject of 'Christ Crucified,'* would serve as a brief summary of all that I had preached

* Preached March 17, 1811, before the University, from 1 Cor. ii. 2.

to them for thirty years; and I wrote a codicil to my will, appointing that an edition of that sermon should be printed immediately after my decease, and a copy be presented to every family in my parish, as a voice to them from the dead; and it is remarkable, that, at the very moment that I was engaged in this office of love, they were, unknown to me, caballing against me in full council, to destroy, if possible, my peace and usefulness through my whole life.

"It may seem strange that, at the end of thirty years, and of twenty years' peace, I should have any enemies left; but most of the old inhabitants had been removed by death, and some of a peculiarly malignant spirit had recently come into the parish; and these, joining with a few of the old inhabitants, who are given over, I fear, to a reprobate mind, drew up a number of articles against me, and sent them to the bishop (May, 1811). The bishop sent me a copy of them, and required me to send him my answer to them. As they were signed by at least forty persons, he conceived that the complaints deserved his fullest consideration; though if he had known the character of the leaders and instigators of the commotion, he would easily have seen, I think, what attention *such* complaints deserved, when urged by *such* persons against a minister whose principles and character were well known, and who had spent his whole ministerial life in the service of that parish. It was impossible for me to answer those complaints without bringing forward many facts, which common modesty would have forbidden me ever to mention, just as the accusations of the false teachers compelled the Apostle Paul to declare many things for the vindication of his own character, which nothing but necessity could ever have induced him to disclose. The bishop, thinking that there were some things in my reply which would invalidate its force, sent to me to explain them; and these explanations rendered my answer so much the more triumphant, so that it was evident that the complainants had not a leg to stand upon. This reply of mine he forwarded (which was right enough) to the parish, for them to communicate their observations upon it, and immediately they exerted themselves to the uttermost to find some flaw in it, but not being able to do so, they never sent any answer to the bishop, nor even returned him my reply, which he had intrusted to them, but pretended that they had lost the document, though it contained half a quire of paper.

"It is a curious fact that the persons, who labored so earnestly to get themselves appointed churchwardens, and whose failure occasioned their petition to the bishop, renewed their attempt the following year; and, as it was a matter of indifference to me who was appointed to that office, I not only desired that nothing might be done to prevent their appointment, but went myself to vote for them. When I came to the vestry, I saw two different lists, as is usual, and took up that paper which was full of names (concluding, of course, that it contained the votes in favor of my enemies), and was proceeding to add my name to the list; but, behold, it was the list of those who voluntarily and unsolicited supported my friends, whilst the other list contained only five names for one of my enemies, and two for the other; these being all the votes they could gain, notwithstanding their canvas; so entirely had they disgusted the whole parish by their treatment of me. If ever God manifested (out of the Scriptures) the benefit of trusting in Him, and committing our ways to Him, I think He did it in this instance; for, had my enemies succeeded, I should have been in hot water all my life by means of their wicked opposition; whereas, through their extraordinary defeat, I have a prospect of carrying on the Lord's work through the remainder of my days in peace. Bless the Lord, O my soul; and all that is within me, bless His holy name!

"The bishop found in this complaint no just occasion against me; but still he wanted to proceed against me, and to put down my evening lectures, which, in my reply, I had vindicated beyond all reasonable exception. He, therefore, wrote privately to the Vice-Chancellor of the University, and desired him to convene the heads of Houses, and to inquire, whether they approved of the young men coming to my evening lectures (there being no doubt what answer would be given to an inquiry so made), that so he might put down the lectures, and cast the odium on them. And now, my soul, say whether there be not a God that ruleth in the earth? Say, whether there be not one who 'doeth according to His will in the armies of heaven and among the inhabitants of the earth, whose counsel shall stand, and who will do all His will?' Yes, I see it on this occasion as clearly as if I had seen the sun stand still on Gibeon, or the shadow go back on the sundial of Ahaz.

"The heads were convened, ostensibly to consult respecting the restoration of Mr. D., of ——— College, to his degree, of which he had in conformity with a Grace of the Senate been deprived, though there was no blame but that of a mistake to be imputed to him. They were all met; and, without one syllable of the *ostensible* business being mentioned, the Bishop's letter was produced, and a written answer of disapprobation was produced with it, and they all rose up to sign it. It happened that one head of a House, a friend of mine, who scarcely ever attends such meetings, was there—was there, I had almost said, by miracle—and it being the first that he had heard of any such business, as that which was now brought forward, he observed, 'That he really had never heard of any evils arising from my lectures, nor saw any harm in the young men attending them; that he had always heard of the extreme care which I had invariably taken to prevent evil; and that, though he did not wish to keep others from signing the paper, he could not sign it himself. He thought that the Bishop had written to make *inquiries* of them, and that it was proper for *them to make inquiries*, before they returned their answer; at least, he felt it incumbent on him to do so.' The propriety of these observations struck the whole company; and they agreed to meet again the week following to give the result of their inquiries, and they parted without adverting for a moment to the professed occasion for which the meeting had been called. The next week they met again; and the same friend being there, not one word of *my* business was brought forward: the original business alone of Mr. D.'s was agitated; and thus the cloud, which had threatened my ministry (two-thirds of which would have been curtailed), was dispersed, even without my knowing that any such business was in agitation. This whole matter was soon mentioned to me by my friend in confidence; and I therefore felt the necessity of increased circumspection; in resorting to which, the crisis before mentioned was produced.

"I have not written the foregoing Memoir as a Life of myself; but only as a record of some facts connected with my public Ministry, the notoriety of which renders them likely to be mentioned after my death; whilst yet there is no man but myself who could place them in their true light, for want of that full knowledge of the circumstances which I alone possess. Had I designed to write a Life of myself, I should have entered into the interior working of my heart in relation to my religious experience, and into a multitude of things known only to God and my own soul; but I have no wish to obtrude upon the public anything relating to myself. If I were to tell them all, or a thousandth part of the evil of my heart, they could not bear to hear it, or be profited by the recital of it; and if there has been anything good in me, it is sufficient for me that God knows it. My whole experience is comprehended in this plain tale; that my innumerable corruptions have supplied me with most abundant matter for humiliation and contrition every day of my life; but the Gospel of Christ has afforded me still more abundant ground for hope in fleeing to the Saviour, and plunging beneath that fountain which was 'opened for sin and for uncleanness;' and to this I have had recourse from day to day, precisely as I did the first moment that I gained a sight of Christ; not coming to Christ, as one who was warranted to do so by any holiness he had attained, but as one whose iniquities could not in any other way be pardoned, and who hoped that God would glorify Himself in saving the very chief of sinners."

EXTRACTS FROM HIS LETTERS.

TO REV. T. THOMASON.

"HIGHGATE, *July* 17, 1812.

"*My dearest Friend and Brother:* "I have been long hoping to see a fleet from Calcutta, in order that I might receive fresh tidings from you, and behold the picture of my dear and honored friend, Mr. Martyn. I trust it will not be long before I am gratified in these respects. . . . I have remembered too, as a token of love, my dear Godson.

"I am as yet in uncertainty, whether I am to be appointed an University Preacher again for next year. I am disposed to think that Mr. Mandell will feel it a duty to his God to propose me; and if proposed by him, there is not much probability of any opposition being made from other quarters. I hope that in this I do not give Mr. M. credit for more zeal and piety than he possesses. As for myself, I do not move a finger in the business. I know sufficiently in whose hands all these matters are. If God say, 'Whom shall I send?' I have the prophet's answer ready. But if He say, 'I have no delight in thee,' I am equally prepared with David's answer, 'Let Him do as seemeth Him good.' How sweet it is to be assured that God reigneth! Well may faith be called '*precious* faith,' when it so composes the mind under all circumstances.

"As for sitting down to write a religious letter, it is what I cannot do myself; and what I do not very much admire, unless there be some particular occasion that calls for it. I love rather that a letter be a free and easy communication of such things as are upon the mind, and such as we imagine will interest the person with whom we correspond. Some indeed, who have a talent for letter-writing, may employ their pen profitably in the more direct and formal way; but it is a thing I cannot do; religion, with me, is only the salt with which I season the different subjects on which I write; and it is recommended in that view by St. Paul, to be used in the whole of our converse with each other. Doubtless when the mind can soar, and we can dip our pen in angel's ink, it is most delightful to prosecute the heavenly theme; but to sit down in cold blood, and say, I must now write a religious letter, is to me an irksome task; or, rather, a task which I leave to those who have talents for it. In a word, religious communications are then most delightful, when they proceed from the abundance of the heart; but all the sweetness of them is taken away, when they are constrained and formal."

"Now let me go to another cause of joy scarcely inferior to the former. On Monday, *the very same day that the people returned to a sense of their duty*, I opened and put up the picture of my ever dear and honored brother, Mr. Martyn. I had indeed, after it was opened at the India House, gone to see it there, and, notwithstanding all that you had said respecting it, to prepare my mind, I was so overpowered by the sight, that I could not bear to look upon it; but turned away and went to a distance, covering my face, and, in spite of every effort to the contrary, crying aloud with anguish. E. was with me; and all the bystanders said to her, 'That, I suppose, is his father.' And I think it probable, that if I *had* been his father, or his mother either, I should not have felt more than I did on the occasion. Shall I attempt to describe to you the veneration and the love with which I look at it? No words that I can write will convey an adequate idea; nothing but your own tender mind can exactly conceive what I feel. I remember (indeed can never forget) the look of a certain lady, when the thought of your going to India was last suggested to her. One might endeavor to describe the mixed emotions that were then depicted in her countenance; but it must have been seen in order to be understood and appreciated; so I should in vain attempt to describe what I feel, and trust I shall long continue to feel, in looking on that image of my beloved friend. In seeing how much he is worn, I am constrained to call to my relief the thought, in *whose service* he has worn himself so much; and this reconciles me to the idea of weakness, of sickness, or even, if God were so to appoint, of death itself. As for your abuse of the painter's device to represent India, I do not at all agree with you; it is done as well as I wish it; and the portrait itself cannot, I think, be excelled. I behold in it all the mind of my honored brother; and if a thousand guineas had been sent me instead of it, they would *really and truly* be lighter than the dust upon the balance in comparison of it. Pardon me if I say, that in the two portraits I seem to have the wealth of the Indies."

FROM A LETTER TO THE SAME.

"Your critique on my Answer to Marsh, I perfectly approve. Vansittart is doubtless a pattern for controversialists; he is a razor—I am a hatchet. But what will you say to Milner? He is like one of those immense hammers moved by steam-engines for the hammering of anchors. I sent one to you the moment it came out. He has actually crushed his adversary to atoms. Of all the men in Britain, that have done good to the Bible Society, there is scarcely one, except the Secretaries, that can vie with Dr. Marsh. In doing all that man can do against it, he has advanced it a thousand times more than if he had written in its favor."

FROM A LETTER TO THE SAME.

"By Mr. Robinson I sent you Dr. Milner's strictures on Dr. Marsh; and I now send you Dr. Marsh's Reply, which has called forth your humble servant again. In a former letter, I expressed my acquiescence in the sentiments, which you so kindly and affectionately stated, respecting my 'Answer to Dr. M.'s Inquiry;' and I did so the rather, that I might encourage to the uttermost such kind and friendly communications. But having taken up my pen again, I must state to you the reasons of my writing in the way I did, and in the way I have since done. Were he a common writer, I should highly disapprove of everything that had the appearance of severity; but when a man brings such sweeping accusations against all the most pious and active Ministers in the kingdom, and endeavors to maintain his ground by such sophistry, such disingenuousness, and by such artifices of every kind—I do think that strong animadversion is proper. How did our blessed Lord argue with such characters? and how did the Apostles? and what directions are given to us, especially towards those who would subvert the faith? Even Timothy, a stripling, was required to 'rebuke them sharply;' and if 'an angel from heaven' were to act so, he must be declared 'accursed.' I say not this to justify *harshness*, but *strength*, and *force*, and *point;* and though Dr. Milner has been blamed by some for the line of argument he has taken, in lowering the imposing weight of Dr. Marsh's authority, I think most decidedly that he has done right; and I think that there is a mistake in the minds of religious persons in relation to this; in that they think nothing should proceed from a religious character but what is soft, and gentle, and persuasive. I think there are times and seasons when he must 'contend earnestly for the faith,' and 'reprove with all authority.'

"The diary of Abdool Messeeh has been highly gratifying to my mind; and I have instantly committed to Mr. Pratt the last two months of it, which he had not received. I am astonished at the *meekness of wisdom* exemplified in that dear man, whom God has evidently raised up for great and gracious purposes. I am quite amazed at what that single individual is doing; and it is no little encouragement to you to see what may hereafter be done by those who may be born to God through you. Mr. Corrie observes to me, that this is the only visible effect of Mr. Martyn's ministry on the natives. But if Abraham had only one child of promise, and that son, too, had only one who was beloved of God; was Abraham a dry tree? So neither must we estimate at too low a rate the success of our beloved Martyn; for this one convert may have a progeny, which in a few years may be numerous as the sands upon the sea-shore."

"You will admire with me the delicate expression which I have received of dear Mr. Corrie's love. Knowing what delight I should feel in the success of Abdool, and considering him as 'a descendant of mine,' through our beloved Martyn, who is my son in the faith, Mr. C. has had Abdool's picture taken, and sent it me, under the idea that it will afford me *in that view* peculiar pleasure and satisfaction. But the truth is, that I feel so utterly unworthy to have any success, that I am rather filled with shame, than with love, when I am informed of any success which God has been pleased to give me. But, peradventure, my sluggish heart may be more stirred up to prayer and praise in relation to India, when I have such a monitor before my eyes. The sight of our beloved Martyn's picture is such a reproach to me from day to day, that I can never keep my eyes fixed upon it for any time. The different effect produced by that, and by my deceased Brother's picture, is curious; I never look at my Brother's picture, but I say, '*dear* Brother!' whereas, at the sight of Mr. Martyn's, I uniformly, though unwittingly, exclaim, '*beloved* Brother!' There is a reverential admiration, blended with love, in the latter case; and it is so rooted in my mind, as to be absolutely inseparable from the sight of his blessed image. It is only from having observed these involuntary exclamations, that I have been led to analyze the feelings which give birth to them."*

TO THE HON. DR. RYDER, DEAN OF WELLS,

ON HIS APPOINTMENT TO THE BISHOPRICK OF GLOUCESTER.

"*May* 24, 1815.

"*My dear Sir:* Whilst all your friends are congratulating you on the attainment of your new dignity, I, though not worthy to be ranked in that number, take the liberty of expressing to you my feelings on the occasion. There are two grounds only, on which I consider the congratulations of your friends due personally to yourself; the one is that, when God has given to you so strong a desire to serve him, He has now enlarged your means of glorifying His name; and the other is, that this honor has not been obtained by any sacrifice of principle, or dereliction of duty on your part; so that you may assuredly expect the blessing of God upon all your exertions in His service. In all other points of view, especially when I consider the difficulties which you will have to encounter through life, so far beyond those which attach to the discharge of the pastoral office in a lower sphere, I feel inclined to think my congratulations due to the Church, rather than to you.

"Nor will you be without trials even from some of your dearest friends; for piety is not always attended with discretion; and you may be sometimes urged to things, which, though desirable in themselves, are not expedient; and if you will not see with their eyes, they may manifest, in a way painful to your feelings, their disappointment and chagrin; and constrain you to seek your comfort in the testimony of your own conscience, and in the approbation of your God."

---

* Mr. Simeon used to observe of Martyn's picture, whilst looking up at it with affectionate earnestness, as it hung over his fireplace: "There!—see that blessed man! What an expression of countenance! No one looks at me as he does—he never takes his eyes off me; and seems always to be saying, Be serious—Be in earnest—Don't trifle—don't trifle." Then smiling at the picture, and gently bowing, he added: "And I won't trifle—I won't trifle."

EXTRACT FROM A LETTER TO THE REV. W. CARUS WILSON.

"I think the great mass of Calvinists (though a moderate Calvinist myself) are wrong. They make a believer to possess that which is in itself *indefectible.* I am persuaded he does not; and have fully considered, and can easily explain, all the passages on which they ground their opinions. Man, to the latest hour of his life, may fall; nor is there anything in him that warrants him to say, 'I *cannot* fall finally.' He is a child in his Father's arms; let those arms be withdrawn from underneath him, and his own weight will precipitate him to destruction. If God have in His secret counsels, unknown to us, determined to keep him from falling, or to restore him when fallen, it will be done; but these secret decrees of God are no rule of action to the believer; the only use he is to make of them is to give God the glory of all the good that is in him, and to encourage him to cleave unto God with full purpose of heart."

EXTRACT FROM A LETTER TO THE REV. T. THOMASON, ON THE MISSIONARY SCHOOL.

"*June* 4, 1816.

"*My beloved Brother:* You will be glad to hear that the Society, which I have for two years been endeavoring to establish in London, for the education of pious young men for the Ministry, is now established; and, I hope, will soon become a powerful instrument in the Lord's hands. The trustees are Lord Calthorpe, Messrs. Wilberforce, Babington, Grant, &c. . . .

"The gentleman, whom I hope to send off for China, is to be ordained next Sunday by the Bishop of ———. Thus he will be ready to go at Christmas. It is astonishing how God has opened the hearts of the Bishop of ——— and the Bishop of Bristol towards me. They do more than could reasonably be hoped for from any Bishop whatever."

MEMORANDUM CONCERNING HIS BROTHER'S LEGACY TO HIM.

"My brother was extremely liberal, and did good to a vast extent. At his death, an exceeding great void would have been made, if I had not determined to accept a part of his property, and to appropriate it to the Lord's service, and the service of the poor. The loss they would have sustained being about £700 or £800 a year, I suffered my brother to leave me £15,000, and have regularly consecrated the interest of it to the Lord; and shall (D. V.) continue to do so to my dying hour. Had I wished for money for my own use, I might have had half his fortune; but I wanted nothing for myself, being determined (as far as such a thing could be at any time said to be determined) to live and die in College, where the income which I previously enjoyed (though moderate in itself) sufficed, not only for all my own wants, but for liberal supplies to the poor also.

"These things are well known at present in our College (Mr. —— in particular, as a counsel, examined my brother's will, wherein there is proof sufficient of these things); but at a future period they may be forgotten; and persons may wonder that, with my income, I do not resign my Fellowship. The fact is, I have not increased my own expenditure above £50 a year; nor do I consider myself as anything but a steward of my deceased brother, for the poor. It is well known that, long previous to his death, I refused what was considered as the best Living of our College; and I should equally refuse anything that the King himself could offer me, that should necessitate me to give up my present situation, and especially my Church.— And I write this now, that if, after my decease, it should be asked, 'Why did he not vacate his Fellowship?' my executor may have a satisfactory answer at hand. It lies in a short space:—

"1. If twice £15,000 were offered me to vacate my Fellowship, I would reject it utterly.

"2. The Legacy I have received I do not consider as mine, but as belonging to the poor and to the Lord; and I am only the Steward, to whose hands it is committed.

"3. The proof of this will be found in my refusal of any Living before, as well as since my brother's death, and in my Account-books, wherein the disposal of this money is regularly entered.

"Witness my hand this 19th of October, 1816.

"C. SIMEON."

LETTER TO THE REV. T. THOMASON, ABOUT THE LIFE OF HENRY MARTYN.

"K. C., *Nov.* 20, 1816.

"*My beloved Brother:* Never did I write to you under such peculiar circumstances as the present. Three whole mornings of about six or seven hours have dear Mr. Sargent, and Mr. Corrie, and your beloved Mother, and myself, been reading the Life of our lamented brother Mr. Martyn. Truly, it has humbled us all in the dust. Since the Apostolic Age I certainly think that nothing has ever exceeded the wisdom and piety of our departed brother; and I conceive that no book, except the Bible, will be found to excel this. In general, the Diaries of religious people exhibit the same thing again and again; but in this there is nothing repeated; and it exhibits such a mind and such a heart, as make him to appear almost like a different species from ourselves; we looked to him as at an almost unapproachable distance. David Brainerd is great; but the degree of his melancholy, and the extreme impropriety of his exertions, so much beyond his strength, put him on a different footing from our beloved Martyn; whilst the imagination of Martyn, and the inexhaustible richness of his ideas, give to his relations an interest superior to anything I ever read. Mr. Corrie's presence, too, has been highly favorable in rectifying some little things, which would have given to some parts an air of inaccuracy. But I must not enlarge; though were I to enlarge ever so much, I should have no fear of disappointing your expectations. The circumstance of Mr. Sargent having so much leisure has been of incalculable benefit; for it has enabled him to throw a lightness over the whole, by connecting every part, and making the transitions easy and natural. . .

"Yesterday was our Cambridge Bible Society Anniversary. It was remarkably well attended, Lord Hardwicke in the chair. I was unfortunately kept away by either a bruise in my foot, or, as Mr. Farish and your dear Mother think, and as I fear, the gout!! My father once had it, and only once; I may therefore have it now, and no more; but in my mind I am rather inclined to think that the time is now approaching when I must descend from my horse to a carriage; and if so I consider it as a very long step towards the eternal world. What may be my views of eternity when it comes very near, I know not; but my trust is in the tender mercy of my God in Christ Jesus; and I can joyfully leave myself in His hands. It has for many years been my delight to contemplate death as close at hand; and the more my mind is familiarized with death now, the more tranquil, I trust, it will be, when the closing scene of life shall have actually arrived. "Ever, ever yours,

"C. SIMEON."

EXTRACT FROM A LETTER TO THE REV. MR. THOMASON ABOUT THE BIBLE SOCIETY MEETING IN LONDON.

"I am just returned from town, where both your Mother and myself spent the Bible Week—the week of Jubilee; she at Dr. Steinkopff's, and I at my accustomed home, Mrs. Cecil's. The *tout ensemble* of the Bible Society was the grandest that we ever yet have witnessed. Such an intellectual feast was scarcely ever spread before. Mr. Money, from Bombay, gave us much interesting information, and in an elegant style; Dr. Mason of America also, in a dry way, arrested and edified the whole assembly. Mr. Wilson's sermon before the Missionary Society was one of the grandest things we have ever heard.—You will be much delighted with it. All the societies had a richer savor of piety than before. The public taste in this respect is daily improving.

"My own health, through mercy, is as good as at any period of my life; and by means of constant and extraordinary caution, my voice in public is as strong almost as ever. But I am silent all the week besides. I think I once told you, that I compare myself to bottled small beer; being corked up, and opened only twice a week, I make a good report; but if I were opened every day, I should soon be as ditch-water. I think I do right in saving myself thus, because it enables me to throw an energy into my public discourses which makes them far more interesting than they would otherwise be. The Gownsmen are sometimes almost one-half of my congregation."

ON LISTENING TO EVIL REPORTS.

"*July* 4, 1817.

"Last night, Mr. D. represented to me in strong terms the (supposed) ill behavior of Mr. ——— to his pupils; and particularly to Mr. B., to whom he refused lately to give his hand.

"The longer I live, the more I feel the importance of adhering to the rules which I have laid down for myself, in relation to such matters.

"1st. To hear as little as possible what is to the prejudice of others.

"2d. To believe nothing of the kind till I am absolutely forced to it.

"3d. Never to drink into the spirit of one who circulates an ill report.

"4th. Always to moderate, as far as I can, the unkindness which is expressed towards others.

"5th. Always to believe, that if the other side were heard, a very different account would be given of the matter.

"I consider love as wealth; and as I would resist a man who should come to rob my house, so would I a man who would weaken my regard for any human being. I consider, too, that persons are cast into different moulds; and that to ask myself, what should *I* do in that person's situation, is not a just mode of judging. I must not expect a man that is naturally cold and reserved to act as one that is naturally warm and affectionate; and I think it a great evil, that people do not make more allowances for each other in this particular. I think religious people are too little attentive to these considerations; and that it is not in reference to the ungodly world only that that passage is true, 'He that departeth from evil maketh himself a prey;' but even in reference to professors also; amongst whom there is a sad proneness to listen to evil reports, and to believe the representations they hear, without giving the injured person any opportunity of rectifying their views, and of defending his own character.

"The more prominent any person's character is, the more likely he is to suffer in this way; there being in the heart of every man, unless greatly subdued by grace, a pleasure in hearing anything which may sink others to his level, or lower them in the estimation of the world. We seem to ourselves elevated, in proportion as others are depressed. Under such circumstances I derive consolation from the following reflections:—

"1. My enemy, whatever evil he says of me, does not reduce me so low, as he would if he knew all concerning me that God knows.

"2. In drawing the balance, as between Debtor and Creditor, I find that if I have been robbed of pence, there are pounds and talents placed to my account, to which I have no just title.

"3. If man has his '*day,*' God will have His. See 1 Cor. iv. 3, the Greek."

ON SUFFERING INJURIES.

"*August* 30, 1817.

"I have this moment heard of a most malignant attempt to injure my character; and I take up my pen to record, to the praise and glory of my God, that my soul is kept in perfect peace. I pity those who delight in the exercise of such wicked dispositions. Little do they think that they injure themselves more than me; and that there is a day coming when the righteousness of the righteous shall be upon him, and the wickedness of the wicked shall be upon him. It is an unspeakable consolation that God knoweth everything and will judge righteous judgment. To Him I can make my appeal, that in the point referred to I am greatly injured; but, whilst I have the testimony of my own conscience and light of my Redeemer's countenance, none of these things do move me, or ought to move me."

On one occasion, when a friend observed to Mr. Simeon: "O, Sir, you don't know what wicked things they are saying of you!" he quietly answered with a smile, "Nor do I wish to know."—"But they are so untrue, Sir!"—"And would you wish them to *be* true?"

TO ONE WHO HAD BEEN URGED TO "PREACH VERY STRONGLY."

"*Dec.* 7, 1817.

"*My dear Sir:* What is your object? Is it to *win* souls? If it be, how are you to set about it? By exciting all manner of prejudices, and driving people from the Church? How did our Lord act? He spake the word in parables '*as men were able to hear it.*' How did St. Paul act? He fed the babes with *milk*, and not with strong meat. As for the religious world, they are as selfish, for the most part, as the ignorant and ungodly. They are not content that you should seek the welfare of others, unless you, *to please them*, bring forward also things which will utterly subvert your end; and if they be but gratified, they care not who is stumbled and driven away.

"You must not be in bondage to the religious world any more than to the ungodly. True, you are not to keep back the fundamental doctrines of the Gospel; but there are different ways of stating them; and you should adopt that which expresses kindness and love, and not that which indicates an unfeeling harshness. Only speak from *love to* man, and not from the *fear of* man, and God will both accept and prosper you. Most affectionately yours."

TO THE REV. T. THOMASON, ON THE CONDITION OF HIS CHURCH.

"*Nov.* 30, 1818.

"*My beloved Brother:* As for my Church, there is nothing new. Those who so greatly disturbed and distressed me are gone; and my Church is sweetly harmonious. As for the Gownsmen, never was anything like what they are at this day. I am forced to let them go up into the galleries, which I never suffered before; and notwithstanding that, multitudes of them are forced to stand in the aisles for want of a place to sit down. What thanks can I render to the Lord for a sight of these things! I am ready to sing my ancestor's song, Luke ii.

"Yours, &c., "C. S."

ON PREACHING.

"Rambling may occasionally produce impression; but its proper tendency is, idleness in you, and lassitude in your hearers. Poetry is beautiful in itself; but if you will come from the mount of God, you will find prose better suited for telling men about their golden calf. First tell a man that his house is on fire, or his father dead, *in verse*, and then interlard your sermons with it; but till then, keep in mind the motto :—

"I'd preach as though I ne'er should preach again,
I'd preach, as dying, unto dying men."

HIS INWARD EXPERIENCE.

In the early part of this year, Mr. Simeon, having accidentally heard that a friend had made some remarks upon his habit of giving expression to his religious feelings, "in sighs and groans," as if it indicated that "all was not right in his experience," drew up the following paper :—

"*Circumstances of my Inward Experience.*—It is now a little above forty years since I began to seek after God; and within about three months of that time, after much humiliation and prayer, I found peace through that Lamb of God who taketh away the sins of the world. About half a year after that, I had some doubts and fears about my state, in consequence of an erroneous notion which I had imbibed from Mr. Hervey about the nature of saving faith. But when I found, from better information, that justifying faith was a faith of affiance, and not a faith of assurance, my peace returned; because, though I had not a faith of assurance, I had as full a conviction that I relied on the Lord Jesus Christ alone for salvation, as I had of my own existence. From that time to the present hour I have never for a moment lost my hope and confidence in my adorable Saviour; for though, alas! I have had deep and abundant cause for humiliation, I have never ceased to wash in that fountain that was opened for sin and uncleanness, or to cast myself upon the tender mercy of my reconciled God.

"With this sweet hope of ultimate acceptance with God, I have always enjoyed much cheerfulness before men; but I have at the same time labored incessantly to cultivate the deepest humiliation before God. I have never thought that the circumstance of God's having forgiven me was any reason why I should forgive myself; on the contrary, I have always judged it better to loathe myself the more, in proportion as I was assured that God was pacified towards me.* Nor have I been satisfied with viewing my sins, as men view the stars in a cloudy night, one here and another there, with great intervals between; but have endeavored to get, and to preserve continually before my eyes, such a view of them as we have of the stars in the brightest night; the greater and the smaller all intermingled, and forming as it were one continuous mass; nor yet as committed a long time ago, and in many successive years; but as all forming an aggregate of guilt, and needing the same measure of humiliation daily, as they needed at the very moment they were committed. Nor would I willingly rest with such a view as presents itself to the naked eye. I have desired, and do desire daily, that God would put (so to speak) a telescope to my eye, and enable me to see, not a thousand only, but millions of my sins, which are more numerous than all the stars which God himself beholds, and more than the sands upon the sea-shore. There are but two objects that I have ever desired for these forty years to behold; the one is, my own vileness; and the other is, the glory of God in the face of Jesus Christ; and I have always thought that they should be viewed together; just as Aaron confessed all the sins of all Israel whilst he put them on the head of the scape-goat. The disease did not keep him from applying to the remedy, nor did the remedy keep him from feeling the disease. By this, I seek to be not only *humbled*

---

* Ezek. xvi. 63.

and thankful, but *humbled in thankfulness*, before my God and Saviour continually.

"This is the religion that pervades the whole Liturgy, and particularly the Communion Service; and this makes the Liturgy inexpressibly sweet to me. The repeated cries to each Person of the ever-adorable Trinity for mercy, are not at all too frequent or too fervent for me; nor is the confession in the Communion Service too strong for me; nor the 'Te Deum,' nor the ascriptions of glory after the Lord's Supper, 'Glory be to God on high,' &c., too exalted for me; the praise all through savors of *adoration;* and the adoration of humility. And this shows what men of God the framers of our Liturgy were, and what I pant, and long, and strive to be. This makes the Liturgy as superior to all modern compositions, as the work of a Philosopher on any deep subject is to that of a school-boy who understands scarcely anything about it.

"The consequence of this unremitted labor is, that I have, and have continually had, such a sense of my sinfulness, as would sink me into utter despair, if I had not an assured view of the sufficiency and willingness of Christ to save me to the uttermost. And at the same time I have such a sense of my acceptance through Christ, as would overset my little bark, if I had not ballast at the bottom sufficient to sink a vessel of no ordinary size. This experience has been now so unintermitted for forty years, that a thought only of some defect, or of something which might have been done better, often draws from me as deep a sigh as if I had committed the most enormous crime; because it is viewed by me not as a mere single grain of sand, but as a grain of sand added to an already accumulated mountain. So deep are my views of my corruption, that I scarcely ever join in the Confession of our Church without perceiving, almost as with my bodily organs, my soul as a dead and putrefied* carcass; and I join in that acknowledgment, 'There is no health in us,' in a way that none but God himself can conceive. No language that I could use, could at all express the goings forth of my soul with those words, or the privilege I feel in being permitted to address the God of heaven and earth in these words, 'Almighty—and most merciful—Father.'

"Hence, then, my sighs and groans when in secret, and which, when least thought of by me, may have been noticed by others. And if the Apostle Paul so felt the burthen of sin as to cry, 'O wretched man that I am! who shall deliver me

---

* Isai. i. 6.

from the body of this death?' (Rom. vii. 24;) if he, who 'had the first-fruits of the Spirit, groaned within himself, waiting for the adoption, to wit, the redemption of the body,' (Rom. viii. 23,) yea, 'groaned, being burthened,' (2 Cor. v. 4;) who am I, that I should not so feel, or so express my feelings; or that I should even wish to be exempt from them? So far am I from wishing to be exempt from them, that I wish and long to have them in a tenfold greater degree; and as already in my daily approaches to the throne of grace, and in my solitude, and in my rides, it is in sighs and groans that I make known my wants to God more than in words, for 'He knoweth the mind of His Spirit speaking in me;' so I desire yet more and more that the Spirit of God may make intercession both in me and for me, 'with groanings which cannot be uttered,' since words would fail to give them utterance. (Rom. viii. 26.)

"But persons mistake, who imagine that groans are expressive only of a sense of guilt; they are often the expressions of desire; as David says, 'Lord, all my desire is before thee; and my groaning is not hid from thee,' (Ps. xxxviii. 9.) And such, I trust, have been many of the groans which I have uttered in secret, and some of which may possibly have been overheard.

"Nor is it on a personal account only that groans are uttered. A Minister who knows what it is to 'travail in birth with his people till Christ be formed in them,' will find many occasions of sorrow, as I have of late years. I have had a people, some of whom have ill understood their duty towards me (Heb. xiii. 17), and have constrained me 'to give up my daily account not with joy, but with grief;' or, as it is in the original, 'with groans.'

"But supposing those expressions of my feelings to have been on a personal account only, and that only from a sense of my unworthiness, I am far from conceiving it to be on the whole an undesirable experience; for by means of it my joys are tempered with contrition, and my confidence with fear and shame. I consider the religion of the day as materially defective in this point; and the preaching of pious ministers defective also. I do not see, so much as I could wish, an holy reverential awe of God. The confidence that is generally professed does not sufficiently, in my opinion, savor of a creature-like spirit, or of a sinner-like spirit. If ninety-nine out of an hundred, of even good men, were now informed for the first time, that Isaiah in a vision saw the Seraphim before the throne; and that each of the Seraphs had six wings; and then were asked, 'How do you think they employ their wings?' I think their answer would be, 'How? why they fly with them with all their might; and if they had six hundred wings they would do the same, exerting all their powers in the service of their God.' They would never dream of their employing two to veil their faces, as unworthy to behold their God, and two to veil their feet, as unworthy to serve him; and devoting only the remaining two to what might be deemed their more appropriate use. But I doubt much whether the Seraphs do not judge quite as well as they, and serve their God in quite as acceptable a manner as they would, if their energies were less blended with modesty and conscious unworthiness. But, whatever opinions the generality of Christians might form, I confess that this is the religion which I love. I would have conscious unworthiness to pervade every act and habit of my soul; and whether the woof be more or less brilliant, I would have humility to be the warp.

"I often in my ministry speak of Job's experience, after God had so revealed Himself to him, as proper for all; why, then, should I not cultivate it myself, and really, truly, deeply, and as before the heart-searching God, 'abhor myself, and repent in dust and ashes?' (Job xlii. 6.) Can I enter into the spirit of that word *abhor*, and not groan? Or, is that a word which is to have no counterpart in our actual experience? —I do not undervalue joy; but I suspect it, when it is not blended with the deepest humiliation and contrition. God has said that a 'broken and a contrite heart He will not despise;' and is that an attainment that is so low and small that I may leave it behind me, as a state that was proper for me forty years ago, but not now? What is meant by a *broken* heart? Would to God that I knew! for with all my groaning I do not know a thousandth part of what it means. I remember to have heard a saying of. . . . and though I do not admire the expression, I do admire the sentiment; and I would not feel my obligation to my Saviour less than I do for ten thousand worlds. Indeed, I consider that this very feeling will constitute the chief felicity of heaven; and that every blessing we there enjoy will be most of all endeared to us as being the fruit of redeeming love. I behold the *glorified* saints *in heaven* falling on their faces before the throne, whilst they sing praises to their redeeming God (Rev. v. 8–14). What, then, should *I* do *on earth?* Yea, I behold even *the angels* who never sinned adoring God in that same posture (Rev. vii. 11). What, then, should *I* do, whose whole soul is but one mass of sin and corruption?

Finally, God himself is light, and I am to be as like Him as I can. But what is light? is it not a combination of different rays—the red, the orange, the yellow, the green, the blue, the indigo, and the violet? Some would think perhaps that they could make better light, if they had the brilliant rays alone; but so think not I; I would have the due proportion of the sombre with the bright; and all in simultaneous motion; and then I think I should more resemble both the created and the uncreated light. At all events, this is my one ambition, to live with one Mary at my Saviour's feet, listening to His words (whilst others are cumbered about the world), and to die with the other Mary, washing his feet with my tears, and wiping them with the hairs of my head."

"P. S. I have not been till lately acquainted with any book, except 'Augustine's Meditations,' that exactly paints all that I approve, and all that I wish to be; Brainerd's Life has too much of gloom and despondency for me. But I think that the Memoirs of my beloved and honored Friend, HENRY MARTYN, come exactly to the point; and his Biographer, the Rev. John Sargent, has marked it with beautiful precision in the close of that Memoir. O! that all the world would study that short Memoir! it speaks what I would, if I were able, speak in the ear of every human being, day and night. May God of his infinite mercy give me more abundantly to experience this heavenly disposition! and may all that I have written be blessed of Him to the producing of this holy disposition in others. Amen, and Amen."

SIMEON'S SKELETONS.

As mention will be made of these in several places hereafter, it may be well to introduce the following extracts from the preface, which are so valuable to ministers:—

"It has not, as the Author believes, occurred to any Divine, *to supply a regular series of Discourses on the most important parts of the whole Volume of Scripture; and to adapt these Discourses, by their general construction, their simplicity, and their brevity, to the special service of the younger order of the Clergy.* It is the particular object of these Volumes, which the Author now humbly presents to the public, to supply this deficiency in Theological writings. And he trusts this labor of love will be regarded by his brethren in the Ministry, not as an act of presumption, but as an humble and affectionate attempt to render their entrance on their holy and honorable calling more easy, and their prosecution of it more useful. . . .

"The Author is no friend to systematizers in Theology. He has endeavored to derive from the Scriptures alone *his* views of religion, and to them it is his wish to adhere with scrupulous fidelity; never wresting any portion of the Word of God to favor a particular opinion, but giving to every part of it that sense which it seems to him to have been designed by its Great Author to convey.

"He is aware that he is likely, on this account, to be considered by the zealous advocates of human systems as occasionally inconsistent; but if he should be discovered to be no more inconsistent than the Scriptures themselves, he will have reason to be satisfied. He has no doubt but that there is a system in the Holy Scriptures (for truth cannot be inconsistent with itself); but he is persuaded that neither Calvinists nor Arminians are in *exclusive* possession of that system. He is disposed to think that the Scripture system, be it what it may, is of a broader and more comprehensive character than some very exact and dogmatical theologians are inclined to allow; and that as wheels in a complicated machine may move in opposite directions and yet subserve one common end, so may truths *apparently opposite* be perfectly reconcilable with each other, and equally subserve the purposes of God in the accomplishment of man's salvation. This the Author has attempted to explain more fully in the Preface to his former Work. But he feels it impossible to repeat too often, or avow too distinctly, that it is an invariable rule with him to endeavor to give to every portion of the Word of God its full and proper force, without considering one moment what scheme it favors, or whose system it is likely to advance. Of this he is sure, that there is not a decided Calvinist or Arminian in the world, who equally approves of the whole of Scripture. He apprehends that there is not a determined votary of either system, who, if he had been in the company of St. Paul whilst he was writing his different Epistles, would not have recommended him to alter one or other of his expressions.

"But the Author would not wish one of them altered; he finds as much satisfaction in one class of passages as in another; and employs the one, he believes, as often and as freely as the other. Where the Inspired Writers speak in unqualified terms, he thinks himself at liberty to do the same; judging that they needed no instruction from *him* how to propagate the truth. He is content to sit as a *learner* at the feet of the Holy Apostles, and has no ambition to teach them how they ought to have spoken. And as both the strong Calvinists and Arminians approve of some parts of Scripture, and not of others; such, he expects, will be the judgment of the partisans of these particular systems on his unworthy comments; the Calvinists approving of what is written on passages which have a Calvinistic aspect; and the Arminians of what is written on passages that favor their particular views. In like manner, he has reason, he fears, to expect a measure of condemnation from the advocates of each system, when treating of the passages which they appear to him to *wrest*, each for the purpose of accommodating them to his own favorite opinions. He bitterly regrets that men will range themselves under human banners and leaders, and employ themselves in converting the Inspired Writers into friends and partisans of their peculiar principles. Into this fault he trusts that he has not hitherto fallen; and he unfeignedly hopes and prays to be preserved from it in future. One thing he knows, namely, that pious men, both of the Calvinistic and Arminian persuasion, approximate very nearly when they are upon their knees before God in prayer; the devout Arminian then acknowledging his total dependence upon God as strongly as the most confirmed Calvinist; and the Calvinist acknowledging his responsibility to God, and his obligation to exertion, in terms as decisive as the most determined Arminian. And that which both these individuals are upon their knees, it is the wish of the Author to become in his writings. Hence it is that he expects to be alternately approved by both parties and condemned by both. His only fear is, that each may be tempted to lay hold only of those parts of his work which *oppose* their favorite system, and represent them as containing an entire view of his sentiments. He well knows the force of prejudice, and the bitterness of the *Odium Theologicum;* and he cannot hope to be so fortunate as completely to escape either. But, even if assailed on all sides, he shall have the satisfaction of reflecting that it has been his wish simply to follow the Oracles of God. The Scriptures and the Church of England have been claimed by each of these two parties, as exclusively favoring their peculiar systems; and if the same comprehensive and liberal character be found in his writings, he shall consider it, whatever may be the judgment of mere partisans, as no small presumption in his own favor.

"There is another point, also, in respect to which it has been his aim not to offend; and that is, in not so perverting the Scripture as to make it refer to Christ and His salvation, when no such object appears to have been in the contemplation of the inspired writer. He regrets to observe, in some individuals, what he knows not how to designate by any more appropriate term than that (which, however, he uses with much hesitation) of an *ultra-Evangelical* taste; which overlooks in many passages the *practical* lessons they were intended to convey, and detects in them only the leading *doctrines* of the Gospel. This error he has labored earnestly to avoid; being well assured that lessons of morality are, in their place, as useful and important as the doctrines of grace. In a word, it has been his endeavor faithfully to deliver, in every instance, what he verily believed to be the mind of God in the passage immediately under consideration; and in the adoption of this principle of interpretation, he trusts for the approbation of all who prefer the plain and obvious comments of sobriety to the far-fetched suggestions of a licentious fancy.

"He wishes much that the practice of *expounding* the Scriptures, which obtained so generally, and with such beneficial effects, at the time of the Reformation, were revived. He has in his present work introduced many Discourses constructed upon this model; and he cannot but earnestly recommend it to his younger Brethren in the Ministry, especially those who preach three times in the week, to reserve at least one of those seasons for exposition. It is his wish, however, to guard them against a desultory manner of explaining the Scripture; and to advise that the leading point of the whole passage be the point mainly regarded; and the subordinate parts only so far noticed, as to throw additional light on that. If this caution be not attended to, the minds of the people are likely to be distracted with the diversity and incoherence of the matter brought before them. But if an unity of subject be preserved, the discourse will come with tenfold weight to the minds of the audience; who will be led, under the guidance of the Holy Spirit, to search the Scriptures for themselves, and to read them with more profit at their own homes. To this it may be added, that it is not necessary the whole passage should be read for the text; let the most striking part of it alone be introduced in the first instance, and then the whole explained, with such remarks as are suited to impress on the mind the truths contained in it. This will be found to have been the course pursued in many of the following Discourses, to a greater extent perhaps than at first sight appears.

"The Author has also sought to render the work useful for families. It has often been a matter of complaint, that there existed few Sermons sufficiently plain and concise for the instruction of Servants; he has therefore filled up the outline of these Sketches somewhat more fully than those in his former Volumes, hoping that Clergymen and others may find them not altogether useless as a *Family Instructor*. . . . .

"In order that the agreement between the Author's views, and what he conceives to be the views of the Church of England, may be ascertained, he begs leave to refer the Reader to the Four Sermons on Deut. v. 28, 29, in which 'The Excellency of the Liturgy' is delineated; and to that on 2 Cor. i. 13, wherein 'The Churchman's Confession' is considered. And to any who may wish to become acquainted with the Author's views of what is called '*Evangelical Religion*,' he begs to recommend the perusal of the Sermons on 1 Cor. ii. 2, and Psalm cxix. 128; which were written for the express purpose of exhibiting, in as clear and comprehensive a manner as he was able, his opinions upon that important subject. More especially, with this object, he would entreat their candid consideration of what he has called an 'Appeal to Men of Wisdom and Candor;' (on 1 Cor. x. 15.) All these Sermons, together with those on the Liturgy, were delivered before the University of Cambridge. These Discourses, it may be added, comprehend all the topics which he considers as of primary and fundamental importance to mankind. On many other points there exists, and will probably continue to exist, a diversity of opinion; and in writing upon the *whole* Scriptures, it would not be expected but that he should occasionally touch on such topics, as they presented themselves to him in his course. But as he has endeavored, without prejudice or partiality, to give to every text its just meaning, its natural bearing, and its legitimate use, he hopes that those who dislike his expositions of the texts which oppose their particular views, will consult what he has written on the texts which they regard as the sheet-anchors of their system; and that, finding him, as he trusts they will, free from party spirit, they will themselves endeavor to shake off party prejudices, and co-operate with him in maintaining and extending that comprehensive, and generous, and harmonious, as well as devout spirit in the Church, which, he ventures to say, it has been one of the great objects of his life to promote."

HIS OPINION OF DR. CHALMERS.

To the Rev. J. W. Cunningham:—

"K. C., *Oct.* 22, 1821.

"*My very dear and honored Friend:* Your person, work, and circumstances, find a deep interest in my heart; and I have much joy in the conviction that they are all indelibly engraven on the breastplate of our Great High Priest, who is touched with the feeling of all our wants and all our infirmities. I trust that your supports and consolations abound *above* all your afflictions; for our God giveth good measure, pressed down, and running over.

"I have seen with much satisfaction the review of Dr. Chalmers's Works. I have received a letter from himself this very day, and not having time to answer it, have conveyed to him an oral reply, carrying my whole heart along with it. Truly, I consider him as raised up by God for a great and peculiar work. His depth of thought, originality in illustrating, and strength in stating, are unrivalled in the present day; and I think he is somewhat less turgid, and intricate, and careless in his language than he was at first. . . . .

"In another respect, he is too sanguine. He does not sufficiently see, that a Chalmers is necessary to carry into effect the plans of Chalmers. But he has a noble aim; and I think will do great good. If we cannot all follow him closely, we may yet tread in his steps; and I trust that many will make the attempt.

"I think, also, he carries too far the complaint about Government making use of Ministers in secular matters. Dr. C. and half a score of others may find it a serious inconvenience. The great mass of Ministers, I fear, throughout the United Kingdom would not engage one atom more in spiritual exercises, or in ministerial labors, if they were to be exempted from all temporal matters to-morrow. Still, if some things are overstrained, (and who ever rode a favorite hobby without going now and then a little too fast?) many things are nobly stated, and come with great power to the mind; and I rejoice exceedingly that you are calling the attention of the Public to them. Such a measure was wanted. Religious people are apt to overlook secular matters, instead of giving them a due measure of attention; forgetting that motto, '*Nihil humani a me alienum puto . . . .*'

"My province is, just to attend to the little things that are before me. Were I to attempt to execute Dr. C.'s plans, my folly would soon appear unto all men. I have often thought that, as *sapientia prima est stultitiâ caruisse;* so *secunda est*, to know, *quid valeant humeri, quid ferre recusent;* and however defective in the first, I have studied carefully, and to pretty good purpose, the second. I make known my little pittance of knowledge, but carefully conceal my ignorance; which is, I conceive, laudably concealed, when you affect not talents or acquirements you do not possess. I intended only to drop you a few lines in answer to your kind note; and behold here is quite a letter; and after all it does not express a tenth part of what I tacitly comprehend, when I sign myself your truly sympathizing and most affectionate Friend,

"C SIMEON."

ON NEGLECTING INSULTS—IN A LETTER TO A FRIEND.

"Perhaps I ought to take some notice of it; but my rule is never to hear, or see, or know, what if heard, or seen, or known, would call for animadversion from me. Hence it is that I dwell in peace in the midst of lions. My blessed Lord, 'when He was reviled, reviled not again; when He suffered, He threatened not, but committed Himself to Him that judgeth righteously.' That seems the right thing for me to do; though some perhaps would think it better for me to stand up for my rights. But to all the accusations that were brought against Him, our Lord made no reply; '*insomuch that the governor marvelled greatly.*' I delight in that record; and God helping me, it is the labor of my life so to act, that on *my* account also the governor, or spectator, may marvel greatly.

"My experience all this day has been, and I hope will yet continue to be, a confirmation of that word, 'Thou wilt hide me in the secret of thy presence from the strife of tongues.' Insult an Angel before the throne, and what would he care about it? Just such will be my feeling, whilst I am *hid in the secret* of my Redeemer's presence."

CHAPTER VI.

HIS VISIT TO IRELAND—STATE OF RELIGION THERE.

"THERE is amongst the Prelates of Ireland an augmented prejudice against the truth. The Primate and the Archbishop of Dublin have withdrawn, and others with them, from the Bible Society and all the Religious Societies. It appeared to me therefore that, through the Divine blessing, I might do good by going there. The bugbear in their minds is Calvinism; by which term they designate all vital religion. You well know that though strongly Calvinistic in some respects, I am as strongly Arminian in others. I am free from all the trammels of human systems; and can pronounce every part of God's blessed Word, *ore rotundo*, mincing nothing, and fearing nothing. Perhaps too I may say, that, from having published sixteen Volumes, and preached for forty years in Cambridge, I may be supposed to give a pretty just picture of the state of Evangelical Religion, such as it really is. On this account I hoped that, however insignificant in myself, I might be an instrument of good; more especially, because in the last year I sent to every Prelate there my Sermons on the Conversion of the Jews. It happened too that they were anxious to have me come over thither; and that Mr. Marsh was actually engaged to go for the Church Missionary Society. With joy, therefore, I accepted the invitation, being myself most willing to go; and accordingly I proceeded with Mr. Marsh, on Monday, April 8, and got to Holyhead on Thursday; and we reached our destined home in good health and spirits on the Saturday afternoon.

"No sooner were we arrived, than Irish hospitality evinced itself in an extraordinary degree. You, who know the precise line in which I walk at Cambridge, will be astonished, as I myself was, to find Earls and Viscounts, Deans and Dignitaries, Judges, &c., calling upon me, and Bishops desirous to see me. Invitations to dinner were numerous from different quarters; one had been sent even to London, and to Cambridge, to engage us to dinner on the Bible-day. But let me enter on what will appear yet more extraordinary on the other hand.

The Archbishop, understanding that foreigners were invited to preach in Dublin, had said that he had no objection to Mr. Marsh or myself; but that he expected the minister to adhere to the Canon, which required the exhibition of our Letters of Orders previous to our admission to any pulpit in his province. Information respecting this had been sent us, and we came prepared; and the Church-wardens were summoned to the Vestry to record and attest the exhibition of them. In the morning of the next day I preached at St. George's Church, to a congregation of 1200, a kind of preparatory Sermon for the Jews; and God seemed to be manifestly present with us. In the evening, I preached at another smaller Church in the outskirts of the City; and had reason to hope that the word did not go forth in vain.

"On the next day (Monday) I dined at the Countess of Westmeath's, and met Judge Daly and many other characters of the highest respectability. Tuesday was the Jews' Society-day. This Society in Ireland takes the lead, and is carried on with surprising spirit. Their Committee meets every Monday morning; and they give themselves to prayer, as well as to the ministry of the various offices that are called for. The Archbishop of Tuam was in the Chair; we met in the Rotunda. It is, however, ill adapted for speaking. The windows were open on both sides, so that the voice was carried out by the wind, and those in front could not hear. I did my best, however; but not without suffering for it for two or three days. They looked to me as the representative of the Society, and therefore I felt bound to exert myself to the uttermost. It was altogether a very interesting meeting.

"The Bible Meeting was the next day. The Archbishop again was in the Chair; and his Address was the finest thing I ever heard. The Primate and the Archbishop of Dublin had withdrawn their names from the Society; the Archbishop of Tuam, therefore, stood on very delicate ground. This he stated; but observed that as they had not declared their reasons for withdrawing, and he could discover none himself, he must continue to uphold it. He spoke with a dignity suited to his rank, yet with the meekness of his Divine Master. Perhaps Paul before Festus will give you the best idea of his whole action, spirit, and deportment. I doubt not but that he will hear of that speech at the day of judgment. After the reading of the Report I left the assembly; for after the exertions of the preceding day I greatly needed rest. Thursday was the Meeting of the School Society; that was in a smaller room, and

Earl Roden in the Chair. It was a most delightful Meeting; and my dear fellow-traveller, Mr. Marsh, produced a vast sensation, as indeed he generally does; such a playful suavity as his I never heard. On the Friday, at the Church Mission Society, the Archbishop of Tuam again presided. If I could have accepted of all the invitations, they would have lasted almost to this time."

PLAYFUL REMARKS ABOUT THE GOLDEN MEAN, OR VIA MEDIA.

To the Rev. Mr. T———.

"K. C., CAMB., *July* 9, 1825.

"*My beloved Brother:* Perhaps you little thought that in what you have said about extremes, *and against the golden mean*, you would carry me along with you. But I not only go along with you, I even go far beyond you; for to *you* I can say in words, what for these thirty years I have proclaimed *in deeds* (you will not misunderstand me), that the truth is *not in the middle*, and *not in one extreme; but in both extremes.* I see you filled with amazement, and doubting whether I am sober, *i. e.*, in my sober senses.

"Here were two extremes; observing days, eating meats, &c.—'Paul, how do you move? In the mean way?' 'No.' —'To one extreme?' 'No.'—'How then?' 'To both extremes in their turn, as occasion requires.'

"Here are two other extremes, Calvinism and Arminianism (for you need not be told how long Calvin and Arminius lived before St. Paul). 'How do you move in reference to these, Paul? In a golden mean?' 'No.'—'To one extreme?' 'No'.—'How then?' 'To both extremes: to-day I am a strong Calvinist; to-morrow a strong Arminian.'—'Well, well, Paul, I see thou art beside thyself; go to Aristotle, and learn the golden mean."

"But, my brother, I am unfortunate; I formerly read Aristotle, and liked him much; I have since read Paul, and caught somewhat of his strange notions *oscillating* (not vacillating) from pole to pole. Sometimes I am a high Calvinist, at other times a low Arminian; so that, if extremes will please you, I am your man; only remember, it is not *one* extreme that we are to go to, but *both* extremes.

"Now, my beloved brother, if I find you in the zenith on the one side, I shall hope to find you in the nadir on the other; and then we shall be ready (in the estimation of the world, and of *moderate* Christians, who love the golden mean) to go to Bedlam together."

MEMORANDA ON VARIOUS OCCASIONS.

On a Bequest for Religious Objects.

"*Feb.* 23, 1826.

"About four years ago, when I was in my blessed work of purchasing Livings, to secure in perpetuity pious and laborious Ministers in them, by the advice of a gentleman, I wrote to Dr. Kilvington, whom I had never seen, to ask some assistance towards it, thinking he might possibly give me £500; and behold he gave me nearly £8000! And now that I am again engaged to the amount of above £10,000, a gentleman, whom I never saw but once, and then only for half an hour, has died and left me, as my informant says, £9000. My poor dear honored and lamented Father thought that I should ruin myself by giving my money to the poor, and therefore left my little fortune in the hands of trustees, to keep me from this apprehended mischief. Behold, this is the way in which God leaves me to be ruined! Oh, what a Master He is! I wonder who ever lost by serving Him? It is sufficient for me to know, that 'what we give for His glory, we lend to Him; and he will repay us again.' But He will not even take the loan; for on both these occasions He has just interposed (as indeed He has on several other occasions) to forestall and prevent the payment out of my own pocket; so that I am still as strong as ever to prosecute the same good work. Who needs prove to *me* the providence of God?"

On receiving Marks of Attention.

"*May* 26, 1826.

"I have thought that I would not make any memorandum of two events, lest it should appear to savor of vanity; but they do in a very striking way evince the goodness of God to me, and may serve to show how He rewards a simple and faithful adherence to Him. I remember the time that I was quite surprised that a Fellow of my own College ventured to walk with me for a quarter of an hour on the grassplot before Clare Hall; and for many years after I began my Ministry, I was a man wondered at, by reason of the paucity of those who showed any regard for true religion. But now, on my open days (Fridays), when I receive visitors at tea, frequently more than forty (all without invitation) come. What an honor is this!

How impossible would it have been for me ever to have obtained it, if I had sought it! But God gives it me unsought."

"Again.—In the month of April I was proposed as a member of the Society for promoting Christian Knowledge; and as it was apprehended that I might be black-balled (for some have been who were far less notorious than myself), there went a host of Bishops and other Dignitaries of the Church, with their friends (about 90 or 100 in all), to beat down opposition, and to vote me in with a high hand. I understand there were but three opponents; and that Mr.——— was peculiarly zealous in my support. Is not this of the Lord?

"Again.—Last week three Bishops did me the honor of visiting me; Dr. Burgess, Bishop of Salisbury—Dr. Law, Bishop of Bath and Wells—Dr. Jebb, Bishop of Limerick; and I accompanied them to King's Chapel, and to Trinity Library, and spent above an hour with them. This shows how much Christian liberality has increased, and is increasing. I am not conscious that I am one atom less faithful to my God than in former days, or more desirous of human favor; yet God is pleased thus graciously to honor me. In former years I should as soon have expected a visit from three crowned heads, as from three persons wearing a mitre; not because there was any want of condescension in them, but because my religious character affixed a stigma to my name. I thank God that I receive this honor as from Him, and am pleased with it no further than as it indicates an increasing regard for religion amongst my superiors in the Church, and may tend to lessen prejudice amongst those to whom the report of it may come."

CHAPTER VII.

MR. SIMEON'S JUBILEE.

We are now come to a period in Mr. Simeon's history, which is memorable, as bringing to a completion the fiftieth year of his residence in the University. In order to commemorate this event in a devout and becoming manner, he requested a select party of his friends to assemble for two days in his rooms for exercises of a social and religious character.

The following letter from one of the most endeared and distinguished of the party invited, expressing as it does so admirably the sentiments which were shared in general on this occasion, will doubtless be read with no ordinary interest.

W. WILBERFORCE, ESQ. TO MR. SIMEON.

"HIGHWOOD HILL, MIDDLESEX, 22*d January*, 1829.

"*My dear Friend:* Ought I to be ashamed to confess, or rather shall I not rejoice, and with thankfulness avow it, that at my time of life, in my seventieth year, I preserve such a warmth of feeling, that, on the perusal of your very interesting letter, and more especially on reading your kind invitation to join the party that will celebrate with you your Jubilee, I was at first kindled into such a blaze as to be quite dazzled by the splendor of my own conceptions, and heated into a hope that I might become a sharer in your Christian festivities. But a little cool reflection sufficed for enforcing on me a more sober view of things, and compelled me to admit that, having been commanded by medical authority to *shut up* during the winter months, I should be taking a liberty with my constitution that would be utterly unwarrantable, if I were to sally forth in such a season as this, though to indulge in the exercise of some of the most generous and even sacred pleasures of which our nature is capable in this imperfect state. I must be content then to join your party in spirit, if not in person; and in offering up my petitions for the various blessings you have enumerated (I thank you for the specification), I shall not forget to return my humble thanksgivings to the Giver of all good, for having enabled you '*to continue unto this day*,' (how much is contained in that brief though compendious expression!) But you are blessed with so much bodily health and vigor, that we may humbly indulge the hope that the Almighty will still grant you a long course of usefulness and comfort. The degree in which, without any sacrifice of principle, you have been enabled to overcome, and, if I may so term it, *to live down* the prejudices of many of our higher Ecclesiastical authorities, is certainly a phenomenon I never expected to witness."

EXTRACTS FROM HIS DIARY ON THAT OCCASION.

Jan. 29.—Curious enough! This day, the day of *my Jubilee*, and of my investiture with the office, was ushered in by the ringing of bells all over Cambridge. It is the day of the King's Accession.

Now, then, let me in a few words give an account of my

Jubilee. Several were kept away by illness; so that my party was not very large at dinner the first day. The first evening was very sweet. I opened *my* views of a Jubilee—(not like the joy of the man healed in Solomon's porch, but like the prodigal, whose joy would be not only tempered by, but almost wholly consisting in, a retrospective shame, and prospective determination through grace to avoid in future the evils, from which God's free mercy, founded on the atonement, has delivered us)—*it was proclaimed on the day of Atonement.* (See Lev. xxv. 9.)

The second day we met at eleven o'clock. I read some portions of Scripture, and prayed generally for the Divine presence. Then Mr. Sargent read, and gave a prayer of humiliation; Mr. Daniel Wilson followed for the Universities; then Dr. Steinkopff for the religious Societies and the Church. We then separated for an hour. Mr. Hawtrey ended with Thanksgiving. Mr. D. Wilson preached the Lecture (at Trinity Church). On the whole it was a season of refreshing to us all; . . . . Blessed be God for this mercy.

MR. SIMEON ON CATHOLIC DISABILITIES.

On the 25th of March, being "Founder's Day" at King's College, a Sermon is annually preached by one of the Society before the University, who assemble in the College Chapel. The Sermon this year was preached by Mr. Simeon, who took occasion to deliver his sentiments on the momentous subjects, then in debate, connected with the passing of the Bill for removing the Roman Catholic Disabilities.

The following is a part of the Discourse :—

"As to the measures which our Government is now pursuing, I condemn them not. I believe from my heart they are necessary, not only for the averting of the immediately impending evils of civil war, but for the forming of a permanent bond of union amongst the widely differing subjects of our distracted empire. But I cannot hide from myself the dangers to which, even by this very remedy, the whole nation will be speedily exposed. That a more familiar intercourse between Catholics and ourselves will be the immediate and necessary result of their introduction to all places of honor and profit in our land, is certain; and we may well expect, in a very short time, to see almost the whole of Britain inundated with Papists. Their priests, of course, will labor by all possible means to diffuse their tenets, and to proselyte our people to their Church. And I think it highly probable that their success for a time will be both wide and rapid; not because of the real force of their arguments, but because of the unprepared state both of our Clergy and Laity to withstand them. Nor do I think that their success will be confined to the lower ranks. I shall not wonder if many who are well instructed in other things, should fall into the snare, and be drawn away by their specious arguments; because, as soon as the mind of any man is impressed with a sense of the value of his soul, he naturally inquires, 'What shall I do to obtain eternal life?' And if there be no one at hand well versed in the truth and excellence of the Gospel salvation, no one to say, '*Believe* in the Lord Jesus Christ, and thou shalt be saved,' he will readily lend himself to those who will flatter his pride, and point out to him a number of rites and services whereby he may conciliate the Divine favor. This is the very essence of Popery; and this is caught at with avidity by the natural man, who, like the Pharisees of old, will rather undertake the most laborious duties, than submit to be saved by grace alone. *This* then renders it necessary for us all to acquire true wisdom without delay. For without *that*, we ourselves shall have no security against the specious arguments of Popish emissaries; much less shall we be able to protect others against their insinuating addresses. But let a person once attain the knowledge of Christ crucified, and come habitually to God through Him, and he will be in no danger of being drawn away by all their subtleties."

MR. SIMEON'S TEA PARTIES.

As it may be interesting to those who never were present at Mr. Simeon's weekly tea parties, to know in what manner they were conducted, the following extract from a graphic and accurate description is here introduced, from a letter addressed to the late lamented Charlotte Elizabeth.

As soon as the ceremony of introduction was concluded, Mr. Simeon would take possession of his accustomed elevated seat, and would commence the business of the evening. I see him even now, with his hands folded upon his knees, his head turned a little to one side, his visage solemn and composed, and his whole deportment such as to command attention and respect. After a pause, he would encourage us to propose our doubts, addressing us in slow, and soft, and measured accents: "Now—if you have any question to ask—I shall be happy to hear it—and to give what assistance I can." Presently one, and then another, would venture with his interrogatories, each being emboldened by the preceding inquirer, till our backwardness and reserve were entirely removed. In the mean time, two waiters would be handing the tea to the company; a part of the entertainment which the most of us could well have dispensed with, as it somewhat interrupted the evening's proceedings; but it was most kindly provided by our dear friend, who was always very considerate of our comfort and ease.

It is my purpose, if you will so far indulge me, to give your readers the substance of some conversations which took place in Mr. Simeon's rooms, on May 3, 1833. This was the most interesting and solemn Friday evening meeting that I ever attended. I never saw the holy man of God more full of the spirit of his Master. His words were distilled as honey from his lips; at least they were very sweet to *my* taste; and their savor, I trust, I have still retained. On that memorable evening, such a deep sense of his own unworthiness rested upon his soul, that he was low in self-abasement before God. All his language seemed to be, "Lord, I am vile;" and his very looks spake the same.

On being asked, "What, sir, do you consider the principal mark of regeneration?" he replied:—

"The very first and indispensable sign is self-loathing and abhorrence. Nothing short of this can be admitted as an evidence of a real change. Some persons inquire, 'Do you hate what you once loved, and love what you once hated?' But even this mark cannot be so surely relied upon as the other. I have constantly pressed this subject upon my Congregation, and it has been the characteristic of my Ministry. I want to see more of this humble, contrite, broken spirit amongst us. It is the very spirit that belongs to self-condemned sinners. Permit me to lay this matter near your hearts. Take home with you this passage: 'Then shall ye remember your own evil ways, and your doings that were not good, and shall loathe yourselves in your own sight for your iniquities and for your abominations,' (Ezek. xxxvi. 31,) and to-night on your beds, or in the morning, meditate thus within yourselves: Loathe?—why, if I loathe and abhor anything, I cannot look upon it without disgust. The very sight of it gives me great pain and uneasiness. I turn away from it as from something abominable and hateful. Have I ever thus loathed and abhorred myself, at the remembrance of my iniquities and abominations? This sitting in the dust is most pleasing to God. When we carry our thoughts to heaven, and consider what is going on in that blessed region, we behold angels and archangels casting their crowns at the feet of Him that sitteth upon the throne, in whose presence the cherubim veil their faces with their wings.

I have been in the company of religious professors, and have heard many *words* about religion; but give me to be with a broken-hearted Christian, and I prefer his society to that of all the rest. In these days, there is too much of talking about religion, and too little of religion itself. On this subject, I remember having read a passage in the life of a pious man, who observed, on his death-bed, 'I have met with many who can talk about religion—with few whose experience keeps pace with their talking.' Permit me again to lay this important subject before your consideration. And that you may be able the better to pursue it, and properly to enter into it, allow me to state to you what have sometimes been my feelings while seated in this chair by myself, shut in with God from the world around me. I have thought thus within myself in my retirement: I now look around me, and behold this apartment. I see all is comfort and peace about me. I find myself with my God, instead of being shut up in an apartment in hell, although a hell-deserving sinner. Had I suffered my deserts, I should have been in those dark abodes of despair and anguish. There I should have thought of eternity—eternity! without hope of escape or release. From all this I am delivered by the grace of God, though I might have been cut off in my sins fifty-four years ago. While engaged in these thoughts, they sometimes overpower me. Were I now addressing to you my dying words, I should say nothing else but what I have just said. Try to live in this spirit of self-abhorrence, and let it habitually mark your life and conduct."

TO MISS E. ELLIOTT, ON THE STUDY OF PROPHECY.

"K. C., *Feb.* 19, 1830.

"*My dear Ellen:* A thousand thanks to you for your kind letter. There is a passage in it which speaks volumes; I will copy it: 'I can perfectly understand that there is a great tendency in many minds to dwell too exclusively on prophetical subjects, and to be led away in consequence from the practical and heart-searching doctrines of the Bible.' My dear Ellen, if your honored grandfather were at your side, he would rise from his chair, and with his wonted ardor would say, My dear Ellen, it is not from *the more practical and heart-searching doctrines,* &c., but from the more *mysterious and fundamental doctrines of the Cross* that they are led aside; from Christ crucified to Christ glorified personally upon earth; from the doctrine which is 'both the wisdom of God, and the power of God,' to a doctrine which is neither the one nor the other; from that which will to all eternity form, as it does already form, the great subject of praise and adoration in heaven, to a doctrine in which no two of its advocates agree, and which, as adding to the honor of God, or the happiness of the redeemed, does not weigh so much as the mere dust upon the balance; from a doctrine which humbles, elevates, refines the soul, and brings 'every thought into captivity to the obedience of Christ,' to a doctrine which fills only with vain conceits, intoxicates the imagination, alienates the brethren from each other, and, *by being unduly urged upon the minds of humble Christians,* is doing the devil's work by wholesale.*

SIMEON ON CONTRITION.

To the Bishop of Calcutta :—

"K. C., *May* 22, 1832.

"*My beloved and honored Brother:* I do not wonder that all are desirous of seeing you before you go, and of obtaining from you a parting blessing. At my time of life, I have no hope of seeing you again till we meet before the throne of our reconciled God and Father. It is doubtless a most joyful thought that we have redemption through the blood of our adorable Saviour, even the forgiveness of sins. But I have no less comfort in the thought that He is exalted to give *repentance* and remission of sins. I would not wish for the latter without the former. I scarcely ask for the latter in comparison of the former. I feel willing to leave the latter altogether in God's hands, if I may but obtain the former.

"Repentance is in every view so desirable, so necessary, so suited to honor God, that I seek *that* above all. The tender heart, the broken and contrite spirit, are to me far above all the joys that I could ever hope for in this vale of tears.

"I long to be in my proper place, my hand on my mouth,

---

* It must not be supposed, from these and similar expressions, that Mr. Simeon discouraged the study of prophecy, for he felt strongly that we "do well to take heed unto it;" and, indeed, he was himself one of the first in modern times to call attention to the subject. His sentiments will, however, be more fully seen from the following passage in a letter to Sir T. B., Sept. 17, 1830. "My complaint is, not that they study prophecy, to whatever it may relate; but that they give it an *undue* measure of their attention (making all the wonders of redemption itself almost secondary to their views of Christ's personal reign on earth), and that they press this their favorite subject with an undue zeal upon the attention of the religious public; making (as Mr. D. has done) a love to all the great principles of the Gospel no better than *idolatry* in comparison of it, and *declaring the reception of their views essential to the salvation of the soul.*"

and my mouth in the dust. I would rather have my seed-time here, and wait for my harvest till I myself am carried to the granary of heaven. I feel this to be safe ground. Here I cannot err. If I have erred all my days, I cannot err here. I am sure that whatever God may despise (and I fear that there is much which passes under the notion of religious experience that will not stand very high in His estimation), He will not despise the broken and contrite heart. I love the picture of the heavenly hosts, both saints and angels; all of them are upon their faces before the throne. I love the Cherubim, with their wings before their faces and their feet. I think we hardly set forth this in our sermons as we ought to do. At all events, for *me*, I feel that this is the proper posture now, and will be to all eternity."

TO THE REV. JOHN SARGENT, ON THE CHARACTER OF MR. THOMASON.

"ISLE OF WIGHT, *July* 19, 1832.

"*My beloved Brother:* The task you have imposed upon me ought to be the most easy and most delightful in the world; for who can know so much of Mr. Thomason, as one who lived, for the space of nearly ten years, a part of every week, in the same house with him? or, who can find such delight in declaring what he knows, as one who was united with him in the bonds of friendship far beyond what is commonly known even in the religious world? But in order to write, one must have a pen, which, alas, I have not. Besides, in Mr. Thomason, though there was every imaginable excellence, there was nothing prominent. Were I to compare him with anything, it would be with the light, in which a great diversity of rays are joined, but no one more conspicuous than another. Towards God, he was distinguished by a simplicity of mind and purpose; and towards man, by a placidity of manner and deportment. I never saw anything of self blended with his actions. He seemed to have one end and aim in all that he did; and what he did was never by an effort, so much as by a habit. In fact, every day with him, from morning to evening, was a kind of equable course, somewhat like that of the sun in a Cambridge atmosphere. He gave a tempered light, never blazing forth with unusual splendor, but diffusing to all around him a chastened influence. Everything was done by him in its season; but in so quiet a way as not to attract any particular attention. There was nothing of elevation, nothing of depression. In this respect there was an extraordinary resemblance between him and Mrs. Thomason. Each executed a great deal in every day; but throughout the whole day, though there was much business, there was no bustle, no parade. Each lived only for the Lord, and to glorify Him seemed to be the one business of their lives. There was not a work of benevolence within their reach, but they engaged in it just as if it had been a domestic duty. The parishes in which they were able to exert their influence seemed as their own family; schools of industry, as well as other schools, were established by them; the poor and the sick were visited and relieved; and all that Christian love could devise was planned and executed with the tenderest assiduity, and most unwearied constancy. If I were to fix on one thing more than another wherein Mr. Thomason was at home, it was in his Sunday evening and Tuesday evening Lectures in his school-room. There the poor were permitted to come, and he was as a father amongst his children, or a pastor amongst his flock. In his addresses, there was an unrivalled simplicity and a divine unction, which left a savor that is not forgotten to this hour. The name of Thomason in Shelford and Stapleford is remembered like that of Schwartz in Tanjore and Trichinopoly; and I doubt not but that to all eternity many will have reason to bless God for his affectionate administrations. One thing I may mention to the honor of both Mr. and Mrs. Thomason, that in all the ten years that I lived under their roof, I never on any occasion heard an angry word from either of them, nor ever saw a different countenance in either of them towards the other, or in either of them towards me.

"Indeed, I should not omit to mention his liberality. He did good to the utmost extent of his ability; so that when he went out to India, he had not wherewith to carry him thither without the aid of friends; and when, after eighteen years' continuance in India, he came home from thence, he had not wherewith to bring him home, without the aid derived to Mrs. Thomason, from taking the charge of several young females during their voyage. Had it pleased him, he might have amassed money both in England and in India; for in England he had twelve pupils, and in India he was in the receipt of a large income; but he was as superior to the love of money as any person, either with or without a family, can be supposed to be.

"But I cannot do justice to his character; that will appear fully, though undesignedly, drawn in his letters both to his Mother and to myself. It is only in compliance with your wishes and commands that I send you this sketch, which I would infinitely rather commit to the flames.

"With most kind regards to Mrs. S., I remain, my dear Brother, most affectionately yours, "C. S."

Mr. Thomason entered into rest Jan. 21, 1829, twelve days after he had landed at the Mauritius, whither he had sailed from Calcutta in the hope of recruiting his health.

"He left an affectionate farewell to those most dear to him, in the following words: 'To my dearest Mother, give my most affectionate love, and may her last days be her best days. To my very dear Mr. Simeon, say I feel unworthy of the great love he has at all times honored me with. Oh, may his bow abide in strength, and may he be, if possible, still more useful in his age!'"—Sargent's *Life of Thomason*, p. 334.

A Monument has been erected to him in Trinity Church, adjacent to that of HENRY MARTYN.

SIMEON AT 73 YEARS OF AGE.

To the Rev. J. H. MICHELL:—

"K. C., *Oct.* 8, 1832.

"*My dear Brother:* Who would have ever thought that I should have to behold such a day as this? My parish sweetly harmonious! My whole Works stereotyping in 21 volumes! and my Ministry not altogether inefficient at the age of 73! Where are all our companions? Cole, Hayes, Luxmoore, Emly, Dampier, Norbury, Butler, Anstey, Bernard, Hayes, Smith, Askew, Moore, Sumpter, Barrow, Cropley, &c.? I saw a fire at Cottenham, which had most unaccountably jumped over two or three houses that were in the very line for consumption. So you, and Goodall, and I have been spared, whilst so many on either side of us have been taken."

TO LADY OLIVIA B. SPARROW, ON HIS RECOVERY FROM ILLNESS.

"K. C., *April* 13, 1833.

"*My dear Lady Olivia:* For fifteen months I went on with my Work, with all the energy and activity of youth, revising and correcting one of my ponderous Volumes every three weeks. But I had no sooner completed the twentieth Volume than the gout came and threw me down, and compelled me to transfer my editorial work to others. But, in fact, all that I was in the least anxious about was completed. I am carried up and down stairs on men's shoulders, and put into and taken out of my carriage like a log of wood. But I can now walk two or three yards alone; and hope, if it be possible, to be helped up to my pulpit to-morrow. I do, indeed, doubt whether it be possible; of that I shall judge better when I get to church. But my judgment scarcely approves of the dictates of my heart."

MEMORANDUM ON THE COMPLETION OF HIS WORK.

"*May* 24, 1833.

"This day God has vouchsafed to me the two richest blessings (next to the enjoyment of himself) that my soul could desire:

"1. I have this day received from the Archbishop of Canterbury his permission to dedicate my Work to him.

"2. I have this day received the last five Volumes, and see the Work complete, the ship launched. This last was the only thing for which I wished to live, *so to speak*, and now I sing my *Nunc dimittis*."

TO THE BISHOP OF CALCUTTA, ON PRESENTING HIS WORKS TO THE KING.

"KING'S COLLEGE, CAMBRIDGE, *July* 3, 1833.

"*My beloved and most honored Friend and Brother:* . . . For fifteen months I continued, with the intervention only of one single day, to revise and correct the press, and in that time finished twenty volumes. Then came a fit of the gout which necessitated me to devolve that labor for the last volume on others. But that volume had been so thoroughly prepared by me, that I could not, so far as I am aware, have altered a single word. It was all finished in sixteen months—twenty-one thick volumes in sixteen months (an expedition never known or heard of in the writings of a private man). I wrote to the Archbishop of Canterbury, who readily permitted me to dedicate it to him; by means of which it will abate prejudice at home, and facilitate the reception of it abroad amongst all the foreign Courts to which I send it. A fortnight ago this day, I had the honor of presenting the Work to his Majesty before the Levee, at a private audience. The King received me very courteously, and told me he should convey them with him to Windsor, meaning that he should have more time to look at them there than in London. To both the Archbishops I presented them. With his Grace of Canterbury I had a long, and deep, and interesting conversation, upon the true character of religion, as suited both to the necessities and capacities of men. He entered fully into my statements, and cordially concurred with me in them. The Archbishop of York was a Fellow of All Souls, together with my brother, Sir J. S. And a curious circumstance occurred. I had presented my books to him the day before I presented them to the King; and whilst I was with his Majesty, his name was announced. On leaving the King, I met him in the anteroom, and he shook me cordially by the hand, and told me he had been reading my book with pleasure. And in two minutes afterwards he was with the King, with the books before him, so that doubtless he would impress his Majesty's mind favorably respecting them. Who can tell what good may result from this? The Queen at least, I hope, may reap some good from them.

"All the foreign Ambassadors have undertaken to transmit them to their respective Courts. Prince Talleyrand has already sent his to Paris. At Cambridge, an extraordinary effect has been wrought. And St. John's College has written me the following letter, which is incomparably the most grateful to me of any that I have yet received.

"'I am desired by the Master and Seniors to return to you their heartfelt thanks for your very valuable present to the Library of St. John's College; viz., "A copy of your entire Works."

"'I am sure you will readily believe, that the Master and Fellows most cordially join in the wish and prayer, you have been so kind to prefix in your own handwriting to the Copy sent.

"'They also sincerely hope that you may be yet a long time spared to labor in the service of our Divine Master.'"

TO A FRIEND UNDER RELIGIOUS DEPRESSION.

"There are two errors which are common to persons in your state: 1st. The using of means, as though by the use of them they could prevail; and 2dly. The not using them, because they have so long been used in vain. The error consists in putting the means too much in the place of Christ, and in expecting from *exertion* what is only gained by *affiance*. There is a passive state of mind—a lying like clay in the hands of the potter—and a casting yourself on the Lord Jesus Christ, content to sink if He will let you sink; and to be marred, if He choose to mar you. This willingness to be saved by Him altogether from first to last, and in His own time and way, and this determination to trust in Him though He slay you, and to praise Him though He condemn you, is what you particularly want. You would fain have *the knowledge* of your acceptance of Him, when you should rather be concerned to *insure* that acceptance. I know not whether this will convey any idea to your mind, but if it do, it will prove of some service to you.

"There is another thing which I would suggest, which is intimately connected with that, namely, that you are too much occupied in looking at yourself, and too little in beholding the Lord Jesus Christ. It is by the former you are to be *humbled;* but it is by the latter that you are o tbe '*changed into the divine image.*' (2 Cor. iii. 18.) You want a greater measure of holiness to warrant your confidence in the divine promises; when it is only by apprehending those promises that you can attain the holiness you are seeking after. (2 Cor. vii. 1.) You must learn to 'glory in your infirmities (so to speak), that the power of Christ may rest upon you.' You are nothing, and it discourages you; but you must be content to be nothing, that Christ may be 'all in all.' I grieve, my dear Madam, that I am not able to counsel you as I could wish; and with earnest prayer to God, that my weak suggestions may not be in vain, I remain

"Your very affectionate and sympathizing Friend,

"C. S."

TO MISS ELLEN ELLIOTT.

"K. C., *April* 3, 1835.

"*My dear Ellen:* You and your sister Charlotte desired me to send you my thoughts on humiliation and contrition, as primary constituents of the Christian's happiness, and absolutely essential to it. But I have written so much upon this topic, that I despaired of adding anything to what I have already spoken. The most important view which I have given of it, is that wherein I have drawn the difference between a wife who has all her days acted up to the duties of her station, and the wife who, after having been taken from the lowest state, has dishonored both herself and the kindest and best of husbands, and been sought out by him again, and reclaimed, and forgiven. Her recollections of the past, and her admiration of the transcendent love exercised towards her, would generate in her mind feelings of which the former woman was incapable, and would give a tone to her conduct more precisely in accordance with our state before God. This will explain to you what I meant, in my last, by 'going on my way weeping,' and by my saying, that the more gracious and merciful God was to me, the more would I loathe and abhor myself, and have my happiness so interwoven with humiliation, as not for a moment to have them separate. On all of this I could speak all the day long; it is so deeply inwrought in my heart as a principle, and so constantly cherished by me as the chief object of my desire.

"But whilst thinking of you in my carriage to-day, a view of this subject occurred to my mind, which, though not overlooked in my Work, I have never treated in a separate form. It is this: That this very humiliation will give to our happiness in heaven a tone that will elevate us above the highest archangel there. The angels can sing the *air;* but cannot from their own experience send forth the deep notes which will soften, and enlarge, and complete *our* songs. I need not say to you that a *chorus* of Handel's far exceeds any mere melody. There is in the chorus a richness and fulness that a simple melody neither does nor can contain. So I should say of the holy angels; their melody is exquisite; but our deep notes they want. They have all the felicity that the contemplation of a Creator and Benefactor can impart; but they cannot look back to a state of guilt and misery from which they have been redeemed; nor can they look upon the Redeemer with our eyes; nor can they see every atom of their bliss bought with blood. These are considerations which will enhance our bliss infinitely beyond any that they can feel, and will give a character to our happiness, of which they can have no consciousness or conception. In fact, they can only add an Amen to the song which we sing; and acknowledge that our blessedness is what they can admire indeed, but not participate. You see I do not touch here on their being made wiser by the Church, and their having only a creature's righteousness, whilst we have that of our Creator; or their forming an exterior circle round the Throne, whilst we form the interior (of these things I have spoken occasionally in my Works); I confine myself to the subject on which you wished me to write: The union of humiliation with our joy; and the aspect of the one on the other. I have merely scribbled in great haste what has occurred to me, but without any order or precision. I thought I had not done well in declining to enter on the subject; and I am not sure that if I delay till to-morrow, I shall not throw it into the fire, as being crude, hasty, ill written, and ill digested. But it shows my love to all who have any blood of the Venns in their veins, and that I am,

"With very affectionate regard, Charlotte's, and Ellen's, and Mary's friend—not to mention your honored Mother's also,

"C. SIMEON.

"Query: If I were offered to change place with an angel, would I do it? On my principles I say, No."

CAMBRIDGE IN 1836.

"Yesterday I preached to a Church as full as it could hold, and partook of the Lord's Supper in concert with a larger number than has been convened together, on such an occasion, in any Church in Cambridge since the place existed upon earth. Before I came to the Living, I attended once at Trinity Church to hear on some occasion a very popular preacher; and, as I then never turned my back upon the Lord's Supper, I stayed during the administration of it, and was myself one of *three*, who, besides the Parson and Clerk, formed the whole number of the Communicants. So greatly has the Church of England been injured by myself and my associates.

"Most affectionately yours, "C. S."

MR. SIMEON'S LAST ILLNESS.

This was brought on by a severe cold. We make the following extracts from his biographer's full and interesting diary of his last moments:—

Saturday (September 24), was his birthday, when he entered his seventy-eighth year. Though he had passed but an indifferent night, he rose early this morning; and when his attendant came to him, he was sitting in a favorite spot before the window to enjoy the first beams of the sun, and employed in writing another letter to Mr. Nottidge, in which he observed, "Of course, my University Sermons are laid aside; if not life itself." On repeating this to his attendant, he added, "What can I expect? I enter my seventy-eighth year to-day. I never expected to live so long; I can scarcely believe I am so old; I have as yet known nothing of the infirmities of age, though I have seen a good old age. I know, however, it will all be ordered well." Soon after, when referring to his journey to Ely, he remarked, "If this is to be the closing scene, I shall not at all regret my journey to the Bishop; it was of vast importance to you all; and I shall rejoice to close my life from such a circumstance."

During the second week of October, when one of his particular friends had called at his rooms to inquire after his health, Mr. Simeon immediately begged to see him, and in a feeble whisper requested him to pray by his bedside. After the prayer, his friend expressed a hope that he was now supported by divine consolations. Mr. Simeon then replied to this effect: "I never felt so ill before—I conceive my present state cannot last long—this exhaustion must be a precursor of death; but I lie here waiting for the issue without a fear—without a doubt—and without a wish." To another afterwards who remarked, "Many hearts are engaged in prayer for you;" he rejoined, "In prayer? ay, and I trust in *praise* too—praise for countless, endless mercies."

On Friday (Oct. 21), all hopes of his recovery were taken away; the gout had at length attacked him internally, and the means used for his relief were evidently in vain; of this he was perfectly aware, and in consequence seemed more than usually calm and happy. The writer was sitting by his bedside, and on making some inquiry as to what had been lately passing in his mind, and of what at that time more particularly he was thinking, he immediately replied with great animation, "I don't *think* now—I am *enjoying*." He then expressed his entire surrender of himself to the will of God, and spoke of his extreme joy in having his own will so completely in unison with that of God, adding, with remarkable emphasis, "He cannot do anything against my will." After a short pause, he looked round with one of his very bright and significant smiles, and asked, "What do you think especially gives me comfort at this time?—The Creation!—the view of God in His work of Creation! Did Jehovah create the world, or did I?—I think *He* did; now, if He made the *world*, he can sufficiently take care of *me*." His restlessness from excessive pain was now so great, that he was continually requesting his position to be changed; but when it was suggested that it would be better to attempt to lie quietly, he said most calmly, "I will do just what you like—I will be guided entirely by what you think best." Shortly after, by way of turning his thoughts to a subject which seemed likely to interest him, I said, "How blessed a prospect is opening before you; to be so soon with the innumerable company of angels, and the general assembly and church of the first-born, and with Jesus, the mediator of the new covenant." Upon this his countenance became peculiarly solemn and grave; and he said nothing, but only looked up most humbly and devoutly. I then alluded to another subject, which I knew would be agreeable to him; and made a remark about veiling our faces, as the Cherubim did, in the presence of God; to this he immediately gave a sign of assent and pleasure. About midnight he was raised up in his bed, and having sent for me to his side, he began to speak, in a very slow and impressive manner, what seemed to us all to be his dying remarks: "I am a poor fallen creature, and our nature is a poor fallen thing; there is no denying that, is there? It cannot be repaired; there is nothing that I can do to repair it. Well, then, *that* is true. Now what would you advise in such a case?" As he made rather a long pause, apparently waiting for an answer, I replied, "Surely, sir, to go, as you always *have* done, as a poor fallen creature to the Lord Jesus Christ, confessing your sins, and imploring and expecting pardon and peace." He answered, in a very determined and joyful manner, "That is just what I am doing, and *will* do." I added, "And you find the Lord Jesus Christ to be very present, and giving you peace?" He instantly replied, looking up to heaven with the most remarkable expression of happiness on his countenance, "O yes; *that* I do!" "And He does not forsake you now?" "No, indeed! *that* NEVER CAN BE!" I observed, "He has said, I will never leave thee, nor forsake thee." He answered by a smile and gentle inclination of the head. Being afraid of wearying him, I then left him for the night.

The day following (Saturday, Oct. 22), about noon, he appeared, if anything, to rally a little; and when he opened his eyes upon us, and saw us standing near him, he began to address us again in the same calm and deliberate manner as before. [To conceive aright of his mode of speaking on these occasions, he should be considered as uttering his words very slowly—generally after long pauses, and at times in a low but articulate whisper.] "Infinite *wisdom* has devised the whole with infinite *love;* and infinite *power* enables me——(pausing) ——to rest upon that power; and all is infinitely good and gracious." I observed, "How gracious it is that you should have now so little suffering." "Whether I am to have a little less suffering or a little more, it matters not one farthing. All is right—and well—and just as it should be; I am in a dear Father's hands—all is secure. When I look to HIM (here he spoke with singular solemnity) I see nothing but *faithfulness* —and *immutability*—and *truth;* and I have not a doubt or a fear, but the sweetest peace—I CANNOT HAVE MORE PEACE. But if I look another way—to the poor creature—O! then THERE is nothing—*nothing*—*nothing*—(pausing) but what is to be abhorred and mourned over. Yes, *I say that;* and it is true." Soon after this he fell into a state of great stupor, which continued till after ten o'clock at night; when suddenly recovering, and being raised up in his bed, he again began: "What is before me I know not; whether I shall live or die.

But *this* I know, that all things are ordered and sure. Everything is ordered with *unerring wisdom* and *unbounded love.*"

As we were afraid of exhausting him, we all left the room. There had been present a larger number of persons than usual, arising from a circumstance which it is only proper to explain. His nurse, apprehending that he was on the very point of death, had suddenly called me in from the next room; and upon my hastening to his side, I was followed by his physician and Curate (who had just arrived), and his three servants. These were all who were present. But not exactly perceiving who were in the room, and not knowing that they were there merely by accident, he soon after sent for me, and in a very serious and affecting manner expressed his disapprobation of what he had observed: "You are all on a wrong scent, and are all in a wrong spirit; you want to see what is called a *dying scene*. THAT I ABHOR FROM MY INMOST SOUL. I wish to be *alone*, with my God, and to lie before Him as a poor, wretched, hell-deserving sinner—yes, as a poor, hell-deserving sinner; . . . . (then, very slowly and calmly) but I would also look to Him as my all-forgiving God—and as my all-sufficient God—and as my all-atoning God—and as my covenant-keeping God. There I would lie before Him as the vilest of the vile, and the lowest of the low, and the poorest of the poor. Now this is what I have to say—I wish to be alone—don't let people come round to get up a scene."

When Dr. Haviland called in the evening, Mr. Simeon addressed him in the most striking manner upon the subject of religion; speaking with a clearness, and power, and dignity, which perfectly surprised Dr. H., though so accustomed to the peculiar energy and characteristic precision of Mr. Simeon's observations on such subjects. He said he had never heard anything before from him comparable to this, for the propriety of the language as well as the importance of the matter.

Early the next morning (Monday, Oct. 24), when I arrived, I found him just raised up, after passing a quiet night; I told him I had, as usual, on the previous evening, addressed a large number of Undergraduates, and had ventured to repeat to them some of his remarks, that they might know the power of those great leading principles he had preached to sustain and gladden the soul in the last hours of weakness. "Yes," said he, "it is to the *principles* I look. It is upon the *broad, grand principles* of the Gospel that I repose—it is not upon any particular promise here or there—any little portions of the word, which some people seem to take comfort from; but I wish to look at the *grand whole*—at the vast scheme of redemption as from eternity to eternity. . . . .

During the greater part of Thursday (Oct. 27), his whole mind seemed absorbed in perfecting a scheme for four Sermons upon his favorite passage in Eph. iii. 18, 19: "That you may be able to comprehend with all saints, what is the breadth, and length, and depth, and height; and to know the love of Christ which passeth knowledge, that ye may be filled with all the fulness of God."

So intensely were his thoughts fixed on the distribution and illustration of this glorious theme, that he declared he thought no higher honor could be conferred on him, than to be permitted to prepare a set of discourses upon it; and added, "This is the grandest subject I can conceive of for a course of Sermons;—I should think a life well spent, even out of heaven, to write and deliver four Sermons upon it in a manner worthy of it."

His nights about this time were generally very restless, and he would employ himself in meditating on such portions of Scripture as particularly displayed the love and immutability and sovereignty of God, or else tended to deepen his sense of sin and promote contrition of heart. But as the time approached for the Meetings in behalf of the Society for the Conversion of the Jews, and for the Anniversary Sermons at his Church, his thoughts soon became engrossed with this great subject, to which he had so long devoted his warmest regards. He wished to deliver, he said, his dying testimony to "its immense importance," and prepared to compose an address to be read to the Undergraduates at their Meeting on the following Monday. Being afraid he might not remember the texts, which he wished to refer to when he came to dictate the address, he ordered his attendant to get his small Bible, and directing her where to find them, he desired her to read them out, and then mark them down; saying, with great emphasis, "*Take care of those texts; they are gold, every one of them.*"

In the afternoon of October 29, he observed to his attendant, as she was sitting by his bedside: "It would be poor work to have to seek Heaven now." She replied: "Yes, dear Sir, your work is now quite done; and what a privilege it is to see the peace you enjoy; and how you are enabled to bear with such patience and submission all your afflictions." She had scarcely ended the remark, before he rebuked her in a tone and language of severity quite unusual with him. She made no reply, intending to explain her words to him at some future time. In about ten minutes, however, in reference to what had just transpired, he said: "Now, bring some paper, and write something down for me directly." Then, in a very serious and deliberate manner, he dictated the following: "If anything laudatory be mentioned before the University by Dr. Dealtry about me, or about my Sermons, I entreat from my inmost soul that I may not have it repeated to me; let me go to heaven as the *vilest sinner in the universe.* So far as respects myself, let me not know there is such a person existing as Charles Simeon; on no account, if any remarks are made, let them be uttered before me."

On the evening of this day we thought he was beginning to lose his consciousness of what was passing, as he no longer took notice of anything, and his eyes had been closed for many hours; suddenly, however, he remarked: "If you want to know what I am doing, go, and look in the first chapter of the Ephesians, from the third to the fourteenth verse; *there* you will see what I am enjoying now." This was the last chapter which he requested to have read to him; but such was his weakness, that it was only when read in a whisper that he could bear to hear it. Another kindred passage of Scripture, the last verse of the eleventh of Romans, was one on which he would dwell for hours together, repeating the words, "For *of* Him, and *through* Him, and *to* Him are all things; to whom be glory for ever. Amen."

During the last few days of his life his bodily sufferings were often excruciating, and his strength so impaired that his voice was scarcely audible. He then observed to his attendant, "Jesus Christ is my 'all in all' for my *soul;* and now you must be my all for my *body*; I cannot tell you any longer what I want, or ask for anything. I give my body into your charge; you must give me what you think necessary." Afterwards, when he had revived a little, he remarked: "It is said, O death, where is thy sting?" then looking at us, as we stood around his bed, he asked, in his own peculiarly-expressive manner: "Do you see any *sting here?*" We answered: "No, indeed, it is all taken away." He then said: "Does not this *prove*, that my principles were not founded on fancies or enthusiasm; but that there is a *reality* in them, and *I find them sufficient to support me in death?*"

The last words I addressed to him were on this night, when I gently took his withered hand, and slowly pronounced the

Benediction: "The Lord bless thee, and keep thee; the Lord make his face to shine upon thee, and be gracious unto thee; the Lord lift up His countenance upon thee, and give thee *peace.*" He faintly answered, Amen; after which I heard him speak no more. During the night he was scarcely conscious of anything around, and on being raised in the morning into the same position as before, he remained thus during the whole of Saturday, and continued apparently insensible to the last. About two o'clock on Sunday afternoon (Nov. 13), at the very time the bell of St. Mary's was tolling for the University Sermon, which he was himself to have preached, after a momentary struggle, he entered into his eternal rest.

Thus graciously did God grant unto him his heart's desire—the most perfect peace, and a "full assurance of hope unto the end." And without weakness or wandering of mind during his severe sufferings, in which patience had indeed its "perfect work"—abounding in love and thanksgiving, he was enabled to testify to the last of the mercy and faithfulness of his God; and so, "having fought a good fight, and kept the faith, he finished his course with joy."

On opening his Will, an intimation was found of his desire respecting the place of his interment. "If I die out of College, I am not careful where my body shall be buried; but if I die in Cambridge, I should wish to be buried in my College Chapel." Accordingly, preparation was made for laying his remains in the Fellows' vault. Many of his clerical friends had expressed a strong desire to be present on the occasion, to offer this last tribute of their affection and respect. These, therefore, were informed of the day of the funeral, but no other persons were invited. It was our desire, in conformity with Mr. Simeon's wish, to conduct everything with as little show as possible. Permission, indeed, had been kindly given by the Provost of King's, for the congregation of Trinity Church to witness the interment of their beloved Minister; and these were admitted privately into the Antechapel. So general, however, was the desire of the members of the University to be present on the occasion, that the funeral unavoidably became one altogether of a public character. These circumstances are mentioned, to show how spontaneous was that remarkable gathering of persons, Heads of Colleges and Professors, and men of all ages and stations and opinions, from every College in the University, who came to do honor to this man of God, in his end.

On the day of the funeral (Saturday) all the shops in the principal part of the town were closed, though it was the market-day;* and, what was an unusual mark of respect in the University, in almost every College the Lectures were suspended. The morning was damp and cheerless, and the gloom around was suited to the feelings of sadness which pervaded that large assembly of mourners. At the appointed hour, the funeral procession began to move from the College-hall, preceded by the Choristers, Scholars, and Fellows, the Provost walking immediately before the bier, and the pall being borne by the eight Senior Fellows. But the following letter, from one of the many distinguished persons present on the occasion, will best describe the scene.

"You know King's great Court and the noble Chapel. The procession round the quadrangle, usual on the burial within the precincts of a College resident, was very striking. The persons who made up the procession, walking three or four abreast, nearly extended round the four sides of the quadrangle. On entering the west door of the Chapel, I was struck by the multitude of persons who filled the nave. Men, women, and children, all, so far as I observed, in mourning, and very many giving proof that they were real mourners by their sighs and their tears. These I understood to be the hearers and parishioners of Mr. Simeon, who had been permitted to attend; and through this sorrowing crowd the procession moved on into the choir. The stall which I occupied allowed me a full view of the interior, and it was indeed a solemn sight; nor was it the least interesting circumstance, on an occasion where all was interesting, to see the young men of the University, as they stood during the service between the coffin and the Communion rails, all in mourning; and all, in appearance at least, feeling deeply the loss which had brought us together, and the solemnity of the service. The vault, in which the body was deposited, is near the west door of the building. Here of course the service concluded. The Provost read most impressively; and, taking under review all the circumstances and accompaniments of the funeral—the affectionate respect for the departed, himself the Luther of Cambridge—the sorrowing multitudes, including several hundreds of University men—the tones of the organ, more solemn than ever I heard them—the magnificence of the building—I should think that no person who was present would ever fail, so long as he remembers anything, to carry with him a powerful remembrance of that day. . . . Turning

* What a change! Once, most of the doors of the pews of his church were locked against him.

to my old recollections, I could scarcely have believed it possible that Mr. Simeon could thus be honored at his death! His very enemies, if any of them lived so long, seemed now to be at peace with him."

The funeral Sermon at Trinity Church on the Sunday Morning was preached by Dr. Dealtry, the Chancellor of Winchester,* from a text which had received a remarkable illustration in the events of the preceding day, "*Them that honor me, I will honor.*"

We must now bring our narrative to a close. For many years previous to this period, Mr. Simeon had been desirous of leaving to his parishioners some token of his regard, which might "benefit them after his death." A Memorandum to the following effect was found in his Will:—

"It is my desire that an edition of the Sermon which I preached before the University, on that text, 1 Cor. ii. 2, be printed; and that a copy of it be presented to every family in Trinity Parish, as a memorial of my pastoral regards, and as the means of impressing their minds with the importance of the doctrine which I preached to them during the whole course of my Ministry."

This last wish of Mr. Simeon was immediately carried into execution; and in the chancel of Trinity Church, directly opposite to the tablets of his beloved *Martyn* and *Thomason*, his monument was shortly after erected by the congregation. It bears this short but expressive inscription, suggested by himself.

IN MEMORY OF
THE REV. CHARLES SIMEON, M.A.,
SENIOR FELLOW OF KING'S COLLEGE,
AND FIFTY-FOUR YEARS VICAR OF THIS PARISH;
WHO,
WHETHER AS THE GROUND OF HIS OWN HOPES,
OR AS THE SUBJECT OF ALL HIS MINISTRATIONS,
DETERMINED
TO KNOW NOTHING BUT
'JESUS CHRIST, AND HIM CRUCIFIED.'
1 COR. II. 2.
BORN SEPT. 24, 1759. DIED NOV. 13, 1836.

---

* Now Archdeacon of Surrey.

www.ingramcontent.com/pod-product-compliance
Lightning Source LLC
LaVergne TN
LVHW020122110826
845151LV00001B/240

* 9 7 8 1 4 2 5 5 4 4 2 2 5 *